Christianity AND THE Images OF Science

For George Croft Barker,
who in living and dying showed the grace,
love, and humor of God.

Christianity and the Images of Science

Granville C. Henry

PUBLISHING, INCORPORATED MACON, GEORGIA

ISBN 1-57312-184-3

Christianity and the Images of Science

Granville C. Henry

Copyright © 1998

Smyth & Helwys Publishing, Inc.
6316 Peake Road
Macon, Georgia 31210-3960
1-800-747-3016

All rights reserved.
Printed in the United States of America.

The paper used in this publication meets the minimum requirements of American National Standard for Information Sciences—Permanence of Paper for Printed Library Materials, ANSI Z39.48—1984.

Library of Congress Cataloging-in-Publication Data

Henry, Granville C.
    Christianity and the images of science / Granville C. Henry
    p.   cm.
    Includes bibliographical references and index.
    ISBN 1-57312-184-3   (alk. paper)
    1. Religion and science. I. Title.
    BL240.2.H46   1998
    261.5'5—dc21

                                98-17459
                                    CIP

Contents

Preface vii

Introduction 1

I. Ancient Science
Its Impact on Orthodox Theology

Chapter 1
Early Mathematical Astronomy 15

Chapter 2
Greek Mathematics 31

II. Classical Science
Its Challenge by Contemporary Science, and Issues of Modern Theology

Chapter 3
Newtonian Mechanics 51

Chapter 4
Evolution 65

Chapter 5
Theological Response to Darwinism 81

Chapter 6
Psychology: The Logic of the Soul 93

Chapter 7
The Soul: A Response to Psychology 109

Chapter 8
Psychology and Determinism 123

III. Contemporary Science and Theology

Chapter 9
The Theory of Relativity 141

Chapter 10
The Self-Limitation of
Mathematics and Quantum Mechanics 155

Chapter 11
Creation: The Big Bang 175

Chapter 12
A Christian Doctrine of Creation 187

Chapter 13
Faith and Reason 203

Epilogue: Two Emotionally Derived Positions 219

Bibliographical Essay 223

Bibliography 227

Index 239

Preface

After trying to speak to scholars through various articles in philosophical, religious, and mathematical journals as well as a few books in university presses, I now attempt a more important task. My goal is to address not-yet professional or scholarly student-Christians who may be in high school, college, or graduate school. In particular, I aim for those Christians who want to pursue a scientific vocation. With little shame, I intend to suggest some radical ideas to them before they get altogether comfortably settled in scientific or theological party lines. Most important, I want to address a problem that can separate Christians from their faith, namely, the perceived animosity between science and Christianity. I have seen too many apparently well-started Christians give up a "childhood" faith to accept what seems to them a "mature" faith in science. Unfortunately, some never return home.

Although these student-Christians and hoping-to-be scientists are a small audience, they could have an enormous impact on the future of the church. My hope is that some few seed scattered in the pages that follow will grow, blossom, and bear bountiful fruit in the fertile scientific minds of young women and men who have not only given their lives to Jesus, but also have a great love for science.

I asked for help and got it in the early writing. Michael Geertsen, Margaret Falotico, and Julie Froehlig—who more recently than I have come through "the valley of the shadow" of academic preparation—gave their dreams as well as their critical faculties to the beginning writing. They got the project started well. As I tightened the content and began to choose emphases, in particular what is called "process thought," I had to consider myself the primary author. Although I may recognize the ideas, phrases, and humor of Michael, Margaret, or Julie, it is now impossible to untangle exactly who said what. I am the one who must take responsibility for the major directions of the book as well as the errors and sometimes folly found in it. I hope these three get some mild amusement or satisfaction when they see their ideas presented without credit, knowing all the while how much I appreciate what they have given to me.

I sent the manuscript to a number of friends and colleagues, both scholars and laypersons, for review. Some responded enthusiastically, some critically, and most not at all. At that point, I realized that the book, like sushi, is not for everyone. Robert Feldmeth, now deceased, checked the sections on evolution. Anthony Fucaloro, in spite of the impossible job of being Dean of Faculty at my institution, read the chapters on physics. John B. Cobb, Jr., read the whole manuscript with an eye to its claims about process thought. No one of these three agreed exactly with my philosophical or theological position, but each indicated I was within the minimal bounds of accuracy in describing their particular disciplines. I thank them for their critical suggestions, but disclaim for them any responsibility for material added recently—much of which they would probably think outrageous.

Introduction

Does God care about scientific theories? Does the Creator experience pleasure, annoyance, perplexity, amusement, disdain, or other complex emotions about the theory of evolution? From our viewpoint, is contemporary evolution compatible with the Bible? How does the latest astronomy fit the Bible's account of Creation? Can quantum physics advance the idea of human freedom? Does Freudian psychology support a biblical doctrine of sin? Does computer science point to the existence of a human soul? Does science itself show the limits of science and thereby promote the importance of other modes of investigation including religion? In short, how does the Christian religion engage science today?

I have tried to answer this question for those of any age who have developed a curiosity, and possible skepticism, about Christianity or its Jewish roots but especially for young adults who study and enjoy science. I have presented technical scientific material, not to have the reader master it, but so it might suggest to her a new perspective on science and religion. For this function, she need only have had some introductory courses in chemistry, biology, physics, or psychology as well as standard courses in algebra and geometry. I believe a restless philosophical curiosity is more important than any background scientific or religious knowledge.

It may seem presumptuous when I present short summaries of contemporary scientific fields while scientists far more able than I spend lifetimes mastering these disciplines. I intend, however, to use these descriptions not just to give a hint and overview of what young developing scientists may have in store, but primarily to show how mathematics, astronomy, physics, cognitive science, evolution, and other sciences are promoting images that engage religion in a new and powerful way. After a century or so of less-than-adequate respect for the Bible, and some outright Bible-bashing, most of the contemporary scientific disciplines are making discoveries and developing theories that complement the religion of the Bible—but not necessarily in the older accepted theological ways.

I use the term "Christianity" to mean the core religious expression of Roman Catholicism, Protestantism, and Eastern Orthodoxy. There are historical, cultural, and doctrinal differences among each of these traditions, but there is also a central essence formed from their common response to the gospel: the good news that God entered history as Jesus Christ, suffered for the sin of humanity a criminal's death by crucifixion, and rose from the dead triumphantly in a bodily human form. A surprising result of God's action in Christ accepted by all Christian communities is that one need not know any science or philosophy to become and remain a Christian. The heart of Christianity proclaimed by each tradition is a relationship *with* God, not knowledge *about* God or the world. The twelve disciples who followed Jesus knew no science and little, if any, philosophy. Most of the church's saints had similar backgrounds. The center of Christianity is its nonphilosophical and nonscientific reality—one that celebrates the love of God and in response loves humanity and the world.

I use the term "science" to mean what most scientists believe is science—with one major distinction. I affirm that every science including mathematics is born with images (insights, intuitions, or models) about the world. At the time these images seem to be necessary to give meaning to the factual, experimental, and theoretical part of science but later can be determined to be inessential or at least replaceable by other images for the proper functioning of science. I call these images the "philosophical aspects of science" or, for this book, simply "philosophy," because philosophers have articulated these images into extended, comprehensive, and sometimes systematic works. They have introduced the distinctions and terminology that now form the means by which scholars examine the issues.

In our discussion of the philosophical aspects of science I shall present the images first and only then develop the philosophical language as necessary to clarify relevant distinctions for the analysis of science and religion. I shall not be interested in nor investigate all the general images used to picture the world by science, or adapted by philosophers, but only those that seem significant for interpreting religion.

As an example of images associated with science, we may ask whether the world is more like a vegetable, say a turnip, or a machine, such as a typewriter. Notice, I am using images in this case to pose alternative views—whether things in general are lifelike or machine-like. The choice of one or the other of these images may have considerable impact on theological understanding. For example, in the turnip image, God is often seen to act like a gardener who cultivates the vegetables, which have an internal life and force of their own. In the typewriter image, God can "punch the keys" causing exact results among things, which always merely follow God's lead but have no real agency of their own.

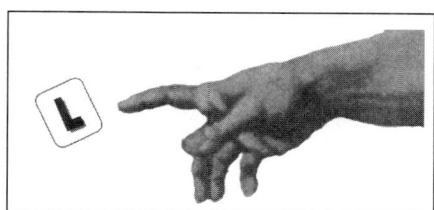

Some who are impressed with the great sophistication of science and philosophy may think these images are foolish examples not really relevant to the science-religion debate. Images of this sort, though not often expressed explicitly, have dominated long periods of science, philosophy, and theology. For example, the organic image held sway during ancient and medieval thought following the philosopher Aristotle and the mechanical image has dominated science since the seventeenth century following primarily the scientist and philosopher Isaac Newton. Neither the mechanical nor the organic images are essential for science, and either image can be replaced by a better one.

Someone told Stephen Hawking that each equation he included in his excellent and popular book *A Brief History of Time* would half the sales.[1] He included only one equation—with apologies. I have included three equations in the text (and some in the footnotes, which the reader can ignore). Two of the three equations are algebraic descriptions of Newton's law of acceleration and law of gravitation, and the third is an equation of a circle. In each instance, the equations are described in words or in geometric images.

Although Newton developed calculus in terms of algebraic symbolism, he described his physical theory exclusively in terms of geometrical imagery—normally those images of plane geometry. I follow Newton in using images of plane geometry: those points, lines, triangles, and rectangles that can be physically drawn on paper or in the sand. With these images I can illustrate the discovery of logic in early Greek thought that had a profound impact on orthodox Christian theology. I can show Aristarchus's assertion of a sun-centered universe and why, in the second century B.C., Archimedes rejected it, thus setting the church on a disastrous course towards Copernicus and Galileo. We can follow Newton's argument from the images of geometry to his philosophical position of mechanism, which has dominated many of the issues of modern theology. With these images I can illustrate Einstein's theory of relativity, which is influencing contemporary discussion of a doctrine of creation.

My point is, this book does not require knowledge of the mathematics of geometry or the mathematics of science. It does require a willingness to grapple with the familiar images of geometry. If you can see a point, line, rectangle, and circle in your mind's eye, you are well within the technical requirements of this book. It is up to me to use these geometrical images, as well as those such as turnips and typewriters, to articulate science and its impact on theology.

The images of science that become philosophical aspects of science are more often than not accepted as simply science by contemporary scientists, who include these assumptions of science as part of science while teaching them as science to students. One need not know or care about professional philosophy in order to be a good scientist, because the philosophical aspects of science are already interpreted within the reigning scientific culture. One of the major tasks in the following pages is to isolate some of the basic images of mathematics and the various sciences and show the philosophical assumptions dependent on them so that readers may have choices about how they might orient themselves to contemporary science.

Even though—like Jesus and the twelve disciples (as well as most scientists)—one need know no technical philosophy to be a Christian (or a scientist), one must grapple with the philosophical aspects of science in order responsibly to engage religion *and* science. This required sensitivity to philosophy is forced on us because the various philosophical perspectives on the sciences, which we interpret as derivative from specific images, have a way of affecting an understanding of religion. I intend to show that images and philosophical perspectives derivative from science have conditioned most Christians's understanding about God, religious history, the divinity of Christ, miracles, the nature of the future, and our souls, as well as other biblical and theological topics. Sometimes these philosophical ideas seem directly to attack Christian faith; other times they support it.

To make any sense of how Christianity does or does not get along with science, we must be able to distinguish these philosophical parts of science from its more factually established base. This activity of philosophical and historical analysis is an art, but like any of the Christian arts of painting, music, sculpture, or even preaching, it generates controversy. There are favorable and hostile reactions to its results in the scientific and religious communities—as there will be to the analysis in this book. The goal is to show the reader some of this activity so that he might practice it on his own. The purpose is understanding.

Although this book is written from a perspective of faith, meaning a self-conscious understanding of loyalty to Jesus and the Bible, it champions what we may call "skepticism," both the skeptic and the ism. My favorite skeptic heroes are Blaise Pascal and Emily Dickinson who in different times and different circumstances used careful, clean, beautiful, and devastating skeptical analysis ultimately to affirm a religious position.

The seventeenth-century mathematician, physicist, and philosopher Pascal participated in a vibrant Christian faith while doing mathematical research to ease the pain of ill health. His statement "It may be that there are true demonstrations; but this is not certain"[2] could be the most skeptical ever uttered. Because of her profound integrity, Emily Dickinson was the only one of her large family (and also one of few at Amherst College) who did not make a profession of faith in Jesus during the great revivals of the nineteenth century in New England. Yet her skeptical poems to Master—God just on the other side of the world she adored—are perhaps the cleanest, most emotional, but nonsentimental, love expressions ever written.

To a degree, we are all skeptics. You and I cannot believe *all* the television commercials. Nor can we accept *all* religious claims. We cannot even give credence to *all* ostensible scientific assertions. As scientists or religious people, we must exercise discrimination and judgment about matters of importance. We choose between the good experiment and the bogus one. We try to determine the true religious experience from the deceptive or merely sentimental one. We seek to decide, literally cut away and then distance, what are to us fraudulent science and religion—because we enjoy the chase of the combination of belief and disbelief, but also because we want the truth. We have to be skeptics about some things in order to believe in others. Any kind of integrity, scientific or religious, requires a fundamental orientation of some disbelief.

One reason for my trying to cultivate an honest skepticism is that I believe our thoughts about the nature of the Bible are often conditioned by common philosophical ideas coming from science. For example, most of the various meanings of infallibility, inerrancy, and truth come from scientific, mathematical, and logical sources that have developed independently of the Bible. (I analyze the inspiration of the Bible in chapter 12.) The claim that the Bible is inerrant is intelligible only when we are clear about what inerrancy means. However, the word "inerrancy" as it is commonly used is not a biblical idea. It is brought to the Bible from outside sources. The point is, you have to exercise care and hard-nosed analysis about ideas you borrow from science and philosophy to express your religion. I had rather interpret the Bible in terms of the Bible as much as possible.

In my personal journey in science and religion I have found that major skeptics about religion, some of whom are avowed atheists, have influenced and stimulated my thought, not only about science, but about religion. They have pointed out aspects of the world or images about science that have modified my understanding of religion that are then interpreted as illuminating the Bible. I find I can be more biblical in my attitudes after wrestling with some of their ideas—and then modifying their philosophical images.

For example, Darwin's insights on evolution have allowed me to understand in a more literal way how God can encounter humans historically. Trying to figure out how God influences the course of evolution in the midst of chance has positioned me better to accept that God deals directly with humans in their limited freedom of choice. Accordingly, my understanding of the events at Mount Sinai where God gave the Ten Commandments or at Calvary where Jesus died on the cross is more biblical than it used to be. Freud's insights into the subconscious have allowed me to accept what I believe to be a more biblical doctrine of sin, to accept that sin is a condition of the human soul determined by past human choices—our own, our parents, and those before we were born. I can give a more literal meaning to that part of the first of the Ten Commandments where God punishes "children for the iniquity of parents, to the third and the fourth generation . . ." (Exod 20:5). However, I do not accept any of the images of determinism and materialism proposed either by Darwin or Freud. There are much better images than these that serve no violence to the true science of evolution or psychology yet allow a more biblical understanding of the Christian religion.

The purpose of this book is to present a new set of images for consideration by young scientists that may allow them a better understanding of science and a more orthodox, or at least biblical, understanding of Christianity. I also seek to protect my relationship with my non-Christian friends and colleagues, for it is they who have most aroused my thinking about appropriate images of science. They are my primary source for the revaluation of my ideas towards Christianity and the stimulus for the wonderful venture in confirming, at least in my mind, that it is true. Besides all this, they are, by and large, forthright and delightful people, and I would be impoverished by their loss. It is for them also this book is written. I often think of them as I write, hoping some proposed image from science or religion might jog them further to see and to accept the grace of God in Jesus Christ.

This book does not attempt to persuade its readers using the disciplines of science or philosophy that God exists, that God is the creator of the universe, or that any of the other accepted beliefs of Christianity are true. Paul Davies in his *God and the New Physics* mounts a sustained argument over hundreds of pages that no cogent case has ever been made, or can be made, to justify any of the traditional Christian beliefs based on science alone.[3] Further, he presents fascinating issues and examples from contemporary physics and astronomy that illuminate what he considers to be traditional religious questions—claiming science can give clearer and better answers to these questions than religion.

Although I disagree fundamentally with Davies on the adequacy of science to explain religious matters, I have no quarrel about his humorous and critical analysis of some beliefs of Christians who seek to justify these beliefs by rational means alone. I follow Saint Augustine who maintained that the essentials of Christian faith are not found through reason, but through commitment. His position "I believe in order to understand" gives reason full function to clarify, explain, modify, and justify beliefs already held. It is in this spirit that I attempt to reason about science and the Christian religion.

You may wonder what I believe about the Bible, and it is only fair to tell you. I'm not sure how God did it, but I believe God is the influential author of the Bible—all the while respecting the humanity of those who wrote about the events of the Bible. As we see both divinity and humanity in the person of Jesus, we see both the finger of God and the human personality of the writers in the Bible. I cannot imagine that God would enter history, suffer, and die for us and then allow the primary written record of the events that show God's love to be deceptive. The Bible has profound integrity and is to be trusted at all levels. Yet it is full of surprises for us in a scientific age. It never speaks exactly, certainly not mathematically, about scientific matters. It even resists in the subtlest of ways any effort to weld it into some systematic logical whole. Why is this the case?

The Bible is wonderfully designed to prevent making it into some kind of idol to be seen as equal in authority to God or Christ. Regrettably, some Christians so emphasize the holiness of the Bible as the Word of God that they appear to elevate it to a position comparable to Jesus. If you ask me whether I believe the Bible is the Word of God in this sense, I would say, "No."

According to the Bible, Jesus is the Word of God "made flesh" (the first chapter of the Gospel of John)—not the Bible itself. The Bible is a written collection of books that is wholly reliable for what it intends. It is, nevertheless, an incomplete expression of the perfection found in "God with us." In my more emotional moments, I might claim that the Bible did not die for us; Jesus did. To set up the Bible as an exclusive authority for a belief in Jesus is wrong, perhaps heretically wrong. The person of Jesus is the only true foundation for Christian belief. In contrast, because it will not honor any person as divine, the religion of Islam does promote an infallible, word-by-word dictated scripture, the Qur'an, as the primary authority of religion. Christianity, however, asserts the unique divinity of a man, namely Jesus, and resists any attempt to equate a written document with him.

I think you will find a sympathetic and reverential handling of the Bible in the chapters that follow. After all, it is the primary document of Christianity and is fully worthy of all respect. I try to understand it literally if possible, allegorically when appropriate, and mythically some of the time. Remember, myth attempts to express truth that cannot be expressed as philosophy, history, or science, and the Bible has much to say that cannot be expressed so conventionally.

I try to show in the following chapters that science and mathematics, whenever they have burst upon human consciousness, have brought images and their attendant philosophical structures with them that seem at the time essential for interpreting the new science or mathematics. It is these philosophical overlays, different in different ages when science changes, that have impacted religion, sometimes challenging Christian beliefs and sometimes supporting them. A philosophical position, such as philosophical mechanism normally associated with Newtonian science or a materialism associated with Darwinian science, may seem initially the best and only way to interpret the strictly scientific theory. As time passes, however, better ways of interpreting science become apparent. I intend to show that some of these "better ways" can often ease the tension between science and religion and may illumine theology and scripture.

In the first chapter I postpone analysis of philosophical positions on science to establish other important theses about religion and science. In the second chapter I explain how basic classical philosophical positions on science were derived in association with images of early mathematics. In the middle chapters I show that the philosophical images associated with Newtonian and Darwinian science can be replaced by better images. In the last chapters I demonstrate how newer philosophical positions articulating the images of substance, time, and space can help interpret quantum mechanics, the nature of random variation in the idea of evolution, and anomalies and paradoxes in cognitive science and mathematics, as well as shed light on the nature of the subconscious in psychology. More important, I think I can show how these ideas may allow us to understand better what Christians believe, not only that God created the world but how God is involved in it today concretely and emotionally.

I hope to surprise you by how literally we may interpret the historical sections of the Bible through some of these new philosophical perspectives. When the Bible says, "God called to him out of the bush, 'Moses, Moses!' " (Exod 3: 4), I interpret God to be a person, there at the particular bush in that time *speaking* to Moses. Because of conceptual difficulties with the physical sciences, much contemporary theology has seen God to be far off in God's relation to us, for example, as one who created the laws that control us rather than one who deals directly with us as felt, heard, and sometimes seen. Other theology in reaction to psychology has made subjective feelings the means by which we reach out to a real but still distant God. I interpret the source of subjective emotions to be from encounters, past and present, with humans and the rest of the animate world, but also with God who is "up front" in history, not "laid back" beyond it. In these historical moments God's awesome power is veiled, less so God's emotions.

This book cannot compete in scope or quality with the superb critical works on science and religion by Ian Barbour[4] and Holmes Rolston, III,[5] who, in my estimation, have given us the best possible books for scholars and their advanced students in the various related scientific and religious disciplines. Nor does it approach the plain historical integrity, and subtlety, of John Hedley Brooke's analysis of historical perspectives on science and religion.[6] Brooke refrains from declaring theses about conflict or harmony between science and religion because he believes they show partisan interests. I heartily recommend Barbour's and Rolston's critical survey and Brooke's attempt at a nonpartisan historical examination.

As an author, I accept the partisan position of the Christian community of faith in order to help solve what has become a religious problem of many Christians in dealing with science. This book is not written for scholars or their students but for Christians and their interested friends who have mastered high school mathematics and are pursuing some scientific career. In contrast with Barbour and Rolston, I do not presuppose the level of scientific knowledge or philosophical maturity that is required to truly appreciate their work. Yet I agree with Barbour, and hope to show intelligibly that process thought is the best philosophical medium in which to express biblical Christianity.[7] In contrast with Brooke, I employ historical theses on the conflict and harmony between science and religion, all the while recognizing the partisan position they serve. Nevertheless, I hope to be neither doctrinaire nor patronizing in my efforts, for I do not wish to obscure the enormous complexity and importance of the material relevant to issues between science and religion, especially to those who may be interested in, and have great respect for, both.

I approach the major problems of science and religion at first historically by means of a brief analysis of the images associated with the scientific revolutions that occurred in chronological order as follows: (1) the discovery of deductive mathematics in the seventh and sixth centuries B.C., (2) the development of mathematical astronomy a few centuries thereafter, (3) the Newtonian synthesis of the seventeenth century A.D., (4) evolutionary theory of Darwin in the nineteenth century, and (5) the contemporary sciences of Freudian and cognitive psychology, as well as (6) relativity and quantum theory in physics of the twentieth century. As mentioned earlier, I begin with mathematical astronomy, rather than the earlier discovery of mathematics itself, because the issues of astronomy seem inherently less difficult than the philosophical positions associated with the images of mathematics, which I analyze in the second chapter.

Notes

[1] Stephen Hawking, *A Brief History of Time* (New York: Bantam Books, 1988) vi.

[2] Blaise Pascal, *Pensées; The Provincial Letters*. *Pensées* translated by W. F. Trotter. *The Provincial Letters* translated by Thomas M'Crie (New York: The Modern Library, 1941) 125.

[3] Paul Davies, *God and the New Physics* (New York: Simon and Schuster, 1983). Davies's position and style are similar to that of Bertrand Russell whom he quotes frequently.

[4] Ian G. Barbour, *Religion in an Age of Science, The Gifford Lectures 1989–1991*, vol.1 (San Francisco: HarperSan Francisco, 1990).

[5] Holmes Rolston, III, *Science and Religion: A Critical Survey* (New York: Random House, 1987).

[6] John Hedley Brooke, *Science and Religion: Some Historical Perspectives* (Cambridge: Cambridge University Press, 1991).

[7] John B. Cobb and David Ray Griffin, *Process Theology: An Introductory Exposition* (Philadelphia: The Westminster Press, 1976). I recommend this book for a beginning look at process thought.

I.
Ancient Science
Its Impact on Orthodox Theology

Chapter 1
Early Mathematical Astronomy

Early astronomy is relevant to the discussion of science and religion because its initial earth-centered position was incorporated into orthodox Christian theology, which was then severely challenged fifteen hundred years later by a new astronomy proclaiming the centrality of the sun. The resulting conflict between the church and some of its own scientists, particularly Galileo, assumed tragic proportions and badly hurt the perception of Christianity's integrity for centuries to come. We study early astronomy to understand the conflict, to see why it was unnecessary, and to develop strategies to avoid similar failures of theology in the future.

Observations of the sun, moon, stars, and planets have been a part of human experience in all cultures since prehistory. The science of astronomy began after the discovery of abstract deductive geometry in Greece by a group of strange and wonderful dreamers during the seventh and sixth centuries B.C. Greek astronomy was quite different from the empirical observations of the Babylonians, Egyptians, and Hebrews, because it could be systematized by mathematical theory. Thus, I call the astronomy we are examining early "mathematical astronomy."

It is hard for us to realize the great impact of the discovery of mathematics on human thinking because, as a result of this discovery, we tend to organize rationally any material that did not have such logical structure initially. Take a glance at the diagrammatic images of "Anaximander's Universe" and the "Old Testament World." They are quite different. One has an obvious mathematical structure; the other does not. The difference may not seem as striking to us as it ought, because we struggle to organize logically for our own analysis any nonmathematical view that to its originators had no initial logical structure. We naturally try to organize the Old Testament view of the world by logical means. It does, however, seem apparent which mode of expression would lead to modern science and which mode of expression would eventually be called "prescientific." We begin the study of astronomy after abstract mathematics was discovered, because mathematics became essential for the presentation and understanding of any true science and set a number of issues for comparing science with biblical religion.

The Flat Earth Theory

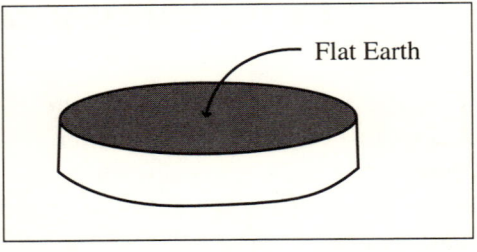

Thales of Miletus, who tradition says predicted an eclipse that occurred in 585 B.C., was the first of the Greek mathematicians and philosophers. Although we do not know much about what Thales thought, we do know that his immediate student Anaximander developed the first mathematical cosmological theory, one that proclaimed a flat earth. Anaximander's flat earth theory is probably the fanciest you have ever seen. The flatness of the earth was the top of a cylinder, as indicated in the picture "Flat Earth."

Anaximander used geometrical imagery to picture what he could not see, namely, the whole earth. Someone would fall off this earth if she sailed to the edge! The cylindrical earth was enclosed, so Anaximander proclaimed, in a sphere of fire. Inside this sphere were dense clouds. The clouds had holes in them: a rather large one, a somewhat smaller one, and lots of little ones. The holes moved in regular patterns. One of them opened and closed. People became very concerned when it or the larger hole closed all the way during an eclipse. These images are pictured in "Anaximander's Universe." How remarkable to develop an elegant mathematical theory, as well as a coherent image, that corresponds so closely to our experience. One could actually see the edge of the world when he looked from a tall mountain. If he could walk around the mountain,

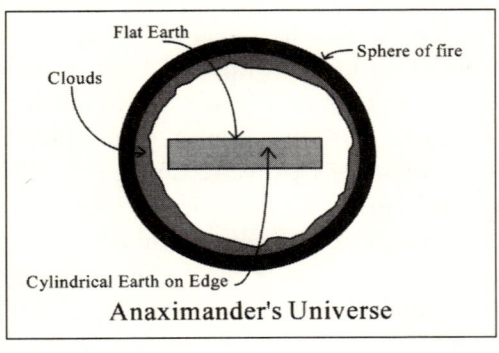

he could see this edge encircling a flat earth. The sun, moon, and stars appeared as lights from the fire shining brightly through the holes, except when clouds obscured them. The moon waxed and waned. Eclipses occurred.

In contrast, the general Old Testament concept of the world was not unified. It was a general collection of different parts—the flat earth, the firmament, the pillars of the earth, the pillars of the sky, and so on[1]—that acted independently of each other but were controlled by the arbitrary delight of God who created them. In this Hebrew perspective, as pictured in "Old Testament World," God understood the universe, but there was no intrinsic mathematical structure to it nor simplified image that would allow us to understand it as an integrated whole.

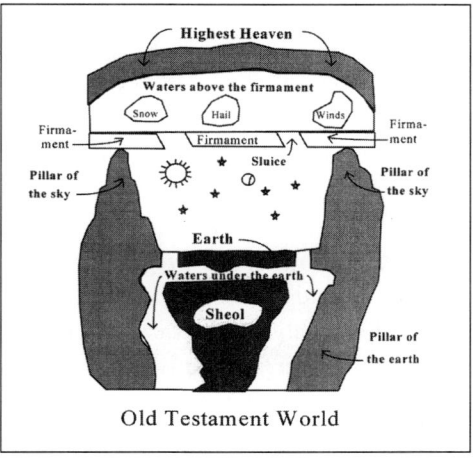

Old Testament World

(We may be surprised to see how well the first chapters of Genesis describe a contemporary mathematical cosmology—one that could not, however, be associated with the biblical creation story until this century. The discussion of this option occurs in chapter 11.) The Old Testament diagram is admittedly a contemporary patchwork of different ideas found in the Old Testament and does not have the internal logical consistency that strictly mathematical diagrams possess. Probably no ancient Hebrew ever had exactly this image in mind. Anaximander, however, did hold something similar to what is pictured for him because of its connected mathematical description.

Of course, no one believes Anaximander's theory about the earth, sun, moon, and stars. Why are we so skeptical about it? Someone might answer: "It's just not true. We all know that. We have seen pictures of the earth from satellites, and the earth looks clearly to be a sphere. We believe that the sun, moon, and stars are physical objects and not just holes. The idea of a spherical fire encircling the earth is just too fantastic to accept." In this case we believe our sense experience as interpreted by what we have been taught, because it seems right to us.

Do we discount Anaximander's theory because of what the Bible says about the earth? Think about this. Be serious now. We probably never questioned what the Bible says about the shape of the earth, because we already believe, indeed we already know, it is spherical. Does the Bible speak seriously about the shape of the world? Is God trying to communicate to us the true state of astronomy? Or does God leave this adventure of discovery up to us? Does the Bible tell us how the heavens go? Or is it primarily interested, as Galileo maintained, in telling us how to go to heaven? Let us examine what the Bible says about the shape of the earth, an issue on which we are already agreed. Perhaps we can learn something about the relationship of the Bible to issues for which some of us may disagree.

There are only two types of references to the shape of the earth in the Bible, one in Isaiah that mentions circularity and the others in Ezekiel and Revelation that point to a flat earth. A single verse in Isaiah claims that God "sits above the circle of the earth" (Isa 40:22). Does this verse from Isaiah refer to a spherical earth, the roughly hemispherical dome of stars above a flat earth, or perhaps a circular flat earth like that of Anaximander? There is little help from the rest of the Bible on the potential for a spherical earth. All stands on this one terse statement that has as its primary intention to proclaim the grandeur of God. There is a reference in Job 26:7 that God "hangs the earth upon nothing." This passage, however, says little about the shape of the earth. Anaximander's flat earth is also suspended in space.

Is there evidence in the Bible that the earth is flat? One verse in Ezekiel refers to the "four corners of the land" (7:2), and two verses in Revelation speak of the "four corners of the earth" (7:1; 20:8). Did these Bible writers believe the earth is flat? Donald B. DeYoung, a conservative biblical interpreter, says, "This false idea is not taught in Scripture!" He contends that the "four corners" actually refer to the cardinal directions: north, south, east, and west. The Bible writers, he asserts, were speaking in the "language of appearance."[2] How did De Young come to this interpretation? Was it from the Bible itself?

There are fifteen uses of "four corners" elsewhere in Bible, each of which refers to some rectangular shape: a table (Exod 25:26; 37:13), a square altar (Exod 27:1-2; 38:1-2; Ezek 43:20; 45:19), a bronze network that was lifted up on four poles (Exod 27:4; 38:5), a rectangular cloak or sheet (Deut 22:12; Acts 10:11; 11:5), a house (Job 1:19), and a court (Ezek 46:21-22). There is no mention of the directions north, south, east, and west in association with any usage of the words "four corners." If we use the interpretative principle that the Bible explains the Bible, it seems clear that the phrase "four corners of the earth" refers to a flat earth that has four corners—certainly not a sphere.

Let us assume for the moment that the Bible does speak of a flat earth in Revelation and a spherical earth in Isaiah. Which one should we choose? The scripture from Revelation may have more authority than the one from Isaiah, because in the book of Revelation, the resurrected and ascended Jesus is showing John directly what is and is to come, whereas the prophet Isaiah is acting only in his "normal" prophetic mode. Yet no responsible theologian or biblical interpreter, Hebrew or Christian, has ever made an issue of a flat or round earth during the last nineteen hundred years.[3] There has been no question about the nature of the earth. It is (roughly) spherical.

Why do we and De Young, as well as all Christians before us, accept this position without question? Why do you think DeYoung would claim on the one hand that "When the Bible touches on scientific subjects, it is entirely accurate" and on the other hand assert that, in spite of the principle that the Bible should interpret the Bible, "four corners" is only a language of appearance? I suspect De Young, like every other biblical scholar, interprets parts of the Bible in terms of what he already believes to be true in science.

The Spherical Earth Theory

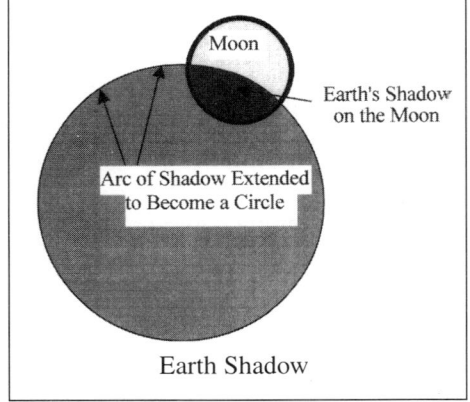

Although the earth seems flat, there is selective evidence that indicates otherwise. Ships gradually drop below the horizon rather than falling off the edge altogether. During a lunar eclipse, where the earth comes between the sun and the moon, one may see the spherical shape of the earth as it casts a shadow on the moon. Many people before the Greeks probably suspected the earth might be shaped like a ball. Some Greeks, however, made a special discovery, simple in its nature, that allowed them to measure the relative size of the earth to the moon. They extended the shape of the earth's shadow on the moon to form a circle, as shown in the diagram "Earth Shadow," thereby judging the diameter of the moon to be roughly one-third of the earth. Notice they were able to grasp the relative size of the moon compared to the earth by a geometrical image—since they could not draw the actual circle in space. A more sophisticated mathematical and philosophical justification of the truth of the image was developed at a later time.

Convinced that the earth and moon were spheres and eager to explore the wonders of the newfound mathematics, a director of the library at Alexandria named Eratosthenes, who lived in the third century B.C., had an idea how to estimate the size of the earth. This idea probably came to him in a flash, but only after he had learned much mathematics and discovered some curious facts. He had read in a papyrus book that at noon on the longest day of the year, June 21, there was a city named Syene, some 500 miles from Alexandria, where sticks or columns cast no shadows. At that time and in that place, the sun was directly overhead. It could be seen as a reflection in the water of a deep well.

Eratosthenes waited until the next June 21 and observed whether shadows occurred at noon in Alexandria. They did. The sun was not directly overhead at the time. It cast a shadow from a stick with an angle of about 7 degrees, as shown in the picture "Sun Ray." What did this mean? Carl Sagan in his book and television series *Cosmos* says, "The only possible answer, . . . was that the surface of the Earth is curved."[4] That is not the only assumption possible. The earth could still be flat, and one could calculate the distance of the sun from the flat earth with a little geometry and trigonometry.[5]

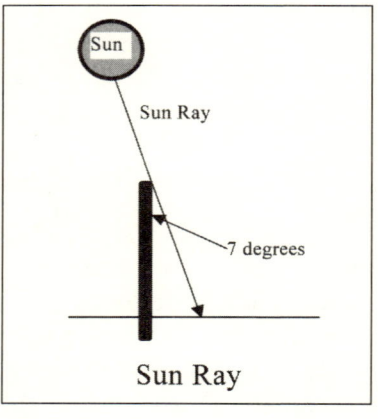

Sun Ray

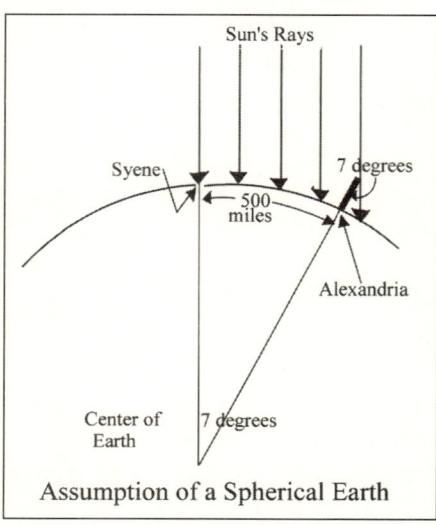

Assumption of a Spherical Earth

It is important to notice at this stage, it is not the mathematics that determines the earth to be a sphere. The mathematics allows one to calculate things, in this case the distance of the sun from the earth, only after fundamental assumptions have been made. Eratosthenes could have made these calculations from a flat earth and come up with the conclusion that the sun is approximately 234,000 miles away from the earth. He did not care about such calculations, because he believed the earth to be a sphere. Under an assumption that the earth is a sphere and the sun is far enough away so its rays come in nearly parallel, the geometry is different. Eratosthenes was able to calculate the circumference and then diameter of the earth to surprising accuracy.[6] I suspect he used geometrical images similar to the diagram "Assumption of a Spherical Earth."

I did not explain the mathematics fully because it is not what is important here. The crucial thing for us to see is that the mathematics allowed these Greeks to spell out the consequences of their assumptions, which were normally conditioned by tactile images. In this case the assumption that the earth is a sphere and the sun is very far away, along with other apparent facts about shadows in Syene and Alexandria, and under the guidance of mathematical knowledge, gives the size of the earth. With that assumption and the knowledge of the relative size of the earth to the moon, the Greek mathematicians could judge the size of the moon. Aristarchus and others of this period, in the third century before the birth of Christ, developed methods to calculate the distance of the moon from the earth and even the size and distance of the sun from the earth. Their work, still under the assumption that the earth is a sphere, was slowly developed into practical navigational tools.

In short, the discovery of mathematics allowed the development of a complex theory about the universe based upon assumptions and images that resulted in a large amount of information about the consequences of the theory. These consequences could often be tested in ordinary experience, thereby tending to confirm or disconfirm the theory. There seemed to be massive confirmation of, and therefore belief in, the assumption that the earth is a sphere. As we have mentioned before, no significant biblical scholar or theologian ever questioned this assumption, certainly not on the basis of the Bible. They may have noted that Isaiah had anticipated a spherical earth, but were quick to comment that the "four corners" was obviously just a figure of speech common to the times. After all, both Isaiah and John had something much more important to say than anything about the mere shape of the earth.

This brief historical survey on the beginning history of astronomy and its relationship to the Bible illustrates a thesis about our understanding of science and religion. I only mention it here; I shall attempt later to illustrate its applicability by other examples.

Thesis 1: Christians normally accept good science. They may then see science as part of theology and contained in the Bible.

This first example has shown that Christians and Christian theology accepted a spherical earth on the basis of the practical scientific discoveries of the culture. In the next section I shall show how this assumption was made a part of theology.

The Earth-Centered Universe

In the fifteenth and sixteenth centuries, enormous controversy developed among Christians about whether the earth or the sun was the center of the universe. The good Christian and scientist Galileo was tried and condemned for heresy and ordered never to teach the sun to be at center. Martin Luther, the founder of the Protestant Reformation, railed against the Christian Copernicus, who had reintroduced the sun-centered theory, as follows: "This fool (Copernicus) wishes to reverse the entire science of astronomy; but sacred Scripture tells us that Joshua commanded the sun to stand still, and not the earth."[7]

Luther's comment is instructive, for it shows that the previous science of astronomy had been thoroughly accepted into Christian theology. Why else would he claim that Joshua intended to speak about astronomy during a prayer in the midst of a battle? Remember, the Israelites with Joshua at their head were in a fierce battle with the Amorites, and Joshua prayed to the Lord: "Sun, stand still at Gibeon, and Moon, in the valley of Aijalon" (Josh 10:12). Does anyone ever seriously consider the scientific structure of the universe, much less proclaim some truth about it, during prayer in a crisis time? I doubt it. I also question whether God was speaking through Joshua about astronomy at such time. Luther could speak of the "fool" Copernicus because he sought to change what everybody believed, including Luther, namely, that the earth did not move. Already "knowing" the truth, Luther felt comfortable quoting a Bible example to confirm it.

The controversy about a *helio* (sun)-centered universe and a *geo* (earth)-centered universe did not begin in the fifteenth and sixteenth centuries. It was engaged much earlier in the second century B.C. by pre-Christian mathematicians and astronomers—and settled for all intents and purposes at that time. Good science became geocentric and was accepted, according to our Thesis 1, into the heart of Christian theology. The early controversy among the scientists about a geocentric or heliocentric universe is a more interesting and certainly a more civil conflict than the one that occurred among the Christian theologians 1700 years later. I shall examine this controversy between the two

Early Mathematical Astronomy

mathematicians and astronomers, Archimedes and Aristarchus, by means of a single sentence from Archimedes's work *The Sand Reckoner*.

Archimedes, born probably in 287 B.C., had great scientific and mathematical authority in his time, further exercised it over the Middle Ages, and maintains it today. He is generally recognized as one of the three greatest mathematicians of all time.[8] He only wrote masterpieces, each one establishing some new area of mathematics and each expressed with a pristine clarity that set the standard for all future mathematics. Archimedes wrote so well that laypersons could understand the basic issues of his thought.

In *The Sand Reckoner*, Archimedes developed a number system—essentially a set of images—that could express any number no matter how large. We now find this task commonplace using a combination of decimal and exponential notation. It was, however, new for Archimedes's day before which very large numbers were often expressed, if at all, by means of ratio. Archimedes introduced both the idea of very large numbers and the symbolism to express them.

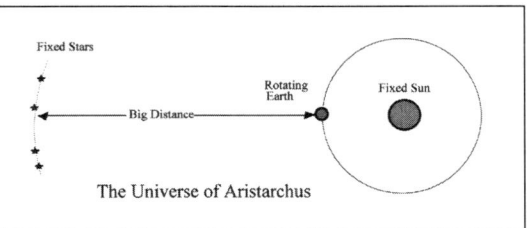

To test the power of his symbolism, Archimedes sought an image for his numbers. A large number would be the number of grains of sand on a seashore. A larger number would be the number of grains of sand on all seashores. An even larger number—this is the number he seeks to express—would be the number of grains of sand that would fill the entire known universe. In order to set the bounds for his large number, Archimedes had to discuss current ideas about the then known universe. In this context he described a recent theory by his contemporary Aristarchus, which we have pictured in "The Universe of Aristarchus."

The description is in two parts. The first part says the sun and stars are fixed and the earth rotates in a circular orbit about the sun. The second part attempts to establish what we might mean by the great distance between the earth (the circle around the sun in which it rotates) and the stars (the sphere in which they reside). We generally believe the first part, except we do not accept that the stars lie in a single sphere. We understand that the stars have different distances from the sun, because we possess both a concept of large numbers and the means to symbolize them. Only Archimedes had this knowledge at the time, a knowledge that was put forward in *The Sand Reckoner*. Aristarchus, however, had to resort to ratio in order to express the second part—there is a great distance between the (circle of the) earth and the (sphere of the) stars.

It was Aristarchus's bumbling attempt to describe large distances by means of ratio that gave Archimedes cause to reject not only the technical description of distance by ratio but also the complete heliocentric theory of Aristarchus. Let us try to untangle Aristarchus's attempt to describe distance by means of ratio and proportion in order to see what he intended to say and why Archimedes did not grasp his intention.

We understand that if distance is described as the ratio between the numbers 15 and 3, we divide 15 by 3 to get a distance of 5. To express the large distance from the (circle of the) earth to the stars, without benefit of the new symbolism of Archimedes, Aristarchus thought he must establish a ratio between two things. These two things are not numbers, but geometrical measures. As mentioned by Archimedes, they are the distance of the stars (in their sphere around the sun) to the sun and the distance of the earth (in its circle around the sun) to the sun. These two measures have a ratio to each other "as the centre of the sphere bears to its surface."[9] The meaning of the surface of a sphere is clear. We can picture it; we can calculate its area. What, however, is the meaning of the center of a sphere? As a point, it has no volume, no surface. Thus, the ratio between the center of a sphere and its surface does not exist. It has no intelligible meaning—at least to Archimedes.

It may have had meaning to Aristarchus because of a conceptual and imaging error derived from the early Pythagoreans. They, and possibly Aristarchus, thought of the unit point as something physical, like an incredibly small round ball. With this image, the ratio between the surface of the sphere and (the surface of its) new center is determinate, a very large number. If we allow the new center of a physical point to become smaller and smaller approaching what we know to be a point, the ratio symbolizing the distance will become larger and larger without bound. I doubt whether Aristarchus had exactly this meaning in mind. He was groping with crude tools to express what he knew to be an enormous distance. Only Archimedes had adequate images to express the large numbers Aristarchus required, a view of numbers Archimedes developed in the very book discussing Aristarchus's theory. Only Archimedes in that day could have understood and championed Aristarchus's sun-centered universe and expressed it in adequate mathematical terminology.

This was one of those very critical times in the history of science, and as it turns out for theology also, when the major figure of science, namely Archimedes, chose badly. He did not deduce badly or generalize badly. Of the two alternate views of the universe, a geocentric one and a heliocentric one, Archimedes by his own volition asserted that the earth is the center of the universe. Why did he make that assertion?

He may have unconsciously argued from his sense experience, or conservatively promoted the familiar assumption. His stated reason for rejecting the Aristarchian hypothesis was, "Since the centre of the sphere has no magnitude, we cannot conceive it to bear any ratio whatever to the surface of the sphere." He concluded, "We conceive the earth to be . . . the centre of the universe."[10] Archimedes apparently rejected the Aristarchian hypothesis because it did not come up to his high standards of mathematical analysis. He did not like the conceptual imaging mistake Aristarchus had made about the nature of a point. Moral: If you ever discover a fundamental truth of the scientific world, you must express it in accurate contemporary style, or it will never be received. Science can be very narrow.

Are mathematicians so narrow-minded, especially the greatest of them, that they reject important new ideas solely because the ideas do not satisfy their sense of proper form? Must we always present new ideas in the images scientists and mathematicians understand? For this most important event in the history of Western thought, cannot we suggest some better emotional reason for Archimedes's rejection of a heliocentric universe?

Suppose you were playing basketball with someone who dribbled around the back of the goal and then shot from outside the regulation playing area and made the hoop. You might cheer her accomplishment, but you would not count the score because she had broken the rules. Basketball is, of course, a game but also can be considered to be an art form similar to ballet. It is a cultural force that drives young players to make the "right moves"—which are closely watched, critically appreciated, and judged rigorously.

When my children were younger, I turned off the popular music on the car radio and switched to something more classical. The immediate reaction from them was negative with a response I now remember: "It sounds as if it's going to get a beat at any time but never does." (In the 1970s, country music would have brought forth the same negative reaction but not the same explanation.) At their age, my children neither understood nor appreciated an art form that is important to a large number of older people. This art form has high standards with many interpreters and critics who evaluate performances. It was quickly judged by children who valued more highly an art medium that spoke directly to them.

Think of Archimedes's rejection of Aristarchus's heliocentric theory as a result of Archimedes's esthetic and rational distaste of considering a ratio between a sphere and a point. He was like children who have their standards about music or basketball players who have their standards about the game. In each case violations of the standards are quickly noticed when they occur, and these violations may be more important than any consideration about skill or "truth." Someone might dismiss the basketball player who could shoot from behind the goal and make a basket, but only at the expense of ignoring a possibly great talent. One can insist on turning off classical (or country) music, but at a cost of potential great enjoyment. Michael Jordan could fail to see the talent of the basketball player, but it would be a major lapse on his part. Isaac Stern could fail to appreciate a brilliant jazz musician, but it would be highly atypical. Archimedes was the only one who could have really understood Aristarchus, but he dismissed him because of an error he perceived in unimportant form. You can almost hear Archimedes say, "Aristarchus doesn't do things my way, and my way is correct," which it was, at least about the nature of a point.

With this boost from the greatest mathematician and scientist of antiquity, who had his blind spots, the earth-centered theory of the universe was fitted well with further adjunct theory and extended to acquire practical utility. Almost all people accepted it as truth. It was the mathematical as well as practical standard for understanding the universe. It became canonized in the second great mathematical and scientific book of antiquity, Ptolemy's *Almagest*,[11] where practical arguments were developed against the heliocentric view. Here is one such argument, though somewhat augmented.

If you move your fist rapidly, you can feel the air going around it. In order for the heliocentric view to explain the apparent movement of the stars, the earth must rotate on its axis once a day. Since we know the size of the earth and the rate of its rotation, we can calculate the velocity at the surface of the earth, which is enormous. If the earth were to rotate, the velocity of the wind at its surface would always be greater than hurricane strength and would always blow in the same direction. We do not observe such winds. Therefore, the assumption that the earth moves is false, and the heliocentric hypothesis is discredited.

In our day we might think it odd that anyone would assume the earth rotated but not its atmosphere. That is because we understand the atmosphere to be local to the earth. If we think of the atmosphere like some unmoving space itself, then the earth rotating in the atmosphere would generate the winds specified by the argument.

The geocentric theory became standard science, reinforcing common sense that the earth does not move. Once Christians believed the accepted science, they used it to proclaim the location of heaven (with God beyond the outer sphere of the stars) and hell (in the center of the earth). They also discovered that the Bible, which appears to claim the earth does not move, confirmed the geocentric position. For example:

> Tremble before him, all the earth. The world is firmly established; it shall never be moved. (1 Chron 16:30)

> The LORD is king, he is robed in majesty; the LORD is robed, he is girded with strength. He has established the world; it shall never be moved. (Ps 93:1)

Should we accept that the very destructive conflict that occurred in the sixteenth century between Christians and Christians—Copernicus and Galileo were Christians as well as Luther and the Catholic theologians—was really an issue between scientific truth and biblical truth? Do the verses just quoted from 1 Chronicles and the Psalms, which are almost the only evidence from the Bible supporting a geocentric position, cause us to reject the contemporary well-nigh universal belief that the earth rotates on its axis? No matter how we take the Bible, I think we could agree that the Bible does not intend to speak primarily about science in these passages.

Why did both the Protestant reformers and the Roman Catholic theologians, who knew the Bible well, react so strongly against Copernicus's restatement of Aristarchus's position? I think there are two major answers, one of them secondary and the other so important that I want to make it the second historical thesis of this book. Here is the secondary reason.

If the theologians had believed that a heliocentric position was legitimate science and was confirmed by experience and measurement, they would have more readily accepted it. This acceptance would have been predicted by the first historical thesis that Christians normally accept good science. Yet, in that day neither theologian nor scientist had the measurements from good instruments necessary to confirm or disconfirm the Copernican sun-centered theory with authority. One of the best examples of this ambiguity was Tycho Brahe's understanding of the universe.

Brahe, through technological innovations in instrumentation, had accumulated the best data available in the sixteenth century about the positions and movements of the stars and planets. After careful consideration in the light of his massive evidence, Brahe asserted that all the planets rotate around the sun, supporting the Copernican theory, with the exception of the earth, which was not a planet. The sun and its whole planetary system, so Brahe believed, rotated around the stable earth, supporting the geocentric theory. We have observed as a secondary reason for the theologians's rejection of Copernican theory: during periods when a new scientific theory cannot be confirmed or disconfirmed scientifically, the new theory does not have the authority to replace an old established scientific theory. The anomalies of the old theory, however, in contrast with the attraction of the new theory, do cause unrest in some scientists and theologians (who in this age were normally the same people).

The main reason for the rejection of the Copernican theory by many Christians, especially the theologians, is now given as an important thesis.

> *Thesis 2. Conflict between science and religion occurs when religion, after accepting science into its theology, engages a new and different science when it arises.*

Christians and their theologians had accepted the geocentric position of the universe for more than fifteen hundred years. Belief that the earth was the center of the universe was based on good authority and was confirmed by massive personal and community experience. This position was accepted as true, believed to be justified by the Bible, written into theology, and championed by classical literature. When the Aristarchian theory proclaiming a sun-centered universe was reintroduced by Copernicus, it appeared to be both bad science and bad theology. It also was seen to conflict with the Bible, but not because the Bible really proclaims an earth-centered universe.

Notes

[1] The diagram was copied with slight modifications from *The Interpreter's Dictionary of the Bible, An Illustrated Encyclopedia*, 4 vols. (New York: Abingdon Press, 1962) 1: 703. Adapted by permission of Abingdon Press.

[2] Donald B. DeYoung, *Astronomy and the Bible: Questions and Answers* (Grand Rapids MI: Baker Book House, 1988) 16–17.

[3] While asserting that "it may be supposed or scientifically demonstrated that the world is of a round or spherical form," Augustine objected to the claim that there were people on the opposite side of the world because there was no historical record in the Bible or elsewhere of their existence. *City of God*, Book XVI, Chapter IX. *Basic Writings of Saint Augustine*, ed. Whitney J. Oates (New York: Random House, 1948) 328.

[4] Carl Sagan, *Cosmos* (New York: Random House, 1980) 14.

[5] There is a right triangle formed with an angle and a side that is known.

[6] One can express the circumference of the earth, symbolized by x, in terms of a ratio between it and the distance 500 miles, which is proportional to the ratio between the angle 7 degrees and the angle of a full circle, 360 degrees. This proportion can be presented as the equation of fractions: $(x/500) = (360/7)$. Solving this equation gives the answer that the circumference of the earth is a little over 25,700 miles.

[7] This quotation is found in many secondary sources, for example: Bertrand Russell, *Religion and Science* (New York: Oxford University Press, 1961) 23. It comes from Luther's *Table Talks*, 1539.

[8] The other two are Newton and Gauss.

[9] Archimedes, *The Sand-Reckoner*, from *The Works of Archimedes*, ed. T. L. Heath (New York: Dover Publications, Inc., original publication date, 1897). 222.

[10] Ibid.

[11] The first was Euclid's *Elements*.

Chapter 2
Greek Mathematics

In the previous chapter I examined the second of the major confrontations between science and Christianity, namely, astronomy. I consider issues associated with mathematics to have caused the first of the engagements between science and Christianity for the following reasons.

The discovery of deductive mathematics in the sixth century B.C. not only preceded the development of astronomy by Eratosthenes, Aristarchus, and Archimedes in the third century B.C., but also provided the intellectual conditions for the successful development of the mathematical aspects of their astronomy. It was these mathematical issues of astronomy that we have shown to be relevant to understanding the conflicts over a geocentric or heliocentric view of the universe, which became important in the relationship between science and religion in the sixteenth century. Although both Greek mathematics and astronomy were developed before the birth of Christ and were available to the early Christian theologians, it was mathematics, not astronomy, that had a profound effect on early, and what became orthodox, Christian theology. The church simply accepted the geocentric universe from astronomy—exemplifying our first thesis. After writing this position into its theology, the church waited until the sixteenth century to engage a conflict over a heliocentric universe, unaware that this was not a conflict between biblical religion and a new astronomy, but between an old science and a new one—exemplifying our second thesis.

During the first and second centuries, however, mathematics engendered images and philosophical perspectives that affected important doctrines of Christianity: God, the soul, the understanding of resurrection, and the problem of faith and reason. Therefore, I consider mathematics not only to be the first historically of the sciences that confronted Christianity, but also the most important of the scientific disciplines to engage Christianity in its developmental stages.

Thesis 3. Any new science is necessarily cloaked in philosophical concepts that can influence religion.

I chose to examine astronomy before mathematics because we could set up the first two of our historical theses in terms of interesting examples—without having to consider seriously what is presented now as our third and last thesis. This is a thesis already introduced in the Introduction that new sciences are born with images, such as the organic (our example was a turnip) or mechanical (our example was a typewriter), that act as powerful assumptions affecting a vision of the world in general and impacting an understanding of religion. These images may be articulated by scientists or philosophers to become what we call the "philosophical aspects of science," "philosophical concepts," or simply "philosophy." Although we looked at geometrical images such as the image of a point in the previous chapter on astronomy, I showed only how these images affected the nature of science, for example, influencing Archimedes to reject the sun-centered universe.

In this chapter, I shall show how images associated with the beginnings of mathematics conditioned general philosophical views about the world that have an ambiguous relationship to science. Initially they may have been necessary to understand the science but later can be modified or abandoned for a different, or sometimes better, philosophical position. In the process, however, these philosophical positions influenced Christian theology considerably, sometimes for the good but often for the bad.

There were three ways the Greeks added philosophical interpretation to their mathematical science, what I call (1) "spiritualism," (2) "the interpretation of unity," and (3) "atomism." We are pursuing this route of analysis of the philosophical assumptions attendant on Greek mathematics not just to gain insight into the development of early Christian doctrine. The philosophical orientations of spiritualism and atomism have an important part to play in the reconciliation of science and religion today, and the interpretation of unity has left its mark on doctrines about God and the soul. These are crucial issues for contemporary theology.

Saint Paul cautions, "No one takes you captive through philosophy and empty deceit, according to human tradition, according to the elemental spirits of the universe, and not according to Christ" (Col 2:8). I take Paul's admonition seriously, for philosophy can in no way take the place of Christian faith. Millions have followed Christ, including most of those in the first-century church without a hint of philosophical knowledge. Others apparently have lost their faith because they accepted what Paul would call "a deceptive philosophy." In order to grapple with the relationship between science and religion, however, it is necessary to understand what philosophical ideas have

Greek Mathematics

been absorbed into theology through science. The only way to keep these philosophical perspectives from being hollow and deceptive is to recognize them when we see them and then examine them for their adequacy and appropriateness. We also may find that some philosophy can have a very creative role in reconciling science and religion. Let us look first at the images and philosophy of spiritualism, one of the three positions influential on early Christian theology that I claim to be derivative from Greek mathematics.

Philosophical Spiritualism

The ideas associated with a philosophical spiritualism are generality, structure, and divinity. Behind these ideas, however, there are more tangible images that illuminate and make intelligible these abstract ideas. Consider the image of all right triangles. The image promotes an idea of generality, namely, the infinitude of all possible right triangles, as well as an idea of the structure of the triangles. This structure is specified by the Pythagorean theorem, which may be stated, *the square on the hypotenuse of a right triangle is equal to the sum of the squares on the other two sides.* Let us look at a crude presentation of the Pythagorean theorem in order to fix the image of right triangles and thereby aid in an interpretation of the philosophical position of spiritualism. Notice, we are seeking to clarify images that present the ideas of generality and structure but not as yet the idea of divinity.

To prove the Pythagorean theorem, we start off with a line of arbitrary length that is divided at an arbitrary point into lengths a and b shown in the picture "Divided Line." Notice, we can fold the line up at its dividing point and create a right triangle with sides a, b, and now c, illustrated in the picture "Folded Line." Construct a square on the unfolded line and join the dividing points creating the shaded triangles in the picture "Square with Triangles." Each shaded triangle has the same shape and area as the original triangle. Now construct another square on the line

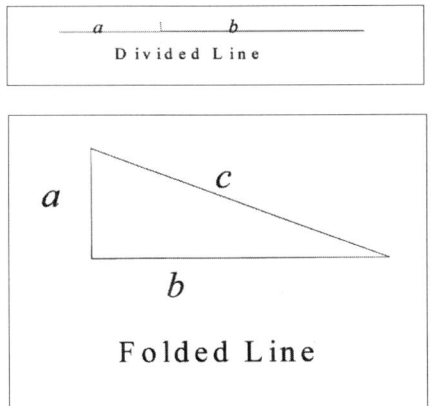

and mark the dividing points *a* and *b* with the same length but with different orientations so that the triangles are positioned as in the picture "Square with Triangles in a Different Order." If we erase the four equivalent triangles from both pictures, we have a square on side *c* remaining in the "Square with Triangles" and two squares, one on side *a* and one on side *b*, remaining in the "Square with Triangles in a Different Order." It

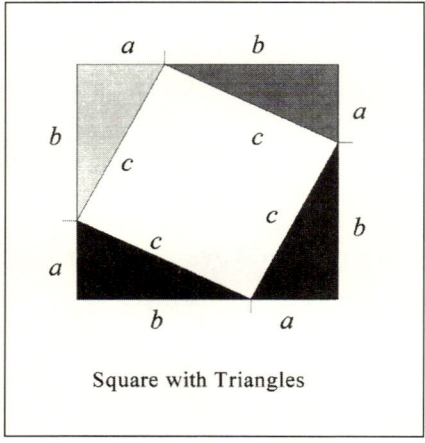

Square with Triangles

is at this point we can see the utter brilliance of the Pythagoreans. They not only argued that the remaining areas are equal; they elevated their reasoning to a general principle that can be expressed by the third common notion of Euclid: "If equals be subtracted (taken away) from equals, the remainders are equal."[1] By accepting this axiom, we will have shown that for any right triangle, the square on *c* is equal to the square on *a* plus the square on *b*.

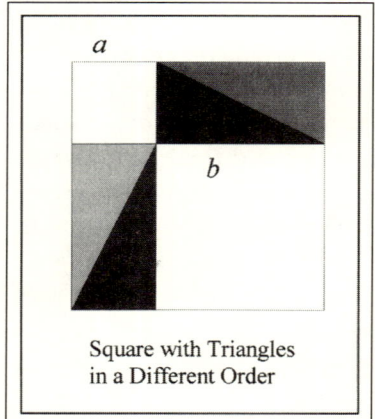

Square with Triangles in a Different Order

We do not easily appreciate the nature or the magnitude of what the early Greek mathematicians did. They achieved a level and quality of abstract generality never before obtained. Assume *any* line of any length whatsoever. Then divide it at *any* point. Their conclusion was: *Any* right triangle has the Pythagorean relationships. To the question "How many right triangles are there?" we would respond, "An indefinite or infinite number of them." The Pythagoreans showed exact structural relations of infinitudes of things. The Babylonians, who preceded them, had discovered the Pythagorean relationships only for a small number of right triangles. There is a great difference between establishing the properties of a few known objects and *all* possible infinity of them. The Pythagoreans not only produced the first mathematical proofs of Western thought but also discovered the techniques of rational analysis necessary for them to be proofs.

Greek Mathematics 35

I have used the image of right triangles interpreted by the Pythagorean theorem to give examples of the primary ideas of a philosophical position of spiritualism, namely, the ideas of generality and structure. I now turn to stories, rather than images, that may illustrate the idea of divinity, which is the third characteristic of the position of spiritualism. These stories are about how the earliest Greek mathematicians (and philosophers) understood the divinity of things associated with their mathematical or philosophical insights. We shall look initially at the Pythagoreans and then the earlier Milesians, who preceded the Pythagoreans historically and who include the first of the Greek mathematicians and philosophers, Thales, as well as his students Anaximander and Anaximenes. First, let us examine stories about the Pythagoreans.

The Pythagoreans deified the individual mathematical objects: the lines, triangles, and some of their numbers, within the medium of logic. When in the mood of logic, they believed they could participate with divine things. Does this sound odd or a bit "spooky" for the original founders of Western deductive mathematics? The Pythagoreans, to our view, were a strange bunch. For one thing, they believed in reincarnation, a theme found infrequently in Greek thought.[2]

Westerners seek eternal life. Easterners who accept the eternal round of birth and death of reincarnation already have eternal life and do not like it. The Pythagoreans, like all who believe in reincarnation, sought some means of transcending birth, death, and rebirth. You may have guessed what it was. Participation with the divine objects of mathematics within the context of logic provided (in the Greek) "ecstasy," literally a "standing outside of" the degrading repeated rounds of birth and death. This Pythagorean mathematical reality offered a way out of the reincarnation cycle and provided a kind of religious salvation. Although we may not identify the experience as religious, we may acknowledge having some of this feeling of ecstasy when we solve a problem logically, say, prove something to be true we had not known before. In this process, however, we can only begin to understand the intensity of religious ecstasy of those who discovered proof itself.

A number of years ago my affable companion, lover, and Christian wife of now forty years took a course on hallucinogenic drugs to prepare herself better to teach and to deal with her junior high school students. Respectful of the importance of reason even for seventh graders, who have been likened to first graders with hormones, she prepared a paper on "Reason, Drugs, and the Pythagoreans." Perhaps more fun than seriously academic, her thesis was that as the hallucinogenic mushroom or bean sources of the Elysian mystery religions began to dry up, the Pythagoreans discovered and substituted mathematical reason in the drug's place as their primary ecstatic source. The point is, Western reason began among the early Greeks not as a practical attempt to manage the physical world but as a means of vibrant, emotional, even religious experience. Now to stories about the Milesians.

All subsequent Greeks attribute the beginnings of both mathematics and philosophy to Thales of Miletus. He contributed a significant dose of generality to practical mathematics, although we do not know exactly what, and established a stunning philosophical generalization that has informed all Western thought since his day. Thales claimed there is one universal substance that underlies and explains all things. This substance, which he called "*arche*," is structured and divine. It is the divinity of *arche* we want to understand. First, let us acknowledge it was probably Thales's implicit attempts at proof[3] that may have led to his assertion of the generality of *arche*. Further, let us attempt to understand this generality of *arche* in terms of contemporary images.

The idea of an *arche* is a presupposition behind so much of our scientific thought today. What are all things composed of? Matter, energy, force fields, or some other discovery or construct of contemporary physics? You may not know exactly which one. Neither do I. We all, however, seem to believe there is some general explanatory matter that makes sense of science.

It might be helpful for us to consider when we began to believe there is a unified essence of the universe. Was it during our preteens? Probably not. Early teens? Maybe. Middle or late teens, likely, with our having some beginning insights into the issue. We may have finally become comfortable with *arche* (without naming it) because the idea of mass became a proper assumption for physics or chemistry. *Arche* was thereby made conventional or practical. No more embarrassment about the intermittent eerie feelings and ideas about some semireligious idea that had tinges of "the unity of all things." Or the feeling that not only my cat and I had some basic bond, but also that I and the grasshopper I squished were joined at a common soul level. We may have noticed that the feeling of a really general substance differed from our childhood ideas of God who exists in the universe (the Bible says "in heaven"). The *arche* does not exist in anything; it is everything.

To get at an appropriate image for the divinity of *arche*, we must look at Thales's students, Anaximander and Anaximines. The students of Thales believed in the existence of an *arche*, but disagreed on its exact nature. Thales thought it was water. His older student Anaximander, whose flat-earth astronomy was presented in the first chapter, said it was *apeiron*, an indefinite or infinite substance of some sort. The most challenging idea came from Thales's younger student Anaximenes. He said that *arche* was air or spirit, that is, it was one and the same, air and spirit.

The original Greek word for both air and spirit is *pneuma*. We have pneumatic tires, for example. Also, the word for spirit in the New Testament is *pneuma*. A literal translation of Holy Spirit is thus "holy air," but not quite. A better translation would be "holy breath," that is, the breath of God. Translating *pneuma* as breath gets close to the meaning of the personal aspect of this *arche*. Many ancient peoples believed that breath is what actually enlivens a body. It is the true subjectivity that characterizes the uniqueness of a person. When dead, the breath and personality depart. For Anaximenes, *pneuma* was also the air that encompasses and contains individual humans. It is outside of human subjectivity. When a person dies, her subjectivity joins the generally objective wholeness of air. Anaximenes attempted to unify subjectivity and objectivity by thinking of breath and air as one, the single *pneuma*, which he declared to be divine. The divine outside *pneuma* is air, and the divine inside *pneuma* is breath. Both are unified as the underlying *arche*, which we could call "spirit."

Anaximenes's brilliance went even further. We have asserted that the *arche*, *pneuma*, is divine. It is also structured. Anaximenes postulated that quantitative changes of *pneuma* allow us to understand qualitative differences. His examples were condensation and rarefaction. Crudely, according to Anaximenes, if you condense air, you get rocks. If you rarefy rocks, you get air. These changes can be described mathematically. Notice that in these few sentences we have expressed what was later to become the genius of modern science: we can exhibit emotional, subjective, and qualitative ideas in terms of quantitative distinctions.

I think the idea of a subjective breath, extended generally to become all things, characterized by mathematical structure, and understood as divine, is the best (certainly not the only) image for understanding philosophical spiritualism and its subsequent development. This image, as interpreted by Anaximenes, says something very new and powerful about religion. If you can describe all things by quantitative changes of *pneuma* (breath, air, or spirit), and if *pneuma* is divine, you can plumb the depths of divinity by rational mathematical means. Notice, I did not say that one can investigate the nature of the Hebrew-Christian God by mathematics. The mathematicians of early Greek thought did not personify *arche*. It was divine, but not a transcendent person. The One Personal God was a unique contribution of the Hebrews. We can understand, however, the desire of Christian theologians, who all used Greek mathematical thought, to explore rationally the nature of the Hebrew-Christian God. This attempt brought forth theology, literally *logos* of *theos*, the logic of God. It also brought forth an intensified problem of faith and reason, which I shall discuss shortly.

In summary, there are three major philosophical doctrines associated with early Greek mathematics that I am labeling as philosophical spiritualism.

- Generality—There is a universal substance, content, or matter from which everything is constructed or by which everything is explained.
- Structure—This universal substance, content, or matter is structured and can be known through mathematics or its logic.
- Divinity—The universal substance, content, or matter is divine. Knowledge of, or participation with, this divinity can impart a feeling of religious salvation.

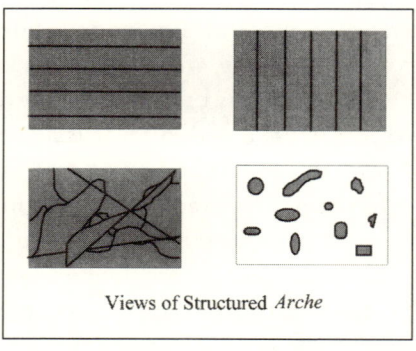

Views of Structured *Arche*

For the first assumption, think of the universe as an empty rectangle and fill it in with a gray substance, the *arche*. Everything in the universe is made of this gray stuff. For the second assumption, think of *arche* as structured in a variety of ways, four of which are symbolically illustrated in the picture "Views of Structured *Arche*."

Notice that the organization of *arche* in the lower right figure consists of individual or separated things (a spiritual atomism). Everything that is, is still *arche*; the "space" between atoms is considered as nothing. This atomism is not a dead atomism of materialism but one in which the atoms have subjectivity or divinity, symbolized by gray. We shall reserve pure black as the symbol for an atom that has no structure, subjectivity, or divinity. Assumption three says that whatever organization applies, *arche* is always (perhaps different shades of) gray in this sense, but never black. There are no basic things that are altogether without divinity.

The position of spiritualism held by the early Greeks was what we might call a "pan-spiritualism." Every thing that is, is considered to be divine, at least in part. This view was not acceptable to Christian theologians, because their God was understood to be transcendent. God created the world separate from God. God does not make up the world with God's very being. Christians therefore rejected pantheism (the Hebrew-Christian God constitutes all things) in favor of a revision of spiritualism that interprets humans and God to each have separate spirits, which are in relation. What about other nonhuman living things? Do they have spirits? Theologians answered hesitantly because they did not want to attribute any divinity to earthly beings, which was idolatry—a violation of the first of the Ten Commandments. The Old Testament historical arena was between God and humans. Nature was not much a part of this venture. Yet any attempt to relate science to Christianity requires some theological analysis of nature.

One way to engage the discussion between science and the Christian religion is to disavow pan-spiritualism or pantheism (everything is divine) in favor of a pan-experientialism (all things have some subjectivity or sentience). In this view some things—namely, God—are divine; others are not. Pan-experientialism contrasts sharply with the philosophical position of atomism that says no (basic) things have subjectivity. I shall describe the philosophical position of pan-experientialism further in later chapters and especially as it is compared with atomism. First, however, let us look at the philosophical interpretation of unity.

The philosophical doctrines that were intimately associated with early mathematics are surprising to most people. We do not today go to mathematics classes and expect to get salvation or even a feeling of exhilaration. These and most other philosophical associations have been clearly separated, at least in principle, from contemporary mathematics and science. This does not mean that they have not laid claim to Christian doctrine in the past or do not influence our theological ideas in the present.

Philosophical Interpretation of Unity

The second philosophical addition to Greek mathematics is what we call "the interpretation of unity." It is about the number one or unit point.

This philosophical theme in Greek mathematics has had an unusual, indeed peculiar, influence on both theology and science, manifesting itself on the one hand in the doctrines of a strictly unchanging God and immortal soul, and on the other hand, in the scientific idea of materialism. Let us look first at numbers, particularly the number one.

We can symbolize numbers by lengths of line segments; for example, the segment └──┴──┴──┘ can stand for the number three where └──┘ is a unit length defined arbitrarily. We also can

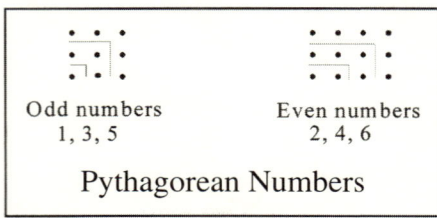

signify the number three by its numerical symbol 3. The Pythagoreans used both kinds of symbolism, except their numerical signs were made up of patterns of numerical points. For example, the numbers 2 and 3 were symbolized as •• and •••. Curiously, the Pythagoreans grouped numbers into gnomons (the pattern ⦂• is a gnomon indicating 3) that resulted in rectangular shapes of numbers to which they gave bizarre interpretations. In the picture "Pythagorean Numbers," notice that the odd numbers when extended always have a square shape, whereas the even numbers when extended have a varying rectangular shape. The Pythagoreans called the odd numbers the "square" numbers, and the even numbers the "oblong" ones. They also called the odd numbers "good," "male," "resting," and "light," and contrasted them with the even numbers that were to them bad, female, moving, and darkness. These numerological attributes of numbers did not take a significant hold in philosophy, science, or Christian theology. One aspect of the interpretation of their symbolism, in addition to their logic, did have profound influence, however—their interpretation of the number one or the unit point.

We interpret the geometrical point as indivisible because it has no dimension to divide. We agree with Archimedes against Aristarchus. The Pythagoreans understood the geometrical point as physically existing but also as strictly indivisible. They extended this characteristic to an arbitrarily defined unit distance, say └──┘, and claimed that it also could not be divided. You should object and say that we can divide └──┘ into halves or thirds or any other division. The Greek mathematicians could not and did not divide a unit line segment into parts, because they had no systematic understanding of fractions. Instead, they would redefine a new unit and say, for example, that └──┘ is made up of two units of size ⌊__⌋. We normally count 1, 2, 3 and recognize the first number to be 1. They claimed that the first number was 2, not 1, because they believed that unity was of an entirely different order than 2, 3, 4. Unity is the means by which we establish and measure the other numbers. By virtue of its use as a standard, it both transcends and gives meaning to the numbers.

Try to imagine what a *physical* point would look like. To our minds, a physical point is a contradiction because anything physical must have some extension, which is exactly what a point does not have. To the Pythagoreans, however, their early conception of a point was physical and *indivisible*—they had not yet grasped the idea of a point without extension. Think of this kind of point as having the size of a period at the end of this sentence. Magnified, it would look something like the picture called "A Point." Now try to think of this point as indivisible. This is hard to do with the enlarged point. A

Pythagorean point, however, may be so small and dense that no one could cut it or smash it. Supposedly, one could not even think about how to divide it. It was seen to have no internal geometrical structure.

I am not saying that these Pythagorean conceptual mistakes dominated philosophical and theological thinking about unity from then on. I am suggesting that whenever philosophers or theologians thought seriously about the nature of unity, which they did with great interest, they quite naturally assumed that unity is strictly indivisible. This happened to Parmenides (a renegade Pythagorean) when he thought about the unity of the world, to Socrates when he thought about the unity of the soul, and to Christian theologians Augustine and Aquinas when they thought about the unity of the soul and the unity of God.

Is your soul eternal? Socrates argued that the soul is eternal for two reasons: (1) It is unified, and (2) as we now know in Greek mathematical thought, unity can suffer no division. No possible division means no possible change. No possible change means that the soul must never decay and, therefore, must be eternal. The soul also participates with the divine mathematical ideas, which also are

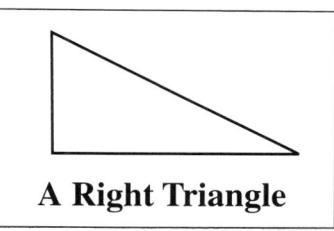

unchanging.[4] Tell me, where is the right triangle pictured on the previous page? Is it strictly on the page? No, what I have drawn is not a true right triangle. The pictured triangle's right angle is not exact; its lines have actual physical width and are not perfectly straight. Furthermore, physicists tell us its molecules are in violent motion. That is not what we mean by a right triangle. If the triangle is not here before us, where is it? The Greek mathematicians (with and after Plato) answered: It is in a transcendent realm where it never changes, unlike the triangle we see that can be erased or folded.

Socrates, Augustine, and most orthodox Christian theologians have argued: If the soul can contemplate, and therefore has company with, such unchanging mathematical ideas, it too can be understood to be immortal—just like the mathematical ideas. We have attempted to show how two images from Greek mathematics, an indivisible point and an unchanging right triangle, have affected the understanding of a human soul. Under these influences, the human soul was understood to be eternal.

Does the Bible affirm an eternal soul? No! The New Testament doctrine is resurrection of the body. There are forty references to resurrection of the body in the New Testament and none to an eternal soul. There is not even a hint that the soul may be eternal. The soul is the personal presence that is part of a mortal body. On numerous occasions Jesus indicates that the soul may be lost or destroyed. Check your concordance (or computer database) to confirm the number of times the Bible refers to eternal soul and the number of times it refers to resurrection, which means resurrection of the body. I think you will be surprised, perhaps astonished, that the doctrine of an eternal soul has been imported to Christian theology by the greatest of orthodox theologians not from the Bible but from mathematical considerations via Greek philosophy.

Quick, do you think God changes? If you were impulsive enough to answer, you probably said "No." We may think variability in human character is a defect. So much more so for God "with whom there is no variation or shadow due to change" (Jas 1:17) and who shows an "unchangeable character of his purpose" (Heb 6:17). Following Greek philosophy about unity, however, Christian theologians went much further than stating that God's character is steady. God, they claimed, like unity, does not change at all in any respect. God is, to use the philosophical word, *immutable*. In their enthusiasm for Greek ideas arising from mathematics, the theologians proclaimed a nonbiblical doctrine, which unfortunately became strict orthodoxy for succeeding generations.

Have you ever loved someone without your being changed by him or her? Do not we get both joy and hurt and a variety of other emotions from caring? A major aspect of love is to undergo modification by the one loved. The gospel is that God so loved the world, God came as human in Jesus and suffered passion on our behalf! And God did not and does not change ever? God has no compassion for us that modifies God one whit? If we have to choose between a doctrine of the strict immutability of God and one that acknowledges God's love, most of us would gladly give up the essentially philosophical position in order to celebrate the experiential one. Augustine and Aquinas, who accepted ideas of both the love of God and God's immutability, had a theologically difficult time reconciling the two. I do not believe they were successful. From a strictly mathematical point of view, the Pythagorean idea of unity was an error. The influence of the idea of unity on a doctrine of God has been confusing and harmful. This was not its only bad influence. When the Greek atomists (next section) considered the unity of atoms, they thought of them, strangely like the orthodox Christian view of God, to be strictly indivisible.

Greek Philosophical Atomism

The atomism of the Greeks differed in one crucial respect from contemporary scientific atomism. The atoms of the Greeks were understood to have no internal structure, whereas the lowest nucleon of contemporary physics has an incredibly rich internal structure whose actual properties are the focus of millions of dollars of research.

Let us try to understand Greek atomism by recalling as an image a familiar print by M. C. Escher, titled Development I.[5] At the top of this print there are gray irregular-shaped pieces, as illustrated in the diagram "Some Atoms." Let us think of these as hard, impervious atoms in motion, guided by an impersonal necessity to collide, stick to, or bounce off other atoms. If one follows zigzag diagonally in this print, the atoms combine in subsequent stages to form a good-looking and active black lizard that then disintegrates, resulting finally in the same formless patches of atoms at the bottom of the drawing.

Some Atoms

I intend this example to symbolize the material atomism of the Greek philosophers Leucippus and Democritus (fifth century B.C.). Their philosophy was born in controversy, for they followed some but threw out other of the major tenants of Parmenides, whom we mentioned briefly as extending the indivisible nature of Pythagorean atoms to apply to the whole world. Parmenides, himself a maverick Pythagorean, rejected Pythagorean multiple mathematical objects and claimed that reality must be exclusively and singly unified, showing Wholeness, that is, without spatial character or any internal activity whatsoever. That the world was unchanging, in spite of its appearances otherwise, was an intolerable position for Leucippus and Democritus who were primarily interested in the sensible experience of things that *move* and have *shapes*. Yet they transferred the properties of the Parminidean Wholeness and Pythagorean points to the interiors of their individual microscopic atoms.

Although they may have an infinitude of different shapes on the outside, the atoms have no interior relations. Inside they have no structure, certainly no divinity and no interesting properties—because they have no properties at all. What kind of structure do you see *inside* the single atom, which we have called "An Atom"? Nothing when you are really inside except plain blackness.[6] As understood by Greek atomists, all things real are combinations of these utterly bland bits of undifferentiated stuff. All activities of the larger bodies are results of the activities of the much smaller ones.

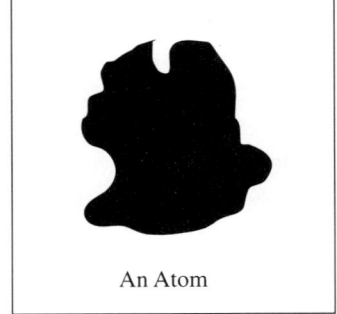

An Atom

Greek atomism is not contemporary scientific atomism. Greek atomism, however, has a certain appeal that modern atomism does not. We are all driven to try to interpret complex things by means of simpler ones. Cells are understood in terms of their chemistry. Chemicals make sense in terms of their molecules, molecules in terms of their atoms, atoms in terms of their nucleons, and nucleons in terms of their—quarks? We are not sure what component of a nucleon gives it the best explanation. We suspect there is no one final particle that can explain the nucleon fully because what we know about nucleons does not explain the atom fully. Atoms do not explain molecules fully, and ultimately molecules do not explain cells and then humans fully. The nucleon seems to be more than the sum of its parts. Certainly the atom is more complex than some combination of its simpler parts. The idea that there may not be any ultimately simple atoms adds a humbling and annoying complexity to our world. No wonder Greek atomism and its child materialism are so popular. Greek atomism has an element of simplicity that is satisfying emotionally. The real world is not always so simple.

Theology

There was very little influence, if any, exerted on the New Testament by the images of mathematics or its attendant philosophical ideas. The New Testament is primarily about what Jesus said and did, and, like any good historical narrative, presents a religious interpretation of the meaning of his life, death, resurrection, ascension, and anticipated coming again by its authors, whom most Christians believe were inspired by God. During the following centuries, however, the Christian religion began to be interpreted by the best of Christian minds, many of whom were well trained in classical Greek mathematics and philosophy. They had no choice but to use the finest of their abilities—and tools—in the service of the Christian religion. Their primary tool, a gift of Greek mathematics and philosophy, which the New Testament writers did not possess, was rational analysis, the direct child of mathematics. And so theology, a Greek word meaning *logos* of *theos*—the logic of God—was born.

The major theologians—Augustine and Aquinas followed by Luther and Calvin—were not just concerned with an abstract knowledge of a transcendent God, but with the meaning of a God who became truly human, suffered for our sins, was brutally executed and rose again from the dead. Because they were challenged by rational criticism, as all theologians, philosophers, and scientists must be, they responded by using reasoned arguments to present the faith. This rational mode of theology attests to the validity of our first thesis. The Christian theologians accepted the best of early mathematics, which was the method of rational analysis and argument, and incorporated it into the very heart of Christian theology.

They ran into major difficulties immediately, and the problem of faith and reason was born. We listed the characteristics of philosophical spiritualism derived from mathematics as:

- Generality—There is a universal substance, content, or matter from which everything is constructed or by which everything is explained.
- Structure—This universal substance, content, or matter is structured and can be known through mathematics or its logic.
- Divinity—The universal substance, content, or matter is divine. Knowledge of, or participation with, this divinity can impart a feeling of religious salvation.

Notice, in this Greek perspective, the proper way to learn about the nature of divinity is through rational analysis. This divinity is presumed to have a structured being that is accessible to those methods that give us knowledge of structure, namely logic (the logic initially developed for mathematics). When theologians use their reason to argue for and to protect the faith, even they begin to slip into the mode that says the results of their reasoning are most important.

When Moses went up on Mount Sinai, was all that happened to him and the people of Israel just a result of his reasoning or thinking?

> On the morning of the third day there was thunder and lightning, as well as a thick cloud on the mountain, and a blast of a trumpet so loud that all the people who were in the camp trembled. . . . Mount Sinai was wrapped in smoke, because the LORD had descended upon it in fire . . . while the whole mountain shook violently. . . . Moses would speak and God would answer him in thunder. (Exod 19:16–19)

Did Jesus just think about the cross and say to his disciples, "I now have the correct ideas about suffering"? Or was he in deep personal anguish during the crucifixion: "My God, my God, why have you forsaken me?" (Matt 27:46). Although succumbing to the techniques of argument, the theologians recognized that there is a mode of encounter with God in history that transcends any logical analysis. Why else would Jesus call on us to act, perhaps to suffer and die, rather than just passively to think and learn? Why do Christians eat and drink of the Lord's Supper instead of merely thinking about or analyzing it? The patterns of how one gets religious knowledge are clearly different in early Hebrew and Christian thought from those of Greek rational and mathematical analysis. Yet both seek a religious reality. The Hebrews and Christians seek encounter with a historically active God. The Greek mathematicians and philosophers seek identification with a structured, though not historically active, divine reality. Any attempt to establish an appropriate relationship between science and religion must engage these two major but differing traditions.

Notes

[1] Euclid, *Elements*, trans. Thomas L. Heath, *The Thirteen Books of Euclid's Elements*, 2d ed. 3 vols. (New York: Dover Publications, Inc., 1956) vol 1, 155, my parentheses.

[2] Empedocles speaks, for example, of a sinner wandering "thrice ten thousand seasons . . . being born throughout that time in the forms of all manner of mortal things and changing one baleful path of life for another." G. S. Kirk and J. E. Raven, *The Presocratic Philosophers*. (Cambridge: University Press, 1957) 351.

[3] Thales may have grasped intuitively some theorems of geometry, such as the side-angle-side theorem of congruent triangles, but it is doubtful he ever produced what we have called an explicit "proof of the theorem."

[4] "When the soul inquires alone by itself, it departs into the realm of the pure, the everlasting, the immortal and the changeless, and being akin to these it dwells always with them whenever it is by itself, . . . and remains always the same and unchanging with the changeless." *Phaedo*, 79d, trans. H. N. Fowler, *Loeb Classical Library* (Cambridge MA.: Harvard University Press, 1958).

[5] M. C. Escher, "Development I," *The Graphic Work of M. C. Escher* (London: Pan/Ballantine, 1973) 16. Permission requested.

[6] Blackness is a symbol for no colors or other relations.

II.
Classical Science
Its Challenge by Contemporary Science, And Issues of Modern Theology

Chapter 3
Newtonian Mechanics

In the chapter on early astronomy I showed how Archimedes, the first of the three greatest mathematicians of all time, conditioned fifteen hundred years of thought and theology by a failure to see mathematically what his contemporary Aristarchus intended. Although Archimedes justified rejecting Aristarchus's theory on mathematical grounds, it was not the mathematics that prompted him to see the universe as earth-centered, but a flawed physical judgment on his part. The community of Christians accepted the erroneous position of Archimedes confirmed by Ptolemy and other astronomers and incorporated a geocentric view of the universe into their theology. This theology was radically challenged by a reintroduction of the theory of Aristarchus by Copernicus more than a millennium later.

In the chapter on Greek mathematics I presented three different but interrelated philosophical positions that were associated with the images of Greek mathematics, what I have called "spiritualism," "the idea of unity," and "atomism." The rationalism of spiritualism had a profound impact on the problem of faith and reason among Christians. The idea of unity affected Christian doctrines of God and the human soul as well as conditioning the philosophical position of atomism. The importance of the assumptions of atomism will become apparent in this chapter.

We now look at Isaac Newton (1642–1727), the second of the three greatest mathematicians of all time, and at his brilliant discovery of the mathematics of calculus that gave intellectual "teeth" to his laws of motion. Then, in a pattern recognizable from the last two chapters, I shall point out a set of philosophical assumptions associated with Newton's science and mathematics that were to many indistinguishable from his mathematics and science at the time. These philosophical attitudes that developed from science had a profound effect on modern theology and even reach to an interpretation of the meaning of the Bible.

As a Christian, Newton wrote more theology than he did mathematics or science. It is, however, his mathematical and scientific accomplishments that are remembered. They have had a more profound influence on our theology today than his strictly religious works.

Newton's Science

The calculus invented by Newton solved two apparently minor mathematical problems: (1) how to find the slope of any line tangent to a general curve and (2) how to find areas bounded by lines and curved shapes different from those described by Greek mathematics. The remarkable thing is, the theory that allowed finding slopes of lines also allowed exact characterization of rates of change including velocities and accelerations. The techniques that allowed calculation of general areas by sums of "infinitesimal areas"[1] also allowed exact calculation of other important physical values such as mass and force. Let us not go further into the mathematical details, but rather point out that Newton's calculus, like other mathematical systems we have observed among the Greeks, can not only clarify the ideas of science but also allow various deductions from physical assumptions.

Newton's physical assumptions included three laws of motion that with the calculus can be simplified into a single expression called the "law of acceleration" expressed: *force is the product of mass times acceleration.* His law of gravitation: *the force of attraction between two physical bodies is proportional to the masses of the bodies and inversely proportional to the square of the distance between them,* along with the law of acceleration, form together Newton's fundamental scientific or mathematical (as distinguished from philosophical) hypotheses about the world. They are the assumptions from which the science of Newton flows and may be symbolized algebraically:

(1) $F = ma$

(2) $F = \dfrac{GmM}{r^2}$

where F is force, r is the distance between two masses m and M, and G is an empirically determined gravitational constant.

Let us see how these assumptions can be spelled out into some consequences. Remember the example from Ptolemy's *Almagest* where the argument was developed that if the earth rotated on its axis, there would always be hurricane winds at its surface blowing in the same direction? We discovered the erroneous assumption of this example; namely, the argument assumed that air enveloping the earth does not rotate with it. Newton's laws allow us to gain the insight that the air should rotate with the earth. How is this so?

The explanation requires examining the meaning of acceleration, which is calculated as the rate of change of velocity. Velocity is the rate of change of distance with respect to time. Notice, I am using ideas of calculus to explain the meaning of fundamental terms, velocity and acceleration. Newton's law of acceleration tells us that if there is no outside force on the air, then there is no acceleration of it. If there is no acceleration, the velocity of the air is constant once it is established. Newton's law of acceleration, however, is talking about velocity in a straight line. Would not the air tend to go in a straight line and escape from a rotating earth as it acted exclusively under this law? The answer is Yes. Why does not the air escape?

The law of gravitation tells that us the air is attracted to the earth. It turns out that the force of attraction of the air to the earth corresponds exactly to the force (caused by the acceleration due to the changing direction of velocity) that would cause the air to fly from the earth as explained by the law of acceleration. Both laws together, with calculus, predict that the atmosphere of the earth should rotate with it. Newton's scientific theory allowed people to notice as a fact that the air of the earth was relatively stable around it, but limited to enveloping the earth. It could not be presumed that air was everywhere and stable in the universe, for this would entail by the same laws the conclusion of the *Almagest* that velocities of winds at the surface of the earth would be horrendous.

This is but one example of Newton's mathematical and scientific structure that seemed to many observers to fit everywhere in the heavens and on the earth. Newton was able to predict the movements of the moon around the earth and the planets around the sun as well as predict where a rock would fall if thrown with a certain force at a particular angle. New planets were "discovered" before they were actually seen because of apparent anomalies in movements of the known planets. A practical physics developed called "kinematics" that described the forces, velocities, and movements of ordinary things. Because the mathematical theory was so precise, both astronomers and terrestrial physicists knew what facts to look for, and when they found them, they became additional evidence of the confirmation of Newton's astronomy and physics.

Newton's astronomy was an extension and modification of the astronomy of Copernicus (and of course Aristarchus). It was not until the publication of Newton's *Principia* that scientists and many theologians became convinced that the Copernican assumptions about a sun-centered universe were at last scientifically confirmed. Should we be surprised that many theologians, including most of the church community in England, accepted Newton's science as true and therefore fit to be included as a part of theology according to our first thesis that Christians normally accept good science? Why did not the church resist more? Probably because Newton's science had exquisite balance of accumulated facts and brilliant theory that, in almost revelatory form, gave clarity and assurance to the truth of the sun-centered universe. Before we consider the theological reaction to Newton's science, let us examine the philosophical assumptions of Newton, which seem to have had an even more intense effect on theology than his science.

Newton's Philosophy

There are two major philosophical orientations of Newtonian science: mechanism and Newton's understanding of the scientific method. Newton argues for what we call his philosophical assumption of mechanism in the Preface to the First Edition of his masterpiece *Mathematical Principles of Natural Philosophy*, commonly called *Principia* from its Latin title. His scientific method is described in his "Rules of Reasoning in Philosophy," which is the title of the beginning section of Book III of *Principia*. Notice, the name of *Principia* clearly claims the book is about natural philosophy, whereas scientists have traditionally recognized it as one of the greatest books ever published about science. By this unconscious device, Newton's philosophical assumptions get thought of, and are taught, as science. I believe we can distinguish the science, which is the mathematics and assumptions such as the laws of acceleration and gravitation (1 and 2 above) from the philosophy, which I now attempt to describe. We look first at mechanism, whose ideal image, of course, is a machine.

Newton presented the science and mathematics of *Principia* normally in geometric form, which was the classical medium of mathematics established by Euclid's *Elements*. Surprisingly, Newton's initial development of mechanism is set forth in *Principia* as an interpretation of the nature of geometry. Newton's argument put simply might go something like this: The world is described scientifically by mathematics. Mathematics is geometry. Geometry is universal mechanics, so what we are describing is mechanical in nature. Therefore, the world we describe by science is a machine. The image you should have in mind is a household or industrial machine such as a windmill or steam engine, not a modern electronic one, such as a computer.

The universal machine is composed of parts, which themselves are also machines made up of the smallest kind of particles. These minimal particles are "extended, and hard and impenetrable, and movable and endowed with their proper inertia."[2] Newton emphasizes the importance of this sentiment by saying immediately, "And this is the foundation of all philosophy."[3] Newtonianism is a kind of atomism. Remember, the atoms of Leucippus were also extended, hard, impenetrable, and movable, but what Leucippus could only name as the reason for the movements of the atoms, Newton could give a supremely sophisticated mathematical description. The emphasis of the Greek atomists was on the atoms and not on the mathematics of their movement. The emphasis of Newtonian mechanics was not on the atoms, but on the mathematical principles that described their movement and the movement of the larger bodies that are the combination of the atoms.

Is it necessary that we associate a mechanical philosophy with Newtonian science? Absolutely not. Newton's contemporary Leibniz, who also independently invented the calculus and developed physical principles complementary to those of Newton, established a philosophical position that was nonmechanical. It emphasized multiple and independent organisms called "monads," which because of their participation directly with God had a kind of divinity or at least subjectivity. These monads were not the grand machine of Newton in which humans (with souls and subjectivity) were an exception to a mechanistic rule.

We may think it is perfectly natural that science is mechanistic. This shows the influence Newton's philosophy has had on us. Science need not be mechanistic. Mechanism is one of a number of philosophical perspectives that can be brought to the mathematical theories of science.

If mechanism seems a natural part of science, the second of Newton's major philosophical orientations, namely, his scientific method, will be even more familiar to us. Put simply, we must go from facts to theories. Newton explains that we must "inquire diligently into the properties of things . . . by experiments, and . . . proceed later to hypotheses for the explanation of . . . things. . . ."[4] In this section Newton claims to be philosophizing, whereas Bertrand Russell (mathematician and philosopher of the early twentieth century) echoing Newton says: "*Science* [my emphasis] starts, not from large assumptions, but from particular facts discovered by observation or experiment."[5] According to Newton and Russell, we start from facts, which are obvious to all, and from them we develop theories. This is straightforward science, the way we have been taught, is it not? We may have been taught science this way, but it is not how contemporary science really works.

Imagine a science instructor standing outside a science laboratory door speaking to students: "Okay guys,[6] there are some facts in there that should be obvious to all of you when you see them. I'm going to open the door and let you in without any instructions. Find these facts, whatever and wherever they are, identify them, agree on them, and then we shall see if we can find some hypotheses that might explain them. Go to it." No matter what Newton and Russell say or what general opinion may think, scientific facts are not always obvious. For a laboratory assignment, students are normally given a detailed instruction manual, told to follow intricately designed procedures, which they did not make up, and only after hard work do they determine, or even notice, any scientific facts. Suppose during a laboratory experiment a laboratory student imbued with the conviction that facts are utterly primary and theories secondary says to his instructor, "I have just disproved the law of conservation of energy because my facts contradict it." I have no doubt what the instructor would say: "Do the whole experiment over again until you get the correct facts."

Facts are not like rocks you pick up and put in a basket, later to ask what they mean. They are not at all obvious, unless we have some philosophical, scientific, or mathematical framework to see them. We hardly know what to look for in examining forces exerted on or by a spring, until we suspect (or are told) that the distance a spring is constricted is proportional to the force applied. Humankind had observed things falling always, but only Newton saw how the apple really fell because he had insight into the mathematical structure of its falling in terms of his theory of gravity. Newton was the first one to see the fact of an apple fall under the force of gravity.

Science, of course, to remain good science must inevitably be compared with human experience of the real world. It differs from philosophy because at least it tries to consider only theories that can be confirmed or rejected by physical evidence. It is not a mere speculative venture but is open to experiments that may challenge its current theories. My point in the discussion about Newton's method, so avidly championed by his followers, is that mere facts are not as obvious as Newton might think or as current education about the scientific method might claim. Sometimes speculative hypotheses come first and by their nature allow us to see facts that are not apparent otherwise.

Physicists require years of education and much laboratory experience before they can recognize certain microscopic events as facts. Faint flickers in foggy chambers that most of us would never notice assume factual importance much beyond their ambiguous appearance. Biologists invoke massive theories to explain the existence and significance of certain bleached bones as facts. Legitimate facts always appear to be theory-laden.

I shall not try to mount a detailed argument at this stage that Newtonian philosophical assumptions about science, namely those of mechanism and the scientific method, are wrong. There is, however, much supporting contemporary historical study and philosophy of science that challenge these positions.[7] Nevertheless, Newtonian attitudes are deeply entrenched in the consciousness of our culture and in the educational system. I intend to return to this discussion when we consider contemporary science. For now, however, I wish to show how these Newtonian assumptions have affected our understanding of the Christian religion.

Newton's Theology

Newton claimed to be a Christian. He believed that God created the world, gave life to every creature, and imposed an obligation on us to treat others justly and mercifully. He believed that God raised Jesus from the dead who as our redeemer should be honored as the Lamb of God. He asserted that Jesus went to heaven but will eventually return and reign. In the interim, he said, God has sent the Holy Spirit to comfort us.[8]

There is an aspect of Newton's Christian religion, shared with the Hebrew tradition preceding Christianity, that aided him in discovering and formulating his science, for it showed him what to look for and how to interpret it. How was this so? God in the Pentateuch (the first five books of the Old Testament), which is the original Torah of Judaism, is seen to be a creator and lawgiver. God created the world and gave moral laws on which the world is supposed to operate. The universe is law-like as imposed by its maker. There are physical laws in addition to moral laws. The Bible gives moral laws. Mathematics gives the conceptuality to express physical laws. Newton sought to discover these physical laws expressed mathematically. For what purpose? Newton claims he did his science to encourage a belief in God, for which, as he says, "nothing can rejoice me more."[9]

A second emphasis of his religion that aided Newton's development of science is the importance Christianity gives to physical things. The gospel expresses an interest of God in this world. God not only made it and declared it good, but "so loved the world" that God visited it in the form of God's Son, Jesus. Christians could look at the facts of this world, however interpreted, without fear, and accept what they have to say. After all, they pay close attention to the very human (as well as divine) Jesus. They accept and honor the physical tokens of his body and blood in the Lord's Supper. They believe in Jesus' physical and bodily resurrection and hope for their own physical resurrection, as contrasted with the Greek idea of an eternal and spiritual life of the soul. They believe that Jesus will return to this earth, not only spiritually, but also physically.

This interest in the body and physical things by Christians finally caught up to a theory-laden abstract science and had one of its finest expressions in Newtonian science. The Greek mathematicians, remember, developed astronomy, whose stars became divine, but had little interest in immediate physical things, which were "shadows" of ideal and divine things. It is instructive to note that until the time of Kepler (1571–1630), the stars and planets were understood to have no mass.[10] Newton had the proper motivation and direction from his religion to look at the facts and experiences of this world in order to develop science.

I do not mean to imply that Newton read his Bible one night and then, because of what he read, discovered gravity the next day. He was a product of a Christian culture that was then more than sixteen hundred years old. Sensitive to the fundamental assertions of Christianity nurtured over the ages—God as lawgiver and creator of a good world, which God participates in through Jesus—Newton was primed to use his mathematical insight to formulate a new science and philosophy.

There was another religious and theological development within Christianity that affected Newton. His matter and "least particles," the atoms, became devoid of any "spirituality" because of fundamental aspects of Christian experience, what we call by the long word "desacralization" (another word is "secularization").

The first of the Ten Commandments insists, "You shall have no other gods before me" (Exod 20:3). The prohibition of idolatry is a declaration that no earthly thing, merely physical or even living, should be given a status of divinity.[11] Thus began a process of desacralization that took away the divinity and spirituality of idols, the living spirits of trees and forests, as well as that of any primal matter—the basic stuff of Newton's philosophy. Furthermore, the victory Jesus had over the powers, authorities, and elemental spirits of this world through his cross (Col 2:15) made it clear to Newton that it was a good thing to oppose a spiritualist philosophical position coming from Greek mathematics. Newton helped atomism triumph over spiritualism. Atoms have no subjectivity or divinity. Atomism has become in this century, however, a hollow victory, for it seems to entail a completely dead universe. Before I outline the theological results of Newton's scientific and philosophical positions, we should continue to look at *Principia* and present Newton's theological positions contained there.

We have found Newton's philosophical positions about science in two places: (1) at the beginning of *Principia* in the Preface to the First Edition and (2) in "Rules of Reasoning in Philosophy," which is the title of the beginning section of Book III of *Principia*. His primary theological statements are found at the very end of *Principia* in the General Scholium of Book III. The major scientific book of Western civilization has a theological section to sum it up! In this section Newton gives a general description of the solar system and then concludes that it must have been created by God.

There are a number of interesting things about Newton's understanding of God. He takes a swipe at any spiritualist interpretation of God as the soul of the world. For him, God is known almost exclusively by God's power as Lord over all. Like absolute time and space, which God created, God is invisible, eternal, and everywhere. Put more practically, "he is . . . all eye, all ear, all brain, all arm, . . . in a manner not at all corporeal."[12] We cannot understand how God exercises God's power.

Theological Reaction to Newton

Suppose you were shipwrecked on a desert island and found a watch on the beach? What would you conclude? Obviously, humans had been or are still there.[13] Watches do not grow naturally in the beach sand. They are machines and must be made by someone. Look around you at nature. See how finely and beautifully everything fits and works together. To the degree you can understand the world as mechanical, you must recognize that it requires—even demands—to be seen as the result of a creator.

This is what is known as a philosophical argument from design. No previous kinds of arguments for the existence of God, say from

Augustine, Anselm, or Aquinas, were ever popular among ordinary Christians because they required a sophisticated knowledge of the philosophical positions of those presenting the arguments. Arguments from design, however, became very popular as the consciousness of the community of Christians accepted mechanism as scientific common sense. Newtonianism had filtered down from the scientists, philosophers, and theologians through the educational system.

The first time I ever saw the "watch on the beach" argument was in a biblical tract handed out on a street corner. Some of us have seen arguments from design in contemporary church bulletins or newspapers. We may have heard Billy Graham use them in evangelistic messages. Arguments from design still have their power but only to the degree that Newton's philosophy of mechanism is still believed to be true about science and the world. A machine suggests more clearly a maker than does a growing plant. We shall look at the reawakening of revised arguments from design developed from (a not necessarily mechanical) contemporary astronomy in chapter 11.

Upon learning of Newton's work, the theologians and other Christians, as they could understand it, flocked to Newton's support. In return, they got an end to the bitter controversy between science and religion over the issue of a geocentric or heliocentric universe. Their champion Newton was a Christian and a believer in the Bible who demonstrated scientifically that their universe was sun-centered. It was also much grander than they ever suspected. Each star could be a universe in itself and potentially filled with living creatures including Christians who are resurrected from the dead.[14] Many thought it was only by the grace of God that Newton could show forth so skillfully the magnificence and majesty of God and of Jesus Christ who participated with God in the creation. With Newton, there was no longer any contradiction or even conflict between science and religion. Science was placed in its proper position as supporting religion. The science of Newton allowed one to see clearly, "The heavens are telling the glory of God; and the firmament proclaims his handiwork" (Ps 19:1).

So emboldened, many Christians began to interpret the Bible in terms of Newton's scientific method. To do that, they had to find "facts" in the Bible that justified the "theory" in the Bible. First, what is the "theory" that must be verified? It is the theology of the divine nature of Jesus Christ. There is no question that the New Testament proclaims the divinity of Jesus. It does so, however, with subtlety, leaving it to the community of Christians under the influence of the Holy Spirit to accept and try to explain it. The church has always considered it a privilege to meditate on the mystery of God in Christ and the wonder of the Triune God. Even when Jesus says, "The Father and I are one" (John 10:30), we are left to try to understand what he meant. Are there happenings or sayings in the Gospels that would help us affirm the divinity of Jesus as well as interpret it for our benefit? Are there facts in the Bible that would allow Christians to argue convincingly to non-Christians that Jesus is the Christ?

The orthodox Christians of Newton's age chose the miracles of Jesus to be the facts that justified and explained his divinity. The Bible says the miracles occurred. We believe the Bible. No one can do miracles of that sort except someone sent from God. The miracles confirm and give the stamp of authenticity to Jesus' statements about himself. This position of the Newtonian orthodox Christians seems reasonable, but it was a drastic mistake for future evangelistic purposes. For miracles themselves were called in question as scientists and mathematicians improved the mechanical universe.

As a Christian, Newton believed in miracles but also required them to fix his universe.[15] His astronomy was not quite right and indicated a universe that was not completely stable. Newton thought that God must repair the universe periodically to keep it going. This meant, of course, that God had not made a perfect universe. As the Newtonian science advanced in the hands of others, the new mathematics did indicate a stable and perfect universe. Some claimed that God was not needed to repair it. God made the universe so well, it did not need God—after the initial creation. The Deists, who included Thomas Jefferson and other founders of the United States, were single-miracle people. God created the universe miraculously and then left it to run on its own. Then came Newtonian atheists, mostly on the continent of Europe, who claimed that the perfect machine had existed forever and was never created. Now God was not needed at all.

The problem in this case is the mechanical universe itself, which ultimately must be understood as a dead universe. Machines as we know them are not alive. If the world is a machine, how do we account for our experience as living beings? Our bodies may be mechanical, but our souls and consciousness as understood by most people, are not. Newton would certainly have agreed with this. To him, God was not mechanical, but spiritual. Newton banned the spiritual aspect from matter and the world but had to allow it in terms of divine and human self-awareness. What then is the scientific or philosophical relationship between the human soul or consciousness and its body? What is the relationship between a spiritual God and a mechanical universe? The Newtonian orthodox Christians answered: miracles. God interacts with the mechanical world through miracles. This answer, however, would require also a miraculous intervention between your soul and body every time you decided to do something.

Enough, enough! The mechanical universe with a nonintegrated spiritual dimension has wreaked havoc in philosophical thought—and Christian development. Many have lost their faith because of the perceived mechanism and materialism of science. And many others have never developed an interest in Christianity because materialism alone seems sufficient. What should we do? I suggest we accept the science of Newton as modified by contemporary physics, especially quantum mechanics and relativity theory, but revise his general images of science and the philosophy dependent on them. You will hear the same refrain in regard to evolution. Accept the science but revise the philosophic images. The same advice will apply to contemporary psychiatry, especially Freudianism, and also with cognitive science and "big bang" astronomy.

We shall look at the relationship between scientific images articulated philosophically and the nature of scientific facts after we explore some of the contemporary sciences in later chapters. For now, however, let us look at the strange similarity between biblical miracles and scientific facts.

The Ambiguity of Miracles and Facts

If the Egyptians had seen God performing a miracle against them when God parted the waters and led the children of Israel through to dry ground, why did they enter the sea to their deaths? In the movie the *Ten Commandments* produced by Cecil B. DeMille, there is no question a miracle is occurring. There are walls of water to the left and to the right in a most unnatural formation with appropriate music and interpretation. In real life when true miracles occur, however, are they evident as miracles to anyone who happens to be present? Or are they seen only by those who have the perspective to see? Do all biblical miracles have this aspect of ambiguity? Let us look at one. The next paragraph is a free paraphrase of John 9:1-38.

Jesus saw a man blind from birth. He spat on the ground and made mud with the saliva and spread the mud on the man's eyes. "Go," he told him, "wash in the pool of Siloam." So the man went and washed, and came home seeing. His neighbors and those who had formerly seen him begging asked, "Is this not the man who used to sit and beg?" Others said, "No, but it is someone like him." He himself insisted, "I am the man." "Then how were your eyes opened?" they asked. He replied, "The man called Jesus made mud, spread it on my eyes, and said to me, 'Go to Siloam and wash.' " "Then I went and washed, and received my sight." "Where is he?" they asked him. He said, "I do not know."

They brought to the Pharisees the man who had been blind. The Pharisees also asked him how he had received his sight. He said to them, "He put mud on my eyes, then I washed, and now I see."

They did not believe that he had been blind and had received his sight until they sent for the man's parents. "Is this your son who you say was born blind? How then does he now see?" they asked. "We know this is our son, and he was born blind, but we do not know how it is that he now sees. Ask him. He is of age; he will speak for himself."

A second time they called the man who had been blind. "Give glory to God," they said. "We know this man is a sinner." He replied, "Whether he is a sinner or not, I don't know. One thing I do know, though I was blind, now I see!" Then they asked him, "What did he do to you? How did he open your eyes?" He answered, "I have told you already, and you would not listen. Why do you want to hear it again? Do you also want to become his disciples?" And they drove him out.

Jesus heard that they had driven him out, and when he found him, he said, "Do you believe in the Son of Man?" "Who is he, sir? Tell me, so I may believe in him." Jesus said to him, "You have seen him, and the one speaking with you is he." Then the man said, "Lord, I believe."

Notice, this miracle of Jesus was not seen as a miracle by all who dealt with the man born blind. His neighbors and parents were not sure what happened. The man knew only that he was born blind but could now see. The Pharisees (an order of Jewish religious leaders) refused to accept that a miracle had occurred and threw him out. The man believed in Jesus only after Jesus told him who he was.

Are all miracles ambiguous? Yes, especially the ones fundamental to Christianity. Does everyone acknowledge the miraculous nature of the Incarnation of God in Christ, the Virgin Birth, the Atonement due to

Jesus' suffering and death by which our sins are forgiven, the Resurrection, the Ascension? These are matters at the heart of faith.

If Newtonian facts are what are evident to all who are present and can observe them, then miracles are not Newtonian facts. Some see events as miracles and some do not, depending on their orientation and faith. The orthodox Christians following Newton made a big error in thinking of miracles as facts. I believe that Newtonians also made a comparable error in considering facts as facts. I suggest that facts are really more like biblical miracles than miracles are like Newtonian facts. One has to have a scientific theoretical orientation and a proper motivation to see facts. Remember the lab experiments.

Notes

[1] This was Newton's calculus of infinitesimals that was declared to be incoherent by Bishop Berkeley but put on a firm mathematical foundation, without infinitesimals, by nineteenth-century mathematicians like Weierstrass.

[2] Isaac Newton, *Mathematical Principles*, trans. Andrew Motte in 1729, rev. Florian Cajori, from *Sir Isaac Newton's Mathematical Principles of Natural Philosophy and His System of the World*, Book III, vol. 1 (Berkeley: University of California Press, 1966) 399.

[3] Ibid.

[4] Isaac Newton, from a Letter to Oldenburg, *Newton's Philosophy of Nature*, ed. H. S. Thayer (New York: Hafner, 1953) 5.

[5] Bertrand Russell, *Religion and Science* (New York: Oxford University Press, 1961) 13.

[6] "Guys" in colloquial California speak includes females and males.

[7] The classic study is that of Thomas S. Kuhn, *The Structure of Scientific Revolutions* (Chicago: The University of Chicago Press, 1962).

[8] Newton, *Newton's Philosophy of Nature*, 66

[9] Ibid., from a letter to Richard Bentley, *Newton's Philosophy of Nature*, 46.

[10] The idea of mass in modern science as quantity of material had not been formulated adequately to allow attribution of mass to the stars.

[11] This prohibition of the first commandment accounts for the main difference between Islamic and Christian theology. Christians believe Jesus was divine. Islam asserts that such a statement is blasphemy, because no person or thing is divine, only God.

[12] Newton, *Mathematical Principles*, Book III, General Scholium, 544–45.

[13] The watch could also have washed ashore, but would still have been made by a human.

[14] Newton, from a manuscript, *Newton's Philosophy of Nature*, 66–67.

[15] See Newton's letters to Richard Bentley, *Newton's Philosophy of Nature*, 46–58.

Chapter 4
Evolution

I have been struck by the tenor of the response from leading biologists and geologists to recent criticism of the theory of evolution by some Christian authors.[1] These scientists do not say, "You don't really understand evolution," or "You haven't been fair in your criticism." Rather, they utter a more heartfelt, "You don't really appreciate evolution." They complain almost wistfully, "How can you fairly criticize us and our beliefs if you don't value what we do?" To which a few Christians respond with unrestrained bitterness, "We think your belief in evolution is not only wrong, but perverse." This is said in spite of other Christians who not only accept the significance of the search for principles of long-term development of biological life, but also believe many tenants of evolutionary theory to be scientifically established—without compromising their faith in a creator God or the inspiration of the Bible.

One of my tasks in this chapter is to remind both Christian believers and those scientists who love their science, "You don't have to believe as true everything you understand—or appreciate." It is quite possible for Christians to say about evolution, "That is an elegant and powerful theory, at least an art form of great value" without accepting as true all or any of the major tenants of Darwinism. If you read a modern textbook in biology, you will see an enormous amount of physical, chemical, geological, biological, and medical information meaningfully tied together by the theory of evolution.[2] I do not understand how anyone can dismiss this link of evolution to hard scientific information, especially if he or she is interested in humane advances in medicine—a cure for cancer, for example.

In continuity with previous chapters, I seek to isolate the scientific aspects of evolution from those that are philosophical. This is predicted by our third thesis that any new science necessarily is cloaked in philosophical concepts that can influence religion. After separating the science of evolution from the images that have bred its powerful philosophical positions, I shall try to understand what merit our two other theses have for explaining the still raging conflict between some conservative Christians and their perception of evolution. This analysis of the historical theses, however, will be presented in the following chapter.

The Science of Evolution

The first major scientific assumption of Darwinian evolution[3] is that organisms produce far more offspring than can possibly survive. If this is not obvious to you as factual, a simple exercise in mathematics may clarify it. Suppose each family has 4 children, and each of the children establishes a family that has 4 children, as pictured in the figure "Generations." The first generation has 2 parents, the second generation has 4 parents, the third generation 8, and the fourth 16. You can easily see that in each successive generation the number of parents double. Furthermore, over any fixed amount of time, the last generation of children will always number more than all of their ancestors put together. Think about this doubling of population every generation. Suppose a town is filled with people. For the next generation, it will take at least that town and another town to hold their children. Suppose the world is filled with people. In the next generation it will take this world and another one to hold their children.

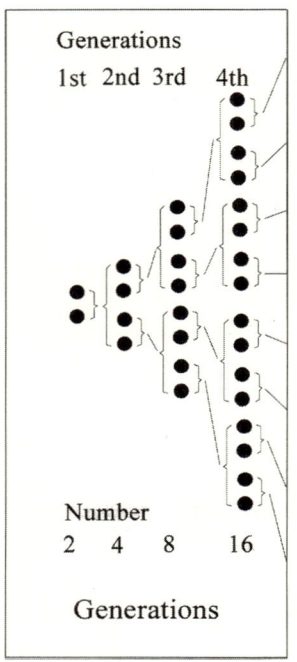

During the reproductive life of an organism, four offspring is a small number. Some organisms have tens of offspring, others hundreds, thousands, some millions. It should be obvious that most have an early death; otherwise there would be no room for further life. If you have cats and kittens, you may not be aware of how many of the kittens die because, after much effort, you were able to give them away. If you live on a farm with a stable cat population, and cannot give kittens away because other farms already have enough cats, you become aware of how many kittens die because of farm dogs, wild animals, disease, and accidents.

The second assumption of evolution is that organisms differ from each other in some ways. All kittens are cats, but each one in the litter differs from the others in some aspects: size, markings, activity, running speed, personality. We are like our same-sex siblings, but there are many differences. There is variation among the individuals of natural populations, even among those in the same family.

The third assumption of evolution is that some of the variation among individuals is inherited. We have some of the mannerisms of our mothers or fathers. Families of cats have family characteristics. There are a number of pure white cats in our neighborhood who ostensibly come from the same extended family. By selective breeding—that is, by choosing which cats mate with cats—one can select patterns that become generally apparent in some families of cats but not in others. Charles Darwin (1809–1882) was quite struck with the power of selective breeding, especially among pigeons.[4]

These three assumptions are indeed assumptions. They seem noncontroversial. They are the kinds of information we would have no trouble calling scientific facts. (Even so, recognize the mathematical theory of exponential growth used to clarify the "facts" of the first assumption. I still maintain that facts are seen clearly only in terms of theoretical structure.) Do these facts tell us something fundamental about the world? Darwin answered Yes, and proclaimed his great discovery of natural selection. Notice, Darwin presents the occurrence of natural selection as an argument from the assumptions.

> As . . . more individuals of each species are born than can possibly survive; and as, . . . there is a frequently recurring struggle for existence, it follows that any being, if it vary . . . slightly in any manner profitable to itself, will have a better chance of surviving, and thus be naturally selected.[5]

A single example: Some mosquitoes give birth to thousands of offspring. Most die when sprayed with an insecticide. A few may survive because they have some natural resistance to the insecticide. Their offspring in the thousands will on average have a higher resistance to the insecticide than the initial population. If these offspring are exposed to the insecticide and the process is repeated, the new population will have greater numbers resistant to the insecticide.

Suppose a person responsible for spraying low-lying coastal sections for mosquitoes comments to his supervisor, "I don't think our insecticides have as much effect this year as they did last year, or even the year before." She might respond, "Have you checked the concentrations in the spray?" At that point the quality of the information of the report that mosquitoes are resisting the insecticide is relatively low. Later the supervisor may say, "I think I know what's happening" and then invoke the theory of natural selection. The report about the mosquitoes seems acceptable, especially if additional information from other coastal sections supports it. A "fact" has been "discovered" in terms of a theory supported by evidence. The fact was questionable until the theory made sense of it. Now its quality is such that the supervisor can take appropriate action, whereas before she was hesitant to do so.

Who has any objection to the use of natural selection to explain phenomena of this sort? We recognize that natural selection is based on assumptions and is a theory we use to understand the world. That is how science works. The assumptions are plausible, and the theory is effective. We do not hesitate to call the theory "science." Few will doubt that it is good science.

The Philosophy of Evolution

Why the great concern about evolution and Christianity? Because Darwin (1) interpreted evolution materialistically and (2) gave a philosophical importance to natural selection it does not deserve. Let us look first at natural selection and later return to a discussion of materialism.

Modern evolutionary theory interprets natural selection as the means by which the fit are constructed, not just the means by which the unfit are eliminated. Natural selection for contemporary Darwinism is the explanation of the creative force in nature. This fundamental force is thought to be extremely powerful but not divine. It is the means by which new species including humankind come into existence. It, not a designing God, is the explanation of Newton's question why animals and people have symmetrical eyes, ears, nostrils, arms, and legs. Newton's response to his question was another "Whence arises this uniformity in all their outward shapes but from the counsel and contrivance of an Author?"[6] In his latter days Darwin believed it could all be explained by natural selection—without God.

If natural selection is *the* means of explaining life, for example, the reason why species arise, then other potential explanations of species generation and differentiation must be minimized. What could some of these other reasons be? Perhaps animals adapt to their circumstances and then pass on acquired characteristics to their offspring. This is Lamarckism (Chevalier De Lamarck, French biologist, 1744–1829), which I do not accept. Perhaps God in association with other agents determines potential boundaries to the random modification of the genetic code, which then causes variations that are inherited. This is a position I do accept but only with careful explanation of the meaning of randomness. In each of these cases, however, natural selection would only eliminate the unfit. It would not be the driving reason why changes occur in populations. In order for natural selection to be the primary creative force, it must be seen to create new features in offspring. Contemporary Darwinism does not accept other explanations that preferentially incline organisms toward adaptations, for then natural selection would not be the main answer.

If natural selection is the cause of change in populations of entities, what is an explanation of the variation among organisms before natural selection takes place? The answer: Variation is random.[7] This idea of random variation became acceptable, and indeed intelligible, only after the work of Gregor Mendel (1822–1884) on genetics. Darwin gave wrong answers, namely that traits from both parents are blended in the offspring. Darwinism began to decline in the latter part of the nineteenth century when critics pointed out that his "blending" theory would not insure variations but destroy them. Darwin never solved the problem of variation, and Mendel's work lay dormant for thirty-five years, only to be resurrected in the twentieth century—when it helped salvage, renovate, and propel the new Darwinism to great success.

Mendel made a remarkable discovery about the nature of variation in organisms by applying a new discipline of mathematics, now known as statistics, to biology. Like Aristarchus, Archimedes, and Newton, he saw regularities from his observations—with peas not stars—that when organized mathematically gave a dynamic new insight into science. As noted earlier, Mendel's relatively simple discovery revitalized the flagging ideas of Darwinian evolution and began the discipline of genetics. I consider Mendelian genetics to be part of the science of evolution, rather than its philosophy, but the analysis of Mendel's contribution is essential to understand the philosophical aspects of randomness.

A plant is true breeding if, when mated with plants like itself, it has offspring like itself. A true-breeding pea plant has only green peas if self-pollinated or cross-pollinated with another true-breeding plant of green peas. Mendel experimented with what happens when a true-breeding green pea plant is crossed with a true-breeding yellow pea plant. To his surprise, the offspring had only yellow peas. When these first-generation peas grew into second-generation plants and self-pollinated, they had both kinds of peas, roughly 1/4 green peas and 3/4 yellow peas. These second-generation peas produced third-generation peas with the following results: 1/4 of the peas were green and true-breeding; 1/4 of the peas were yellow and true-breeding; the remaining 1/2 of yellow peas produced plants that had both yellow and green seeds.

What is happening here? Mendel recognized this puzzling situation in pea plants and then solved it by certain assumptions, which I express using contemporary terminology.

Pea color is determined by a factor now called a "gene." Each genetic character is produced by two variants, called "alleles," one provided by each parent. I symbolize this idea by showing a gene as composed of two alleles in the diagram called "Genes of an Organism." A true-breeding plant with yellow peas will have both alleles yellow producing, which are symbolized *YY*. A true-breeding plant with green peas will have both alleles green producing, which are symbolized *gg*. When the plants are cross-fertilized in the parent generation, the yellow pea plant supplies the *Y* allele and the green pea plant the *g* allele, for possible combinations of *Yg* or *gY* in the offspring genes. When the offspring plants self-pollinate, the alleles separate and combine randomly into genes that still have only two alleles. The possibilities of combination are *YY, gg, Yg, gY*.

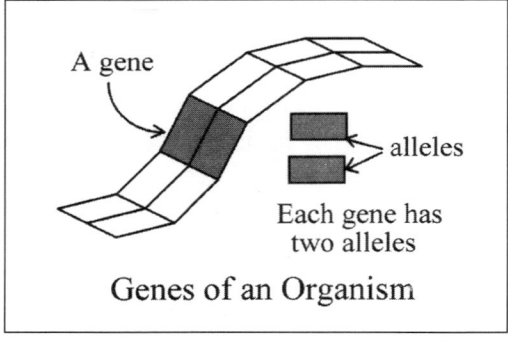

We can get the feel of the random nature of genetic selection of alleles by tossing two coins. Each of the two coins, like a gene, will have two positions, which might be heads *H* and tails *t*. The four possibilities, similar to the allele combinations, are *HH, tt, Ht,* and *tH*. If you actually toss the coins and keep tabs, you will have roughly 1/4 of each combination *HH, tt, Ht,* and *tH*. We interpret our experience with coin tossing and our understanding of randomness in this case to apply to allele combinations. With random selection among alleles, we also should have genetic combinations of *YY, gg, Yg,* and *gY* in roughly equal numbers.

Why then in the second generation do we get all yellow and in the third generation 3/4 yellow and 1/4 green? Mendel assumed yellow is dominant and green recessive. For each *YY, Yg,* or *gY* combination, we get yellow seeds. Only for alleles *gg* do we get green seeds. This explains why the first generation is all yellow, since its only genetic possibilities are *Yg* or *gY*, and the second generation has 1/4 yellow for each of *YY*,

Yg, and *gY* and 1/4 green only for *gg*. It also explains why all the green seeds are true-breeding and only 1/3 of the yellow seeds are true-breeding.

We have examined the random properties of only one character, the color of peas either yellow or green. When we examine other characters, say whether peas are wrinkled or smooth, in association with their color, the analysis gets more complicated. We would be working with the random association of alleles with at least two genes rather than one. Yet the statistical assumptions of Mendel, seen in simple form above, still hold. You can imagine the complexity of modern genetics when a gene is interpreted to be a small part of the fundamental genetic structure of deoxyribonucleic acid (DNA),[8] which is composed in mammalian form of approximately 100,000 genes. The situation is made even more complicated (and more interesting) because genes can replicate and add to themselves, travel from one location to another, and be modified by mutation. Each of these genetic changes can produce different effects. In short, the simple assumptions of Mendel give an organization and clarity to this enormous amount of information and ground the discipline of biology in mathematical principles—from which one can make predictions.

As I have attempted to point out in previous chapters, I show my belief again that mathematics has been and continues to be not only influential in science but also in the relationship between science and religion. Yet the mathematics in this case is quite different from the calculus of Newton or the geometry of the astronomers. This mathematics has elements of chance and is dependent upon an intuitive idea of randomness. The secret to understanding evolution in a compatible way with Christianity is to interpret randomness intelligibly and throw out strict materialistic determination altogether. If we retain randomness in the universe, but dismiss materialism, we have an opportunity to present a philosophical interpretation of evolution that allows theism. This will come later. Let us now look more carefully at the meaning of randomness.

The philosophical and mathematical idea of random events is based on common experience. What do we mean by a random flip of a coin? Generally, we mean that we cannot predict whether we will get a head or a tail. Suppose, however, in a flip of a coin, it disappeared in midair. Would we call that a random event? Probably not. Most likely we would begin looking for whoever (or whatever) may have taken the coin. Nor would we consider it a random event if in the throw of a white die with black dots, it unexpectedly turned green with yellow dots. Again, we would think the situation was quite "strange," not familiarly random. Such an event would be outside our expectations of the white die showing a 1, 2, 3, 4, 5, or 6 by means of black dots. I give these examples to show that the explanation of randomness is not just an initial arbitrary state A that does not allow us to predict a later arbitrary state B, but that the states A and B must be part of some generally understood pattern. What we do mean by randomness is that given the pattern and the preconditions, we cannot know in advance which among the possibilities of pattern will occur.

This is a key point. Randomness has meaning in terms of a pre-accepted structure. It is not just anything you can imagine happening. A particle may move randomly, but within the constraint it will move in some direction, where directions are explained in terms of geometric or other mathematical structure. In a meaning of random movement, we do not normally allow the particle to disappear here and reappear there, unless we have carefully stated this as a possibility (as may occur in quantum mechanics). There is a clear meaning to the idea of a random number between 0 and 1, but this meaning is dependent upon the elaborate structure of the real numbers. Randomness in variation of organisms is normally explained today in terms of random variations of genetic structure, which is highly complex. To repeat: You do not get structure out of randomness. Randomness has meaning only in terms of structure.

Evolution does not ask us to believe that we can get order out of pure chaos through random variation and natural selection. Rather, it asks us to believe that classes of organisms with a certain structure can over considerable time evolve through their offspring into classes of organisms with a different structure. We are still asked, however, to accept that highly complex organisms, such as a living cell, evolved from the random activity of much less complex entities such as molecules—of course, appropriately selected by the environment. We may balk at this because we have little experience of structures of greater complexity coming from much less complex structures except through the agency of intelligent design.

We know that humans can design computers, but computers do not evolve by themselves from random variation and natural selection. Monkeys typing randomly on a keyboard do not give us Shakespeare plays; Shakespeare did. The brilliance of evolutionary theory is that it never asks us to accept such large jumps as the transition from sand (silicon) directly into computer (silicon) chips, or the production of a Shakespeare play from excited monkeys, or the evolution of *homo sapiens* from other mammals, without clarifying some of the smaller steps that are (ostensibly) more rationally acceptable.

For example, there are basically two kinds of cells: (1) single-celled bacterial organisms called "prokaryotes"; and (2) cells that constitute all other forms of life, including humans, called "eukaryotes." The prokaryotes, whose DNA has no encompassing nucleus, are much simpler than the eukaryotes, which contain a number of membrane-surrounded organelles, one of which is a nucleus. Many biochemical processes are similar in the two cells indicating from the theory of evolution (and other supporting fossil evidence) that the eukaryotes are derived from the more ancient prokaryotes. How did eukaryotes evolve from prokaryotes by random variation and natural selection? There are two theories: autogeny and serial endosymbiosis.

Autogeny proposes that the cell plasma membrane "inpocketed" to surround its DNA with a membrane forming a nucleus, as well as creating the other enclosed membranes from which the various organelles evolved. We illustrate this in the picture "Inpocketing of Cell Membrane." This evolution occurred in a process similar to the original evolution of the prokaryote cells.

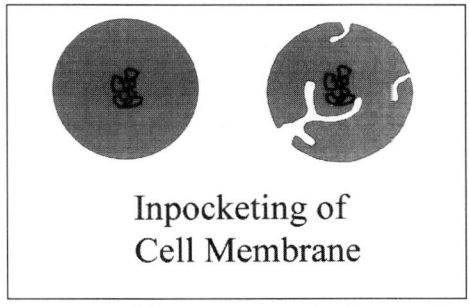
Inpocketing of Cell Membrane

Serial endosymbiosis proposes that with many prokaryotes coming in random contact with each other, some of the larger ones engulfed the smaller ones, which then evolved to perform particular functions in the host bacterium. Which theory is more attractive from an evolutionary standpoint? The one that sees the smallest steps brought about by random variation and natural selection. The already existing structures of engulfed bacteria can modify their function more easily than can random variation and natural selection recreate the structure from the beginning inside the host bacterium. No wonder there is a great effort to find appropriate confirming evidence for the serial endosymbiosis theory.

You can understand the motivation of choosing the smaller steps rather than the larger ones by having to decide whether you will modify existing motors in a small way to perform specific functions in a larger machine or whether you will try to build each and every motor from scratch in order to perform the required functions. The main purpose of the theory of evolution is to achieve intelligibility—meaning, if you like—from among a wide variety of information. The core ideas of random variation and natural selection seem intelligible only if we understand their application to small changes.

If large variations occurred, say on the order of differences in species, natural selection would again only have to eliminate the unfit. It would not have had any part in creating step by step the larger change. Small changes over time are how natural selection is supposed to make big differences in organisms. We obviously have big differences in organisms. So we must have had a very large number of small changes. Conclusion: Evolution has taken a very long time. The earth is very old. The universe appears even older, say on the order of fifteen to twenty billion years.[9]

The earth is old, a position that is not just derived from the theory of evolution. One can marshal very strong evidence for an ancient age of the earth from geology, chemistry, and physics. Frankly, in my judgment, the evidence from these sciences is far stronger than the suspect schemes of genealogy counting used by some biblical scholars to claim an age of about 6,000 years for the earth. I think these Christian claims are unfortunate, for they seem to assert it is the Bible that speaks about the age of the earth rather than a position about the Bible derived without much consideration and held onto tenaciously.[10] The Bible talks about "ancient times" and "ancient days," and God is even called "the Ancient of Days" in the book of Daniel. The Bible does not speak about any exact age of the world. What it does say, however, is that God preexisted any world and created all worlds in terms of a personified wisdom (Prov 8) later identified as Christ. "He was in the beginning with God. All things came into being through him, and without him not one thing came into being" (John 1:2–3). A discussion of God's initiation of the universe is contained in chapters 11 and 12.

In short, I believe that the current theory of evolution is at least an artistic creation that brings astonishing meaning and depth to the enormous data of biology and geology as well as some physics. Its central core of random variation (appropriately interpreted) and natural selection (in proper balance) seems well-grounded in factual data. Its philosophical orientation of materialism, yet to be discussed, remains suspect. Yet no one is going to displace the ideas of random variation and natural selection from the imagination and affection of millions of people, including many Christians, by claims that the theory is not altogether true.

Of course, it is not true absolutely, just as Archimedian and Ptolemaic astronomy were not true in this sense, but were eventually replaced by Copernican and Newtonian theory. Newtonian theory was not exactly true and has been replaced by relativity theory and quantum mechanics. Even Darwin's initial theories on variation were wrong and have been superseded by those of Mendel. Truth, however, is only a partial issue in science. Only attractive theories that give esthetic satisfaction in acquiring meaning are even considered as options to present truth. The theory of evolution is certainly in this category. Yet, if the history of science is any guide to the future, we should expect it to be replaced by an even more attractive theory that seems closer to the truth.

A Christian's response should be to understand and appreciate the theory of evolution while looking for, and forward to, the "new" evolutionary theory (possibly called by a different name). You do not have to believe everything you understand or appreciate. In particular, you do not have to, and I assert should not, accept the strict materialism currently associated with the theory of evolution.

Materialism

What is materialism? It is an orientation that gives primary status to matter—on which mind or spirit are seen to be dependent. It is often associated with mechanism because machines are composed only of material parts. Newton was a mechanist, because he believed that any good explanation was mechanical (geometrical), but he was not a complete materialist, because he did not believe that mechanism could explain everything—God, mind, spirit, and the soul, for example. In our descriptions of chapter 2, Newton was an atomist as far as the world was concerned and a spiritualist as far as God and the soul were concerned.[11] Evolution has had great success with mechanical explanation, which is its genius. Its greatest triumph of mechanical explanation is the genetic material DNA, which is described as acting like a machine. It reacts chemically—although pictured mechanically—with RNA (ribonucleic acid), which specifies chemically—again interpreted mechanically—certain proteins, etc. Here again is the primary image of a machine affecting philosophical attitudes towards a major science.

Although the current standard orthodox formulation of evolution is materialistic, it is not completely mechanical. The changes in genetic structure (thought of as modifications of mechanical DNA) that occur when one species is seen to evolve from an earlier one cannot be described in strict mechanical fashion. They involve random variation and natural selection. These changes cannot be plotted by a classical deterministic mathematics such as calculus but only presented in the newer mathematics of probability and statistics. Nevertheless, the image of random variation accepted by contemporary evolution is one that does not involve purpose of any sort. We assume naturally that the idea of randomness is not purposive. When we throw a die, we do not expect our intention to affect the outcome. Certainly the die itself has no purpose.

Yet in the larger picture, purpose is involved. Someone made the die so that it would have the random properties we expect. Actually, a great deal of effort is spent to insure that dice have standard random properties—that the dice are true. Here are the two images we need for understanding randomness in evolution. Materialistic evolutionary theory understands randomness in terms of the throw of a pair of dice where each event is seen as unpredictable and without purpose. This idea of randomness is extended to all relevant random events of evolutionary theory, as well as articulated philosophically. I propose a more appropriate image for evolution. It is the design of dice where purpose is involved to insure their randomness when thrown.

In evaluating the place (or lack) of purpose in evolution, Stephen Jay Gould sums up the orthodox position as follows: "Darwin argues that evolution has no purpose,"[12] a statement indicating a philosophical extension of our image of a throw of a pair of dice where randomness without purpose is paramount. Gould's next sentence, "Individuals struggle to increase the representation of their genes in future generations,"[13] shows there is at least some purpose in evolution. Purpose, however, does not conflict with randomness. For example, in selecting reproductive partners where, as we all know, there are many aspects of choice involved, humans set the bounds of potential genetic combinations within which randomness operates. Notice in this case the appropriateness of the design of dice image. It shows a situation where the possible limits of the "throw of dice" are set, but within which the "throw is random." The choice of a marriage partner establishes the "design of dice" within which the "throw of dice" randomness of sperm-egg contact occurs.

I have argued previously that randomness has meaning only in terms of structure. That a throw of a die is random makes sense only if the possibilities of the throws 1 through 6 are evident. I assert that the image of the design of dice is more relevant to evolution than the throw of dice image, because the image of the design of dice includes the ideas of both the structure of possibilities and the random events that may satisfy the possibilities. The design of dice image also admits a much easier interpretation of God's activity in evolution as well as more general relations with the world and humans. God, with other agents, may set limits on the possibilities of events within which there may be genuine random activity. The image of the design of dice is very fruitful for a number of philosophical and theological ideas, especially freedom of choice—but we shall examine these ideas at a later time.

Summary

We have said the science of evolution involved historically three indisputable assumptions: (1) organisms produce far more offspring than can possibly survive, (2) organisms differ from each other in some ways, (3) some of the variation among individuals is inherited. We gave Darwin's argument from these assumptions for natural selection, which is summarized and tightened by Steven Jay Gould as follows:

> On average, offspring that vary most strongly in directions favored by the environment will survive and propagate. Favorable variation will therefore accumulate in populations by natural selection.[14]

In addition, we consider the science of evolution to include Mendelian genetics and its presentation in terms of contemporary statistical theory.

The characteristics of what we have called the "philosophy of evolution" are: (1) an overemphasis on natural selection as the creative force of evolution, which entailed (2) an understanding of randomness in terms of the image of the throw of dice (not the design of dice), and then (3) materialism. I think I may have the logical transition wrong here. It should be materialism first, the nature of randomness second, and an emphasis on natural selection third. Materialism insists foremost that any purpose in the world should be seen as secondary and furthermore as derivative from material things. If there is no purpose, randomness must be seen as in the throw of dice image, not the design of dice image. If there is no design in materialism or randomness, one must find it by seeing natural selection to be the creative force of evolution.

My fundamental point is, materialism is not necessary for an understanding of evolution. Some other more appropriate philosophical position, say based on the design of dice image, can and should be put in its place. We shall examine some of these philosophical positions after we look more carefully at other contemporary sciences.

Notes

[1] For example, Stephen Jay Gould's review "Impeaching a Self-Appointed Judge" in *Scientific American*, July 1992, 118–21, of *Darwin on Trial*, by Phillip E. Johnson (Washington DC: Regnery Gateway, 1991). Gould's judgment that "The book, in short, is full of errors, badly argued, based on false criteria, and abysmally written" seems based more on Johnson's attitude towards evolution than it does on the quality of the book.

[2] See, for example, *Biology: The Science of Life*, 3d ed., by Robert A. Wallace, Gerald P. Sanders, and Robert J. Ferl in which they state, "We believe that biology is best understood in terms of its development through evolution and adaptation, so we have tried to weave our discussions around these twin themes throughout the book" (New York: Harper Collins Publishers Inc., 1990) vii.

[3] I am following distinctions between the scientific aspects of evolution and its philosophical aspects that were made by Stephen Jay Gould in his Prologue to *Ever Since Darwin, Reflections in Natural History* (New York: W. W. Norton & Co., 1979) 11–17.

[4] Charles Darwin, *The Illustrated Origin of Species* (New York: Hill and Wang, 1979) 53–56.

[5] Ibid., 47.

[6] Newton, *Newton's Philosophy of Nature: Selections from His Writings* (New York: Hafner, 1953) 65.

[7] Contemporary evolutionary theory maintains that there are two sources of variation, mutation and genetic recombination, both of which are said to be random.

[8] A gene is a segment of DNA that (through RNA) specifies a protein.

[9] I understand that recent information from the orbiting Hubbel Telescope may indicate a possible age of about 8 billion years.

[10] The emphasis on genealogy as a clue to the age of the universe began with Cambridge University Vice-Chancellor John Lightfoot, who in 1642, the year of Newton's birth, published his calculation that the universe began September 17, 3928 B.C. A few years later, the Anglican archbishop of Ireland, James Ussher, claiming error in Lightfoot's calculation, declared that the correct date was October 3, 4004 B.C. Lightfoot responded with a minor correction, adding additional information that Adam was created on October 23, 4004 B.C. at 9:00 A.M.

[11]Newton was not a typical spiritualist, for he emphasized the priority of God's will rather than his existence as some spiritual substance.
[12]Stephen J. Gould, *Ever Since Darwin, Reflections in Natural History* (New York: W. W. Norton & Co., 1979) 12.
[13]Ibid.
[14]Ibid., 11.

Chapter 5
Theological Response to Darwinism

If history supports our second thesis that theology conflicts with a new science after identifying with an old one, we would expect a severe reaction to Darwinism among those Christians who accepted Newtonianism most completely. Response in England and the United States, especially among conservative Calvinists and their Fundamentalist descendants, was quite extreme. It was less so on the European continent among Roman Catholics, Lutherans, and Eastern Orthodox who still felt more comfortable with Plato and Aristotle than with Newton.

Rather than outline a theological history of the various theological parties and their reactions to evolution, I prefer to choose as a case history a single movement in American Protestantism. This movement calls itself "Creation Research" or "Creation Science." I want to show on the one hand the extent to which these conservative biblical Christians are Newtonian and to examine on the other hand how their Newtonianism affects their attitude towards evolution and the Bible. My primary source is the book *The Twilight of Evolution* by Henry M. Morris, now in its twenty-fifth printing.[1]

A cultivated and developed Newtonianism was the dominant understanding of science by scientists through the nineteenth century. As such it thoroughly conditioned our "common sense" for the twentieth century. Only near the end of this century does relativistic, statistical, and quantum mechanical physics begin to challenge our old way of seeing the world. To describe our Newtonian outlook, we may only have to consider what is comfortable about our beliefs.

Let us try to put ourselves into the perspective of a Newtonian Christian. In this viewpoint God and the world are different, and both are very real. The world is law-like and has the familiar image of a machine. Like a machine, its parts are separable. An electron is not a proton, oxygen is not aluminum, a snake is not a rabbit, and an ape is not a human. Also like a machine, one part does not change or grow into another. A spring does not modify itself to become a wheel. An ape does not change into a human. Stability is dominant. Any change occurs within clear bounds. A baby may become a mature woman. A mature woman may give birth to a male child. Yet the female baby, the mature woman, and her male child are all humans. The woman does not give birth to an ape. Species are separable and distinct. A new species of animals or plants does not develop out of an old one.

For Newtonians, time and space are objectively real. Everything physical exists *in* space and *in* time, because space and time exist prior to and independently of things. History is about what really happened in an absolute space and time. Since space and time exist apart from things in general, what really happened is separable from human emotion or perspective. Therefore, if the Bible and science disagree about historical events, one (or both) must be wrong. In this Newtonian perspective, we should not say that the Bible sees it one way and science sees it another way and leave the issue there. It is possible, though perhaps difficult, to find out exactly what happened—because in this Newtonian perspective something really did happen in the strictest objective sense.

For Christian Newtonians, God acts through miracles. God created the world. God caused a virgin to bear a child. God raised Jesus from the dead. God miraculously inspired the Holy Scripture, which tells us among other things what happened historically in the past. God gives eternal souls to babies. Even human rationality is a kind of miracle, a communication of the human mind and soul with God; we cannot explain reason as coming only from a mechanical universe.

Morris is Newtonian foremost because of the kind of science he accepts. He is typical of conservative Protestant Christians who embrace the great authority of classical science. To him and others of this movement, science is the discipline that grows out of facts established by experimentation and presented finally in laws that after exhaustive testing can be declared as unquestionably true. Morris asserts that Christians *should* accept the results of established science, a statement that is stronger than our first thesis that Christians normally *do* follow good science.

Morris believes that contemporary evolution is very bad science. It is really not science at all, because it has not been empirically verified by adequate experiments. It is rather a philosophy, and a dangerous one at that. Morris believes that two laws at the heart of classical science contradict the theory of evolution. They are the first and second laws of thermodynamics, which he states are "proved beyond any scientific doubt whatever."[2] In this regard Morris is correct. These laws are at the foundation not only of classical physics, but also of contemporary relativistic and quantum physics.

The first law of thermodynamics can be stated simply as that of conservation of energy, which can neither be created nor destroyed but only changed to different forms. When we drop a ball, its potential energy due to its position above the floor translates into energy of movement, called kinetic energy, which is highest right before it hits the floor. The energy of movement is translated into some small amount of heat because of the friction of the ball with the air and its internal friction when it is deformed as it hits the floor. Upon recoil, the ball's kinetic energy is changed back into the energy of position. The ball does not bounce as high, however, because the heat energy is not converted to positional energy but warms the ball and its environment slightly.

We have mentioned potential, kinetic, and heat energy. These are but three forms of energy. There is energy of work. The work done in pushing a body a certain distance is the force of the push times the distance pushed. Also there are electrical and electromagnetic energies; the energy results of various nuclear forces; mass that can be converted to energy; and thermodynamic, chemical, light, sound, and other forms of energy. The law of conservation of energy relates all these kinds of energy in an elegant mathematical formulation—by equating them. (For example, the potential energy of the ball when released is equal to the kinetic energy at the bottom of its fall plus the heat energy expended.) The law of conservation of energy is one of the highest of generalizations of classical science as well as the foundation of contemporary science. I certainly agree with Morris and accept the first law of thermodynamics as fundamental to science.

The second law of thermodynamics states that in any of the transformations of energy in a closed system governed by the first law, there is a necessary decrease of usable energy. Another way of expressing the same law is to say that entropy, which is usable energy depleted from the system, increases. Things tend to move towards disorder, to run down. The food we eat for energy becomes waste, which does not have the same energy potential for our consumption as the original food. One can have an increase of usable energy locally, say by eating food, but only at the expense of the larger environment, which is polluted by the waste. Pollution of the common environment by unusable heat or other forms of energy is a necessary consequence of the second law. Things and situations in general are "wearing out." Complex order becomes more random disorder. The second law of thermodynamics is as fundamental to contemporary science as the first.

If evolution declares that things go from simplicity to complexity, from relative disorder to significant order as in the evolution of simple cellular organisms into the multicellular complexity of humans, we can see how evolution would seem to contradict the second law of thermodynamics. In evolution we have an increase in order. For entropy we have a decrease in order. Morris has found an apparent contradiction in the relationship between physics and evolution—but only if we ignore the fact that the earth is not a closed system. The sun pours energy into the world system to fuel evolutionary complexity while burning itself out slowly, according to the second law. If evolution is universal, each star is also a source of energy for evolution while conforming to the second law of thermodynamics.

Morris is also Newtonian because of his attitudes about the nature of history. Newtonian history is what happens in absolute time and space. Since time and space are strictly independent of things and events, what happens in history is independent of any perspective. Because the Bible is divinely inspired and contains descriptions of historical events, the Bible is telling us exactly what happened. It is what happened that is important, not perspectives on it. Newtonian absolute time and space have become common sense. It is history as "most of us understand history."[3]

Morris not only claims that evolution is completely discredited by the second law of thermodynamics, he further insists that the Bible as it gives an objective history is the guarantor of the second law. According to Morris, each of the three major facts of biblical history—the creation, the fall of humanity, and the flood—confirm the second law of thermodynamics and contradict evolution. Why does the Bible seem compatible with the second law of thermodynamics and against evolutionary theory?

God created the world initially with all its inhabitants and declared it to be good. It was good—no death or decay—until the sin of Adam and Eve. After that, God put a curse on the physical earth. Since then, the second law of thermodynamics has held sway with its consequent deterioration of the environment—physical, mental, and emotional. Men earn their living by the sweat of their brow. Women have pain in childbirth. The whole earth is in distress due to God's curse on it. This travail is explained in scientific terms by the second law of thermodynamics. The law of entropy is a physical expression of the results of sin, a sin entered into historically by the first humans. Parenthetically, it was the third great fact of history, the flood, that explains the fossil record.

The Bible further tells us historically, according to Morris, that God finished God's creation on the seventh day and rested. God is currently maintaining the universe by the first law of thermodynamics "so nothing further is being created nor is anything being destroyed" but is allowing it to deteriorate by the second law since "there is everywhere in the world a tendency towards death and decay."[4] God rested on the seventh day and is *still* resting. There is no new creation. The analogy Morris uses is of a great clock symbolizing the universe that was "originally wound up by God"[5] at creation but that is winding down slowly. Notice the Newtonian mechanical imagery supported by an extended Newtonian science. God will eventually re-create a new universe at the end of the age, but between the original creation and the final one, God exercises only maintenance, which is symbolized scientifically by the first law of thermodynamics.

Christian Fundamentalism, which Morris represents, is primarily a theology of Calvinism (John Calvin, 1509–1564) adapted to a Newtonian perspective. The original predestination of Calvinism, by which God is understood to have predetermined what is to happen in the world, became associated with the initial creation of the world that then worked itself out according to law—divine law expressed as Newtonian law. The world and history are so well planned by God, there is no need for any creation after the first. Later Calvinism modified the original Newtonian Orthodoxy by de-emphasizing contemporary miracles, especially those that might signify a new creation. Miracles may occur, but they are all part of a divine plan that is working itself out in regular, lawful, and predetermined fashion. There is nothing radically new.

Is this what the New Testament says? Is not the heart of the gospel that God has entered history as a truly human person Jesus Christ? Can God do that within the same old framework of the old history? Do not Jesus' miracles show God at work in a new way? What about Jesus' bodily resurrection? It was (and is) a body different from all human bodies. Is not the new birth of believers a new creation? "So if anyone is in Christ, there is a new creation: everything old has passed away; see, everything has become new!" (2 Cor 5:17). Claiming there is no new creation misses the fundamental biblical assertion of God's grace.

Evolution and the Three Historical Theses

Let us review the historical theses as related to scientific upheavals studied so far with careful attention to the Darwinian revolution. Our first thesis claims that Christians normally accept good science and write it into their theology. Our second thesis explains conflict between science and religion as conflict between a new science and an old science now hallowed and obscured as theology. Our third thesis recognizes that a new science is necessarily cloaked in philosophical concepts that can influence religion.

We have seen the first thesis exemplified when Christians accepted (1) the logic of Greek mathematics as one of the methods of theological analysis; (2) the philosophical ideas of unity from Greek mathematics that were applied to a doctrine of an eternal soul and an immutable god; (3) the spherical earth from Greek astronomy; (4) the geocentric universe as confirmed by Archimedes; (5) the Aristarchan and Copernican sun-centered universe as established ultimately by Newton; and (6) Newtonianism with its emphasis on a mechanical universe, the primacy of facts, a spiritual God who governs by strength of will, and miracles.

Not all Christians, however, have accepted all of the science most scientists believe in. Not all theologians approved of Greek logic for an analysis of God. Certainly the church did not accept readily the sun-centered universe, but proceeded to the trial of Galileo over the issue. And, of course, we witness the ugly contemporary confrontation between evolutionists and some biblical Christians over what should be taught in public schools. Why does the first thesis seem to fail in these important cases?

There are three reasons, two of which involve the second and third theses. The third reason depends on an additional minor thesis we have expressed as follows: During periods when a new scientific theory cannot be confirmed or disconfirmed scientifically, the new theory does not have the authority to replace an old established scientific theory.

Let us look at the minor thesis first. We have indicated that during the century and a half between the assertion of the sun-centered hypothesis by Copernicus and the publication of Newton's *Principia*, the factual evidence was ambiguous for deciding between the earth-centered and sun-centered universe. As an example of this confusion, Tycho Brahe, who had the most accurate astronomical readings available, thought that all planets revolved around the sun except the earth—which was at the center—and that the sun and its planets revolved around the earth. During that time scientists chose, often passionately, between an earth-centered or sun-centered theory for esthetic or other reasons. This minor thesis is one of the reasons many

Christians today do not accept the theory of evolution. The fossil evidence alone, which indicates on the surface only stability of species, is not adequate to confirm, without question, an understanding of the transition of one species into another.

We have illustrated the second thesis in a previous chapter by claiming that the church rejected the sun-centered universe because it had taken to its heart the earth-centered universe, written it deep within its theology, and saw it to be expressed by the Bible. When faced with the challenge of the new science, the church saw it to contradict the Bible and orthodox theology, even though the Bible says almost nothing about the issue.

In this chapter we have shown that certain groups of American Protestants, including many Fundamentalists, found evolution difficult to accept because they had become quite Newtonian. The Newtonian presuppositions had been well adapted to their theology and formed the background for their understanding of the Bible. We indicated how Morris, as representative of these groups, used Newtonian science as an argument against evolution. The new science of evolution became suspect because it did not conform to (presuppositions of) the old Newtonian science, which had been thoroughly integrated into a theological perspective. Our second thesis is one explanation why evolution was not accepted readily by these groups, as should have been predicted by the first thesis, which claims Christians normally accept good science.

The main reason why many groups of Christians have rejected evolution is given by extending our third thesis, which says that science brings with it philosophical concepts. Most Christians throughout the ages of the church, in accordance with the first thesis, have accepted good science provided it does not come with offensive images associated with philosophical interpretation. The church theologians rejected the early atomism of the Greeks, derived as we claim from an association with mathematics, because it was not philosophically favorable. Atomism became theologically agreeable in Newtonian philosophy, however, only after it was minimized in favor of the theistic positions.

The main reason why most Christians have questioned evolution, and some have rejected it altogether, is its nonacceptable materialistic philosophical perspective. Some theologians have rejected both evolutionary science and its attendant philosophy because they were unable appropriately to distinguish the two. A reconciliation between the science of evolution and theology can occur with a new and appropriate philosophical orientation, which I shall suggest for consideration in subsequent chapters. We want any new general philosophical orientation—and the images that drive it—to be relevant not only to evolution but also to relativity theory, quantum mechanics, cognitive science, and psychology.

The Bible and Evolution

Morris's scientific criticism of evolution was a challenging position for its time, first presented in 1962. I have criticized him for misapplying the second law of thermodynamics by falsely viewing the earth as a closed system. To say the least, I do not see any appreciation of the artistic quality of evolution by Morris. There are, however, some areas in which I agree with him.

Trying to focus only on the "bare facts," Morris claims with considerable justification that neither the fossil record in itself nor any other acceptable unambiguous scientific evidence leads directly to a belief in the transition of one species into another. If anything, the fossil record confirms the fixity of species. I do not disagree with him on this matter nor with his statement that the Bible should "be taken as basic and as absolutely and literally true."[6] I believe in a divinely inspired Bible, which is described more carefully in chapter 12. My challenge to Morris and to many other biblical Fundamentalists who deal with science is, *they do not take the Bible seriously enough*. They do not accept the Bible in its plain statements when these statements challenge their fond rational way of understanding the Bible.

I have already given an example in chapter 1 where DeYoung claims that the Bible never speaks of a flat earth, although in the Revelation of Jesus to John, John as inspired by Jesus speaks of the "four corners of the earth." Each of the other fifteen uses of "four corners" in the Bible refers to a flat rectangular figure of some sort. Never in the Bible does "four corners of the earth" refer to the four directions north, south, east, and west—as DeYoung claims. Is this taking the Bible seriously, or is it bringing a nonflat interpretation of the earth established by science to the Bible? Morris makes similar assertions about matters he sees to be in the Bible that I do not think are in the Bible at all. For example, he claims that the doctrine of God's creation of the world out of nothing, *ex-nihilo*, by means of God's speaking word, is taught explicitly in the Bible. Furthermore, he denigrates all other ancient cultures because they did not develop and could not understand an *ex-nihilo* doctrine.[7]

What does the Genesis record say about creation of the world?

> In the beginning when God created the heavens and the earth, the earth was a formless void and darkness covered the face of the deep, while a wind from God swept over the face of the waters. Then God said, "Let there be light"; and there was light. (Gen 1:1–3)

Notice, before God spoke the words of creation "Let there be . . . ," there was already a formless earth, a surface of the deep, and waters.[8] Some biblical interpreters say that the negative language of these first few verses of Genesis, as well as other places in Scripture, indicate creation out of nothing. That is not what the Bible says. The philosophical idea of creation out of nothing could only be cogently expressed after mathematical and Greek conceptuality had arisen. Christian theologians with philosophical skills had no difficulty in reading the doctrine of creation *ex-nihilo* back into Genesis. If you consult Bibles with the Apocrypha, you will find in 2 Maccabees 7:28 a nonphilosophical statement about creation of the world out of "what did not exist." I do not think, however, that Morris or others in his camp wish to make a doctrine of creation from nothing dependent exclusively on an apocryphal source. They prefer to see it in Genesis, even though it is not there explicitly.

Please do not think that my disagreement with the way some Christians use the Bible shows any attempt to discredit the Bible. As a Christian, I find myself in continuity with Christian believers throughout the ages in asserting the Bible to be the chief written document for participation in the faith. It is, of course, not the exclusive source of support for the Christian life; there are activities of prayer, communal worship, Eucharist, generosity, and others. I believe it to be an infallible guide to faith and practice. I have no difficulty in accepting it to be perfectly inspired by God.

Perfect in what sense? Perfect certainly not as a guide to perfect rational schemes, modeled on science or Greek philosophy, which can be brought back to the Bible to claim as its exclusive interpretation. One aspect of the Bible's perfection is that it confounds *any* rational philosophical system brought to it, unless such scheme is held tentatively. If God had intended to speak rationally (in terms of Greek philosophical thought) or scientifically (in terms of scientific theory), God would have done so. That God did not do so and spoke in an ancient prephilosophical and prescientific cultural mode causes us to ask, "Why?"

God did not want the Christian religion, as contrasted with the rationalism of Christian theology, to be accepted as a mere mode of thought. If we could participate with God completely through reason, it would not have been necessary for God to become incarnate in Jesus Christ. If we could achieve forgiveness of sin by rational means, Jesus would not have chosen to suffer and die for us. If we could participate with God fully by studying Eucharist, we would never need to take into our bodies Jesus' body and blood. All of these events are transrational and causative; in no way can rational philosophy approach them. Neither the Bible nor the Christian religion is primarily about knowledge.

The Bible is designed by divine inspiration to frustrate any rigid logical scheme brought to it, because thinking of the Bible as knowledge can obscure its true message—the love of God for the world. God's love, compassion, judgment, and wisdom are communicated best by personal relationship, within the church and with God directly, rather than by conceptual knowledge including theology. Untold numbers of noneducated Christians throughout the ages have participated in a love-and-justice relationship with God through the unique inspiration and excellence of the Bible. Most of them would not have dared to suggest that other Christians are exempt from God's favor, since they understood that any favor extended to them was by God's grace alone.

Morris and many Fundamentalists bring their narrow schemes to the Bible, it seems, in order to exclude other Christians from the faith. Morris believes that Christians who accept any portion of evolutionary theory are deceived by Satan. One cannot be a Christian and an evolutionist. Is this really what the Bible says? Absolutely not! The Bible is very open about science. No past science fits it exactly. No contemporary science gives us exact truth. The theories of science have always been a part of Christian theology. They are important to Christianity for the future, whether we recognize their presence or not. We shall greatly need the guidance of currently young Christians who appreciate science, particularly evolution, and who wish to participate in the adventure of relating science with the religion they love.

I wish that Morris and other Fundamentalists who have such rigid views on evolution, and also about those Christians who accept some parts of evolutionary theory, could accept the sentiment of the verses of "Amazing Grace," original and added, including this one:

> 'Twas Grace that freed my mind to wake
> From narrow ways that hide
> The world of wonder God did make
> Who speaks and breaks our pride.[9]

I wrote this verse as a response to my frustration over divisive differences among Christians about the issues of evolution and in hope that it might aid in a reconciliation of the separated parties.

Notes

[1] Henry M. Morris, *The Twilight of Evolution* (Grand Rapids: Baker Book House, 1963).

[2] Ibid., 33.

[3] Charles Caldwell Ryrie, *Neo-orthodoxy* (Chicago: Moody Press, 1956) 51. Quoted by Morris, 24.

[4] Morris, 36.

[5] Ibid.

[6] Morris, 66.

[7] Ibid., 75–76.

[8] Hugh Ross notes that if the perspective of Genesis 1:2 is from the point of view *under* the cloud cover, then anomalies of the Genesis account vanish. God created the initial cosmos as indicated by Genesis 1:1, but further creation took place as seen *from* earth. Hugh Ross, *The Fingerprint of God* (Orange CA: Promise Publishing Co., 1991) 165-66.

[9] The hymn "Amazing Grace," written by John Newton (1725–1807) when he was in his sixties, has over the years taken on a life of its own and accumulated verses to itself from various sources.

Chapter 6
Psychology: The Logic of the Soul

In previous chapters I have presented the essentials of the sciences studied and then shown the images from which philosophical positions about the sciences were derived. I then examined these philosophical positions to see how they affected the Christian religion. In this chapter the goal is the same, though the procedure is slightly different. Rather than look first at what we now call "scientific psychology"—the discipline that derives from experiments in psychology—we examine the older philosophical psychology—the body of ideas influenced by previous interpretations of the sciences, particularly mathematics. These two historical phases of psychology are both systematic because they use a mature logic. They follow on what we call presystematic psychology including that of the Bible.

The Greek words *logos* and *psyche*, which make up the word "psychology," mean respectively "logic" and "soul." In presystematic psychology there was no *logic* of the soul because there was no well-developed logic. Soul was understood simply as that which kept humans alive and therefore separated from the body at death. For example, Jesus spoke of those who could "kill the body but cannot kill the soul" but also warned against those who could "destroy both soul and body" (Matt 10:28). Psychology as the logic of the soul, or as further refined by the Greeks to be called "the study of the mind," has been cultivated since logic and philosophy began in early Greece. Christianity has adopted some of these well-formed doctrines of the soul.

We are interested in pursuing an understanding of the soul that was developed before contemporary experimental psychology began, what we call "the classical doctrine of the soul," and particularly in examining any influences the images of mathematics had on ideas about the soul. Then we shall examine the nature of the current science of psychology and its negative impact on the classical doctrine of the soul in Christianity. Finally, as a theological response in chapter 7, we shall begin to lay the foundations for a revised doctrine of the soul that is adequate biblically but also makes considerable sense within contemporary psychology.

Our three theses have relevance in the following way. In accordance with the third thesis, we attempt to show that philosophical ideas of the soul have been engendered by the discovery of mathematics in the Greek era and expressed by philosophers Plato and Aristotle and then by the theologian Augustine. In the modern era, new discoveries of mathematics affected ideas of the soul, which were expressed by mathematicians and philosophers Descartes and Leibniz. We call the view of the soul from Plato through Leibniz "the classical doctrine of the soul." The philosopher Hume promoted a different understanding of the soul, what we call "the associationist doctrine of the soul," because, for Hume, what was left of the soul was an association of sensations or ideas.

Reflecting our first thesis, Christian theologians accepted some of the ideas of the classical doctrine of the soul into Christian theology and then saw them as derivative from their religion. In accord with the second thesis, when the new science of experimental psychology emerged with its attendant philosophy following an associationist doctrine of the soul, it challenged the old ideas of the soul dependent on the old mathematics. As expected, significant conflict over the nature of the soul then occurred between psychologists and theologians.

Mathematics and an Idea of the Soul

I remind the reader of mathematical images, a Pythagorean point and a right triangle, we have already used to illustrate doctrines of God and the soul in chapter 2. A point, symbolizing unity, perhaps viewed by the Pythagoreans as about the size of a period at the end of a sentence, illustrates that unity has no internal divisions and never changes. If the soul, understood initially to be merely the enlivening principle of the body, is thought also to be unified, then it also can be seen as having no modifications. If the soul does not change, it does not decay or disappear at death. It is naturally eternal. We contrasted the Greek idea of an eternal soul with the New Testament and early Christian belief in resurrection of the body.

The true right triangle is not on the page where pictured, nor could it be anywhere in the real world; because, as pictured, its sides are neither straight nor its angles true. Its lines are not lines but fine and irregular solids. For Plato (427–347 B.C.), the true triangle understood by the mind is in a realm apart from this physical world and never changes. When the soul understands this transcendent triangle by participating with it, the soul "remains always the same and unchanging with the changeless."[1] The soul is also confirmed by this image to be eternal.

Plato, who was much influenced by these and other mathematical images, held that the soul had three parts. In a long passage in Book IV of the *Republic* where he compared the similarity of the soul with the state, he claimed that the soul was composed of mind, spirit, and desire. Mind, however, was clearly the superior of the other two faculties, for it named the immaterial substance of the soul that survived death of the body, whereas the other two faculties—spirit and desire—died with it.

Aristotle's idea of the soul was driven more by biological images than those of mathematics. Souls were more like vegetables than triangles. Plato's divisions of the soul—mind, spirit, and desire—were, as Aristotle said, different ways of life—which as self-originating always sought a goal. Vegetables and all other living things have goals, and hence, souls. He acknowledged that animal souls are more complex than vegetable ones, and that human souls are more complex than animal souls, because, among other things, humans have minds. For Aristotle, mind itself is defined in terms of life. It is self-origination guided by rational goals. It is at base the vegetable or animal soul, with a higher faculty—reason. Aristotle's philosophical position is a kind of atomic spiritualism rather than a materialistic atomism. He did believe in individual substances, vegetables, for example. His individual substances, however, had a complex interior structure and sought their fulfillment though goals. In short, they were alive. In contrast, the atomist's ultimate substances, the atoms, had no interior structure. They were dead.

The Christian theologians borrowed ideas about the soul from both Plato and Aristotle, but added something very significant even to the philosophical discussion. It is difficult for us to realize, being heir to and familiar with the intense subjectivity of these theologians, that the earlier Greek philosophers had little if any concept of consciousness. Theirs was a public world. Truth was understood to be objective. The Christian theologians, particularly Saint Augustine (354–430), turned inward to explore the matters of personal sin and salvation. Conscious introspection became a source of knowledge and the means of revelation. To find God, one must go deeply inward as led by God through prayer. After that, one may also discover the nature of reason by private access to the subjective structures of consciousness. This introspective exploration of the rational soul is quite different from Aristotle's more objective understanding of a soul as a self-actuating substance that pursues a goal.

In spite of his great discoveries of spiritual subjectivity, Augustine was still influenced philosophically by images from mathematics. He used them in the same way Plato did to show that the soul is immortal. In his treatise *On the Immortality of the Soul*, Augustine argued from the unchangeable nature of mathematics to the eternal nature of the soul. The argument (simplified) follows.

Anything that contains something eternal, that is, unchanging, cannot itself be noneternal. The soul contains mathematical knowledge, which is eternal. Therefore, the soul is eternal. We symbolize this relationship geometrically by the picture called "Soul." The soul cannot be totally destroyed without destroying the mathematical truth. Thus, the eternal existence of the mathematical truth entails that the soul cannot be destroyed. The argument rests on the

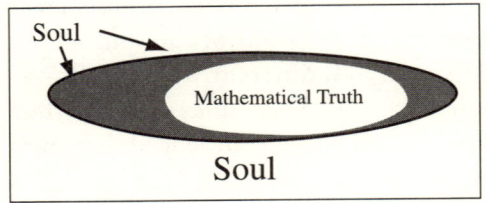

assumed unity of the soul; that is, the soul is unified and cannot be divided. For if the soul is composed of parts, the existence of part of the soul that is mathematical truth would only guarantee that the part of the soul that continues to live is the mathematical truth. This conclusion would be unacceptable, for it would take away the remaining subjectivity of the soul, since mathematical truth was still viewed as objective.

Following Plato and Aristotle, Rene Descartes (1596–1650) accepted an eternal soul but added an important new dimension. He showed that Augustine's intensely subjective soul conditioned by religious considerations could be affirmed to exist by procedures modeled on those used by mathematics. Descartes sought to reinforce by scientific means what was the orthodox Christian view of soul, seen then as supported by the Bible.

Recall our discussion of the Pythagorean theorem in chapter 2. We showed that given any right triangle whatsoever, we could construct two squares of equal area each containing four identical right triangles to the original triangle. When we erased the four equal triangles from the equal square areas according to the Euclidean maxim "if equals are subtracted from equals, the results are equal," we found that the square on the hypotenuse of the original triangle was equal in area to the squares on the other two sides—a statement of the Pythagorean theorem. The characteristic most appreciated by Descartes of a proof of this sort, indeed of all mathematical presentation, was that once begun and followed carefully, the results were without doubt, that is, indubitable.

Could there be a procedure modeled on mathematics for obtaining indubitable truth in philosophy?

Descartes answers "Yes" and gives his method (simplified) as follows. Accept only that which is presented clearly and distinctly. Divide difficulties into as many parts as possible. Begin with simple parts in order to understand the complex matters. Finally, make logical transitions so complete and reviews so thorough that we may be assured of omitting nothing.[2] This method is so vague, it has borne little fruit—except when used by Descartes. After denying the existence of the world, his own body, God, and even some mathematical truths, Descartes discovered that whenever he thought about anything, he must exist. This sentiment when expressed in Latin is his famous *Cogito Ergo Sum*, "I think therefore I am." From this one essential truth, Descartes could then argue for the existence of God and the physical world. The Cartesian highly personal and rational soul was discovered, not by an Aristotelian examination of the world of humans and animals, nor by an Augustinian quest through prayer, but by a rational procedure of doubt and insight modeled on mathematics.

Because the soul could be perceived without any reference to physical things, including one's own body, Descartes asserted it was a thinking substance completely independent of any physical (extended) substance. Thus was born Descartes's radical dualism: there are only two kinds of things, thinking substance and extended substance. The human body as extended substance is a machine that is controlled somehow by the soul, a thinking substance. Descartes thought that animals did not have souls; thus, they were only machines.

Gottfried Wilhelm Leibniz (1646–1716) thought that animals had lower grade souls. Indeed, he believed that all things had some kind of a soul and developed a philosophical position without Descartes's strict dualism. For our consideration, Leibniz's central contributions to the idea of a soul are about the soul's continuity. Each of us believes (rather strongly) that we are the same person now that we were a minute ago, or last week, even though many things may have happened to change us. As we change, our souls change, but we have the same identity. Even as we change, we seem to do so imperceptibly. Each state of the soul is continuous with past states. There seem to be no gaps in our consciousness, but a continual flow. Leibniz, as co-discoverer of the calculus, used it to understand the soul, in contrast with Newton, who used calculus to describe the mechanism of the world. How did the calculus help Leibniz to understand our experience of the continuity of the soul's flow? What are the images from mathematics he applied to the soul?

Reconsider the problem of finding the area under a curve—one of the two mathematical problems that precipitated the calculus. Begin by approximating the area by rectangles (shaded), as pictured in the diagram "Area Approximated by Large Rectangles." The height of each rectangle is determined by its leftmost side, which is the height of the curve.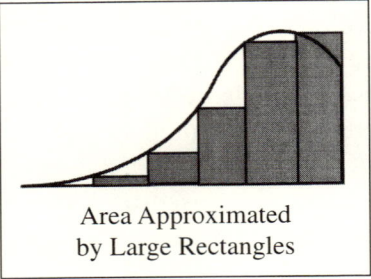

Area Approximated by Large Rectangles

The sum of the areas of the rectangles is not the area underneath the curve, but can be made to approach the area more exactly by increasing the number of rectangles—a process that automatically decreases their individual area, as shown in the picture "Area Approximated by Smaller Rectangles."

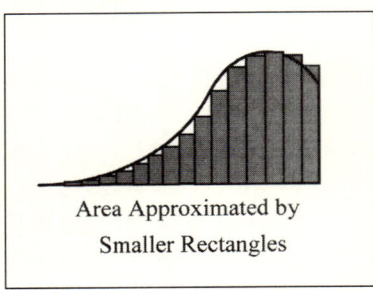

Area Approximated by Smaller Rectangles

Suppose we keep up this process. The individual rectangles get narrower and narrower. As their number increases, their sum approaches closer and closer to the area we want. Visualize an individual rectangle as its width gets smaller, as shown in the picture "Smaller Rectangles." I had to draw the smallest one as a line because of the resolution of my printer. We may still see it in our minds as a very small rectangle. How small? Surely the area of the decreasing rectangle can be made smaller than any pre-assigned number. Can it be made smaller than any positive number whatsoever? Both Leibniz and Newton thought at one time the answer to the last question was "Yes." They both accepted (tentatively) the existence of infinitesimals, quantities not zero but smaller than any number. In this view, one could add an infinity of infinitesimal areas to get a finite area.

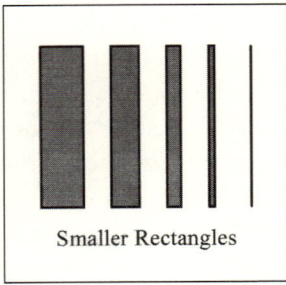

Smaller Rectangles

Why would both Leibniz and Newton accept such a confusing and ultimately contradictory idea of infinitesimals when it was not required by their mathematics?[3] The answer: Both men used infinitesimals to discover new legitimate mathematics and science. They were what we call images—mental pictures that were useful for the discovery, presentation, and understanding of mathematics and science but are not essential to their nature. The logical consistency of infinitesimals was questioned early on, but they were finally banished from the study of calculus by the development of more rigorous mathematics in the nineteenth century.[4] As originally understood, they are no longer used for the teaching of calculus.[5] They had a profound effect, however, on the considerations of Leibniz about the soul.

Think of getting the area underneath the curve above by an accumulation of infinitesimal areas. These infinitesimal areas are so dense that they cannot be added one by one, step by step (as in our graphic examples), because for any infinitesimal area, its neighbors are so close that none can be considered a next one. To show that, consider any infinitesimal area at a and assume there is a next one at b. The number b cannot be the next one, since there is a number between a and b, namely, $(a + b)/2$. As we add infinitely many densely-packed infinitesimals, the area changes smoothly and continuously as governed by a rational rule, in our case the function itself, without any gaps or stages. This is a model of the soul, which has its individual identity defined by its own rational principle. Though always identified as the same soul, it changes imperceptibly and continuously. Although we can notice that our current state of consciousness is different from five minutes ago, just as an infinitesimal area can be different from one a finite distance away, we seem to experience our present state of consciousness as an unbroken flow, in a pattern similar to the continuous connection of infinitesimal areas that were used in the early calculus.

The classical idea of the soul, which we have considered as influenced by mathematical developments, shows the soul to be a substance, existing through space and time, that is, unified, eternal, deeply subjective, continuous and, at least in humans, conscious. This view of the soul, which is accepted today in much practical theology, was challenged philosophically by English philosophers Hobbes, Locke, and Hume. Hobbes (1588–1679) sought to describe the mind and soul in terms of physical motion. His naive mechanical theory of mind was beset with many difficulties, such as an explanation of consciousness and the apparent unity of the soul. John Locke (1632–1704) developed a much more influential and appealing system that can be analyzed in terms of yet another mathematical image—the acts of counting.

What happens when we count the four objects in the picture "Objects"? Locke would claim that we receive a sense impression from each of them including their shape and color on the passive and blank slate (tabula rasa) of the mind. Once inside the mind, the active spiritual substance (similar to the classical soul) intuits from them ideas, whose further manipulation gives knowledge. In our example, an idea of unity derived from the sense experience of each of the four objects is combined with the others by the soul or mind in the act of counting to get the number four. Notice, the number four in this account is not innate to the human mind but created by it. It is not transcendent and eternal, as was the right triangle of Plato. It offers neither a guide to nor an assurance of an eternal soul. Indeed, the philosopher Hume would claim that it offered no assurance even of the existence of a soul.

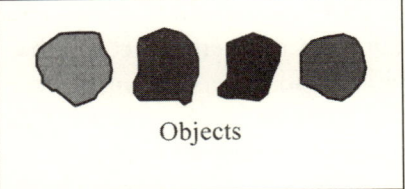
Objects

David Hume (1711–1776) believed that all true ideas were derived from simple impressions that occurred on the mind. As he looked inward, however, he saw no idea of the soul that compared in simplicity or intensity with the idea of, say, one of the objects pictured. The soul became for him, not the agent that associated the ideas of unity to get the number four, but at best an association of ideas itself, such as the number four. The soul was something developed out of the impressions, not something that sat back and viewed them. Hume changed the study of psychology. Psychology became no longer the logic of the soul, but the logic of the association of the ideas of consciousness—since there was no substantial self or soul to study.

Results from Cognitive Science

There is a legitimate challenge to the existence and nature of the classical soul in contemporary psychology. This mystery, almost paradox, comes from many areas but particularly from cognitive psychology. Simply put, we seem to experience subjectively an observer (what we might call a soul) of our internal experience. Yet we cannot find this soul objectively by any experiment. Since psychology is now based on public experiments, and not subjective introspection, we have little choice but to assert that the soul no longer exists in the domain of professional psychology. Let us look at some research on the brain confirming this position.

The brain is most interesting when it is alive, not dead. To examine the nature of the soul, should it exist, and its relationship to the brain, we must examine the brain when the soul presumably is present. Although we can get pertinent information from autopsies, recently developed techniques for studying brains in action have given significantly new and surprising information.

One fruitful study is an analysis of the perceptions and abilities, tested experimentally, of people who have had specific localized injuries to the brain primarily from stroke or accident. The location of the injury can often be determined by sophisticated X-ray techniques called "CAT scans" (Computerized Axial Tomography). Based on these many studies, it is clear that certain portions of the brain control certain functions of the body. For example, damage to a region of the left frontal lobe called "Broca's area" results in an unimpaired ability to understand but considerable difficulty in saying words to express ideas, whereas damage to what is called "Wernicke's area" does not affect the mechanical abilities to say words but severely restricts the ability to understand them.

Another technique uses the "PET scan" (Positron Emission Tomography), which can illuminate on a screen areas of a living brain that are using more fuel, specifically are more active. By this method one can plot the different areas of the brain that are involved in different activities: reading, talking, dreaming. Physicians can use the PET scan as a diagnostic tool to find regions of the brain that may be abnormally active or inactive, indicating a stroke, a tumor, or perhaps a psychological disorder.

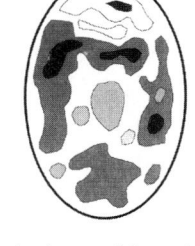

Active and Inactive Regions of the Brain Viewed in a Section By a PET Scan

In addition, psychological experiments that are nonintrusive to the brain have been developed to assess the functions and differences between the left lobe of the brain and the right lobe. The different functions of the lobes of the brain, the left dealing with more temporal matters and the right dealing with more spatial matters, for example, were discovered from patients whose connection (the *corpus callosum*) between the lobes had been surgically severed to help their severe epilepsy. One has to be a clever designer of experiments to distinguish the different functions of the two brain lobes in normal people because of the rapid communication between them. The left lobe knows something of what the right lobe has done, discovered, or recommends rather quickly, and vice versa. The picture we have of the brain so far is of various portions that communicate with each other, each of which controls various activities. Who is in charge? To whom (what), if anyone (anywhere), do the various parts report? Where is the self or soul in the brain?

One method of seeking to find the region of ultimate control in the brain (where the self or soul may reside) is to pursue the hierarchical control functions to their ultimate source. The brain operates as a kind of chain of command where some areas control other areas, which direct lower areas, which determine functions of behavior. This principle of hierarchy seems to be the standard throughout the nervous system. The routes of control can be illustrated by cutting the paths of communication between regions of lower and higher functions in experimental animals.

A cat whose brain is severed so that it has only its hindbrain and spinal cord still has individual trunk movements but cannot coordinate them to walk. If the cut is made so that the animal has use of its midbrain, hindbrain, and spinal cord, it can stalk a prey and kill and eat it. It does not seem to associate these activities with hunger. It may be starving, but will not search for food. If the animal is deprived of some functions of its cortex by cutting the brain at a higher level, it may organize its acts towards some purpose such as finding food when hungry. It does not, however, have its full personality and cannot operate effectively in complex situations. The top of the hierarchy in these experiments with cats, as well as humans, seems to be in the cerebral cortex.

Where in the cortex? The answer is paradoxical: sometimes somewhere, other times nowhere, and yet other times everywhere. Some experiments indicate that the controlling region of cats and humans is in one part of the cortex at one time and another part at another time. Other experiments show that some hierarchies do not even reach the cortex. And some experiments show that the whole cortex seems involved in the action. The point is, there are many different hierarchies interacting continuously, with one hierarchy seemingly in charge at one time and another in charge at another time. What does this information say about the center of control of the brain, the seat of the soul, the true you and I who are experiencing consciously the things around us? It says, should such a soul exist, it at least moves around and may even jump around.

An Agent in the Brain?

Although our internal experience indicates consciousness flows without gaps, contemporary cognitive experiments indicate that brain activities that produce consciousness are not continuous. They start and stop, react and rest, assume and give control to other functions of the brain. And they have discernible lapses and gaps. The startling factor is that consciousness—which, if accurate, should reflect the buzzing, jerky reality of the brain—is "filled in" by the brain to make both spatial and temporal experience *seem* continuous. Let us do a short experiment.

Close your left eye and stare at the left X in the top line with your right eye. If you adjust the book forward or backward slightly, you will see the O disappear. Then with your left eye still closed, look at an X in the bottom line in roughly in the same position as the X above it. Do you see any X's disappear to the right?

```
           X                              O
XXXXXXXXXXXXXXXXXXXXXXXXXXXXXXXXXXXXXXXXXXXXXX
```

The O vanishes because its image is falling on the eye's optic nerve, which has no receptors for reporting light. What do you see in the rather large "hole" where the O disappeared? Most of us see the same white background around it. Because the brain is receiving no information from that space, it seems to paint the same whiteness over it. When you look at the line of X's below, do you not see X's continuously with appropriate white space above and below? Your brain does not alert you that there is a large breach in your vision. You may have never noticed this rift until now. The brain, which is remarkably creative, makes the visual field seem continuous when it obviously is not. It will make white space, X's, or even more intricate patterns appear when there is no actual evidence coming to it that they are there.

Consider the diagram called "Pink Donut"[6] (see back cover). If you examine it closely, you will see that the space between the red squares is white, like the other spaces, and not pink as it appears. In this case, the brain fills in a color where it is not. We have caught the brain seemingly trying to make an area outlined by red lines to be a whole, even though this area is chopped up into discontinuous white sections.

The brain also tries to overcome temporal gaps in the mechanism of seeing. When we read, the words in our visual field seem stable over time, even though our eyes jerk from one position to the next. This page appears the same as it was a second ago. Using sophisticated technical methods, we can change the words in a paragraph after the eye starts moving and before it settles into a new position. Will we see the changes? Eyetracking experiments confirm the answer is "No." If you are a participant in the experiment, the page you are reading will look like this one—unchanging, rigid. If you are looking over the shoulder of a participant, you will see the words of the page rapidly changing. For the participant, her consciousness presents the page as constant over time, which it is not. In our ordinary reading, though our eyes jump from one position to another and the information comes to our brain in fits and starts, we do not notice it. The page always looks stable in time and space.

These experiments, and many others, show that the experience of dominant stability and continuity in our consciousness is an illusion that is quite tightly protected by the brain. Although the activities of the brain are jerky, discontinuous, and full of gaps (physicists say they are "quantized"), we see this world as a seamless piece in time and space. This active temporal and spatial organization by the brain is not its only function of showing disparate data as a whole.

Not only does the brain show our experience as continuous in space and time, it seems to present *all* of our experience in terms of its own background organization. That the brain offers our experience to us in organized wholes, and not in bits and pieces, has been pointed out convincingly by Gestalt psychology, pioneered by Max Wertheimer (1880–1943), Kurt Koffka (1886–1941), and Wolfgang Köhler (1887–1967). The genius of Gestalt psychology is in its experiments and images, of which we shall use only one.

Look at the white vase in a black background in the picture "White Vase." This is Edgar Rubin's famous example of how we see a picture in terms of a whole structure, a Gestalt, and not just in terms of its individual parts. Although the parts are exactly the same, with a shift of the vase to become white background for the black figures, we can see two people looking at each other. Notice, we see either the vase or the two people, not both  vase and people at the same time. The brain changes the orientation so that we see one or the other. The lesson here is this: we see things in general in terms of the context formed by the brain, and not just in terms of the visual data that impinges on the brain. The brain is very active in how we see.

Does this activity of the brain suggest, after all, there may be some controlling entity there, some undiscovered or undiscoverable soul, that at times supervises, other times merely influences, and yet at other times is influenced by the mechanical and electrical functions of the brain? Some scholars believe there is an argument for the existence of a soul (or mind) in the brain supported by the psychological experiments. Most cognitive scientists, however, as well as some Christian theologians, accept the fact that we have lost our (classical) souls. This belief is motivated by significant evidence, but primarily suggested by the current images of computers.

The Image of Computers

Alan Turing (1912–1954), who established the nature, scope, and limitations of computers in a single short article,[7] single-handedly began the discipline of computer science. In seeking the simplest ideal expression of a computing machine, Turing turned to human experience. He observed that in terms of the state of our consciousness and stimuli from our environment, we react, which leads to our experience of a different state of consciousness.

Turing radically simplified this description of human experience to apply to his machine, called a "Turing machine." He clarified exactly what he meant by a state of a machine (not consciousness), which was just a name or number, say 3. He declared that the stimulus to a Turing machine is its reading of a single letter of the machine's alphabet on a tape. He asserted that the Turing machine's action is to move left or right on its tape or print a letter of its alphabet. The different state of a Turing machine was, again, simply a name or number. All this happened on a machine defined logically in Turing's mind that could read letters from a tape, move left or right or print on the tape in terms of its state and letter read, and finally go to a new state. This machine was controlled by a Turing table, consisting of quadruples of symbols, each of which was, as we might expect: the initial state, the letter read, the action to be taken, and the new state. To find out what a Turing machine would do next, one would find the state it is in and the letter read, which identifies the appropriate quadruple in the Turing table, and read off what action it will take and what new state it will be in. A Turing table is a description of a procedure the Turing machine will accomplish. It is like a computer program that controls a computer.

What kind of procedures can a Turing machine do? Can it add or subtract or do other complex mathematics? Can it play the violin if given appropriate mechanical appendages? Can it perform the full activities of the human brain? Turing became convinced that his simple ideal machine, given an appropriately complex table, could do any specified procedure whatsoever that was well defined. This astonishing thesis, now known as the Church-Turing[8] thesis, has become a foundation of computer science and logic.

Turing went even further. He defined (the table of) a Turing machine that could read the table of any other Turing machine and perform its action. This meant a single Universal Turing Machine (UTM) could be constructed that can perform any well-defined procedure whatsoever. If someone could describe exactly how the human brain worked, a program (table) could be written (with great difficulty) so that the UTM would act like a human brain. Are there such Universal Turing Machines in existence today? Yes, and these UTMs are far easier to run and understand, as well as being much faster, than the original ideal UTM. Every desktop computer today that has a modern operating system and runs contemporary computing languages can act as a UTM. Even our ordinary personal computers could act with full human rationality, should we discover with clarity what the procedures of the brain are and write appropriate programs that represent these procedures.

The scope of computers is known. The problem of what computers can do now and in the future has been solved. As symbol-manipulating machines, computers can solve any problem for which there is a clear procedure for doing so. They can receive information from their environment from various input devices—for example, keyboards and cameras—translate this information into symbols, solve the problem symbolically, and then take physical action as its output symbols precipitate exact physical action. To repeat, if we could discover exactly how the brain works, and write clear procedures simulating this activity, we could create an electronic brain that mimics human rationality. This electronic brain would be incredibly slow as run by contemporary machines. The human brain is still, by far, the fastest (and most powerful) computer.

We believe the human brain to be at least similar to a computer, because we can now mimic many of the brain's functions by computers. Computers running expert systems software simulate many complex human skills. Computer chess programs can sometimes beat human grand champions. Computers, however, are also similar in construction to the human brain. The heart (central processing unit) of the most powerful computers is composed of simple gates that are either on or off. Combinations of these gates can give us all the logical functions that allow us to manufacture a general machine that can perform any well-defined procedure. We can construct these gates electronically and observe their action in simple cases. The active agents of brains that correspond to gates in computers are neurons, which themselves are either resting or discharging—either on or off.

Current computer technology provides a powerful image to suggest humans are soulless machines. It reinforces the psychological experiments that show no central controlling substance in the brain. Never do we observe any soul, subjectivity, or consciousness in the collections of gates in computers. Never do we observe any soul, subjectivity, or consciousness in any small collection of neurons. The current discipline of artificial intelligence flourishes in the art of making machines that can reproduce intelligent human activities. Yet as the discipline expands, the fact and mystery of consciousness, as well as the soul and self, become even more pointed. What and where is consciousness in a machine? What and where is the self in a human? From the cognitive science perspective, the answer is often heard that consciousness and soul emerge (somehow) from the complexity of interactions of the gates and neurons. Yet how can we get subjectivity in the whole brain if we cannot observe it in any of its parts?

The computing image also answers the question of why centers of control in the brain seem to move around. Different activities of the brain and body are controlled by circuits whose interaction with each other take different routes and therefore occupy different physical places at different times. It answers the question posed by Gestalt psychologists why experience has meaning only in terms of whole structures. The whole is the coordinating controlling software that interprets the sensation data. One sees the white vase only in terms of the governing software of that experience. A different programming control shows the whole to consist of two black faces looking at each other. It answers the question why the brain is active to "fill in" colors and space and to show our experience in time to be continuous. These are just activities of the programs of the brain created by evolutionary processes and not some soul substance.

It seems that the classical soul of the philosophers and theologians is dead, replaced by images from computers and reinforced by contemporary psychological experiments. Yet such a negative conclusion cannot be held with much satisfaction. I am surprised by literature in cognitive science, whose very purpose is to show there is no observer in the brain, falling into usage that is only appropriate for an observer in the brain. These "Cartesian slips" (from Rene Descartes, who advocated a substantial thinking substance) are often pointed out with some embarrassment by other cognitive scientists. Very few of us are satisfied with understanding the brain as a machine and nothing more. In our non-academic moments we have an experience of personal subjectivity. In our personal relationships we have experience of our own self and the selves of others. In our religious experience, we have experience of our souls. How should theology react to this serious challenge from science?

Notes

[1] Plato, *Phaedo*, 79d, trans. H. N. Fowler, *Loeb Classical Library* (Cambridge MA: Harvard University Press, 1958).

[2] Condensed from Descartes's "Discourse on the Method," Part II.

[3] The mathematics was about operations on series of terms presented algebraically and the insight that one could get sums of things (integration) as an inverse process of finding rates (differentiation).

[4] Bishop Berkeley challenged Newtonian infinitesimals as logically incoherent. Dismissing infinitesimals, Weierstrass and others put calculus on a firm foundation.

[5] A way of defining and including a new concept of infinitesimals was discovered by Cohen in this century.

[6] H. F. J. M. van Tuijl, "A New Visual Illusion: Neonlike Color Spreading and Complementary Color Induction between Subjective Contours," *Acta Psychologica*, 39: 441–45. Reprinted with kind permission from *Elsevier Science*-NL, Sara Burgerhartstraat 25, 1055 KV Amsterdam, The Netherlands.

[7] Alan M. Turing. "On computable numbers, with an application to the *Entscheidungs-problem*," *Proc. London Math. Soc.*, Ser. 2, 42: 230–65.

[8] The Church-Turing thesis was announced formally by Alonzo Church who arrived at it after consideration of mathematical problems independent of Turing machines.

Chapter 7
The Soul: A Response to Psychology

In the last chapter I presented a part of contemporary psychology that engaged a classical doctrine of the soul through cognitive experiments and the image of the computer. We have yet to speak about behaviorist and psychoanalytic psychology, which we shall postpone until chapter 8. It seems important to respond theologically and philosophically at this time to the apparent abandonment of the idea of the classical soul in cognitive psychology while the issues are fresh in our mind.

In accord with our third historical thesis that science promotes philosophical perspectives, we have shown that a philosophical understanding of the human soul emerged from human experience and became clarified by ideas from mathematics. Christians accepted this classical doctrine of the soul into their theology in accordance with our first thesis. Now, this philosophical, as well as theological, idea of the soul has become untenable in cognitive science because of recent experiments, as well as because of a dominating image of computers. We should not be surprised to see a conflict between the Christian religion, which claims that some assertion of a real soul is necessary, and cognitive science, which claims it is not. This discord is in accordance with our second thesis, because Christians, who accepted the classical doctrine of the soul influenced in part by science, find themselves uneasy with the new science over the issue of the soul.

What should a proper theological reaction be? One could claim that a classical doctrine of the soul is true to the Bible and therefore try to defend it against the evidence and images of contemporary science. I am not persuaded by these attempts, because the old arguments for the classical soul do not have appropriate cogency against the fresh and stimulating results from psychological experiments. Also a careful examination of scriptural assertions shows that the classical doctrine of the soul misrepresents the biblical position in a number of ways, especially as the classical soul is seen to be some eternal spiritual substance that can exist independently of the body. The Bible says nothing of such a spiritual substance and is more inclined to identify the soul with the body, although it does not (of course) state this position in exact philosophical language.

The Christian claim is that the Incarnate God came bodily as the baby Jesus, was painfully crucified in the flesh, physically died, and was buried as a body—and had a bodily resurrection. Jesus also gave us physical bread and wine as a symbol and reality of his body and blood in the sacrament of the Lord's Supper. There is a very earthy emphasis in the biblical narrative about human souls that is de-emphasized in the classical doctrine of the soul. For example, consider the often-used euphemism about death as a "passing away." "We regret to inform you that Professor Smith passed away last evening." The background understanding of this usage is of a spiritual substance that leaves the body and "passes away" somewhere. Such usage seriously detracts from the reality and meaning of physical death. Christians never speak of Jesus as passing away on the cross. Jesus *died*. The great dignity of the Christian religion resides in his actual physical and bodily death.

A better way for theology would be to establish a philosophical doctrine of the soul that would be closer to the biblical position—especially if such a revised doctrine of the soul could also help clarify contemporary psychological experiments. Let us be careful, however, to keep our goals well set. We do not want to do philosophy of science for the singular benefit of philosophers or scientists. We are not prepared to try to influence the nature of practice of science. We are not trying to engage the philosophical community over the fundamental nature of metaphysics. We only wish to examine perspectives on a classical doctrine of the soul that tend to lead one away from a biblical position and also conflict radically with contemporary cognitive science. We seek a new position that is both biblical and makes sense within contemporary science. These are admittedly grand words in this last sentence and are uttered with some hesitation. The goal, however, is worthy of attention because it seeks reconciliation and understanding between the biblical Good News and the brilliance of contemporary science. We should not be timid in this venture, for its importance is considerable.

What are some of the biblical and theological requirements for a soul? Foremost, the soul must exist. A soul is mentioned on numerous occasions in the Old and New Testaments. In addition, the soul is understood to be deeply subjective. It is an arena in which conscience, and the awareness of sin, judgment, and forgiveness are felt. It also has a fundamental experience of continuity with itself. It recalls its past decisions and their consequences. It can be self-critical. It can have an ongoing relationship with God through prayer. Although the New Testament emphasizes resurrection of the body, and not an eternal soul, the resurrected Jesus is presented as having a new body (See Luke 24:37-43, John 20:19, and 1 Cor 15:42-44). The soul of the new body has continuity with its own past. Jesus, for example, remembered his friends. Notice we have kept all the characteristics of the classical doctrine of the soul, with the exception of its naturally eternal nature. Even this remaining robust doctrine of the soul, with its existence, its subjectivity, and its continuity with itself, is effectively challenged by contemporary experiments in psychology. There seems to be no room in the image of a computer for this or any other kind of soul.

The Soul as a Sequence of Events

We need to examine carefully exactly what in the biblical doctrine of the soul is challenged by psychological experiments. In spite of the evidence and images of the last chapter, I do not think contemporary psychological experiments reflect adversely on an existing, observing, deciding, subjective, and continuous soul. What they do challenge is a philosophical assumption about the soul—and the nature of being in general. The psychological experiments present evidence against the idea of a soul continuously existing as a substance through space and time. This dominant and currently held philosophical assumption is not taught in the Bible, nor is it seriously questioned by the philosophical proponents of the classical position on the soul. We seek to challenge and revise this classical idea of a substance by asserting that true substance is a sequence of events, which in their singularity do not exist through space and time. We are now beginning to introduce ideas from a contemporary philosophical position called "process thought."[1]

To show the distinctions between a classical idea of substance and what we propose, consider the image of a person walking and the image of a motion picture of the person walking. We think of the actual person walking as more real than the filmed picture of her walking because, among other things, the film consists of distinct frames in which the image of the person is at rest in each frame. When shown in rapid sequence, the filmed person *appears* to be walking, although we know that in the time between frames there is no substance shown of the filmed person. The actual person, under current assumptions, exists between the frames, and indeed is considered to subsist continuously through the places and the times she walks. The filmed version, however, consists of a sequence of picture events that are shown (almost) instantaneously, and these events as shown do not exist continuously through time.

The distinctions between the filmed person and the actual person, however, are not as radical as they might seem. In watching an actual person walking, we see and feel her in terms of the discontinuous processes of our nervous system. The eyes do not see continuously because they jump from place to place and do not see carefully as they move. Even when the eyes are stable, the information received by them comes in bunches and is transmitted to other areas in the brain in fits and starts. Remember the eye-tracking experiment where words were changed in a text when the eye started moving, but the page always appeared stable. The brain gives the impression of the stability of the page as well as the concreteness of a person walking through space and existing through time. We know, however, that neither the page nor the person walking need be continuous in space and time. Multiple experiments have shown us otherwise.

There is no direct and conclusive scientific evidence that a substance exists through space and time. Indeed, contemporary physics, which we shall examine later, gives much evidence to the contrary. The classical doctrine of a substance is an assumption about reality in general—a massive and dominant one—that has been held tenaciously by some theologians, philosophers, and scientists since the beginnings of rational thought. We challenge it because of the awkwardness it entails for the existence of the soul in contemporary science. Psychological experiments indicate there is no thinking or feeling substance—as substance is defined classically—in the brain. Yet we all experience ourselves as thinking and feeling selves. Christian theology requires the existence of a human soul. I believe we can rediscover our existing souls for the benefit of religion and science by a philosophical shift in focus.

I propose that the walking person, as well as any substance, consists of distinct events, each of which does not make transit through space and time. Movement is registered in our experience by perception of the sequential nature of the events that occur in distinct places and times but do not in themselves move. The motion picture takes pictures frame by frame of a walking person who herself—so we assert—also consists of successive events, which we call person events. The person events occur far more rapidly than the motion picture frames. The solidity we think we observe in the person and not the moving picture is due primarily to our knowledge of how the projection machine works and our less well-known understanding of human perception. If we did not understand the mechanics of the projection camera, we might never know that distinct pictures on the film were being shown. We forget about our knowledge of projection most of the time when we watch a movie. Because we do not yet know the full mechanics of our bodily perceptual system, we do not naturally assume that substance consists of distinct events. We follow our experience and the massive attempt of consciousness to present things as continuous and assume that substance exists through space and time. Because of this assumption, scientists, philosophers, and theologians have established their disciplines so the assumption is hardly ever questioned. I acknowledge that this new idea of a substance is difficult for Christians and scientists, because it is so unfamiliar.

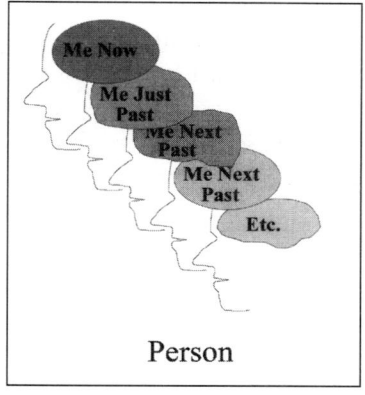

Person

Although person events considered objectively are distinct and discontinuous, they are known subjectively as our ordinary presented experience in the moment. My current person event is the totality of my immediate experience—right now. It is symbolized as Me Now in the diagram called "Person." Past predecessor events are labeled *Me Just Past*, *Me Next Past*, and so on. I propose that an event of this sort, viewed from the outside, will take up a distinct part of space and last through a small finite period of measurable time. It will occupy some region of the body, normally in or including the brain.

Spatio-temporal regions of the brain generally do not overlap, but the spatial regions may. That is, two events may occupy the same spatial region but occur at slightly different times. A subjective event in the brain may include spatially many other events including some parts of the hierarchy of nerve events that are influencing it. These person events may also move around sometimes here, sometimes there, sometimes including the whole brain—even extending from the brain to other parts of the body. In this perspective, the true you, which we can still call a "substance," is a sequence of these subjective events. Your soul is this sequence of soul events. In the diagram "Person," it would be symbolized by the many shaded regions, each representing a central or soul event. Notice, the soul in this interpretation is not naturally eternal. It can be born, live, and cease to exist.

The reluctance we may have in accepting the idea of a soul as a sequence of distinct events may be due to the difficulty in giving up the idea that the rest of the brain and body, which support soul events, are old-fashioned, hard, existing-through-time, substantial events. The image we have to overcome is of the soul as a fitful, wispy spirit in the throes of a hard, uncompromising machine. Understanding the soul as a "ghost in a machine" is a bad idea for any philosophical or theological position. The reality I seek to propose is of a concrete soul event that is, if you like, more real than the body events that support it—the molecules, nerves, circuits, and mechanical brain—because it is the dominant event of the whole bodily complex of events. This event as following on past bodily and soul events can be seen and touched objectively in the guise of the body, although as a soul event it never shows its full subjectivity to an outsider. It may appear as (part of) the body, or we may feel it directly. In short, the events of the soul are physically as real as any other existing things. I can speak literally and truly about having feeling-glimpses of the soul of my human friend or my cat.

The soul, even as distinct events, has continuity with itself. We may have an experience with our soul as far past that is more intimately connected with our current experience of our soul than we have of any experience of present or near past physical things. For example, I may feel the same joy or hurt that I felt as a child more intensely than I now experience the things I may be seeing. Christian experience involves a subjective life of the soul whose profound connection seems essential to the heart of the religion. How do we account for the sense of timelessness of the soul of which the Christian mystics speak in their more profound experiences of God? How do we account for the experience we may have of the transcendent God who becomes involved in history and physical time—and encounters the soul? How do we account for the history of a soul that knows conversion, judgment, and forgiveness in the rough and tumble of ordinary life? Are there not aspects of our experience, religious and secular, that show there is more in this life than what is bound to and explained by physical time?

In answer, I propose there is a fundamental distinction between time as measured in the physical sciences and the kind of developmental structure that occurs within a single soul event. We have a sense of subjective transition, an internal and different kind of time in our inner experience from that measurable by clocks. Consequently, we say that the internal growth of a soul event is nontemporal even though there are some aspects of its development that occur "before" others. By analogy, 1/2 comes "before" 3/4 without any necessary time sense attributable to order in the real numbers. (There is order in the real numbers without any temporal counting.) We can say that a soul event in its process of development synthesizes causal influences received "initially" without requiring any temporal sense of before and after. It is this subjective nontemporal "time" in which the development of each singular soul event takes place. It is this internal process that has no physical time calculation that can give us a sense of the soul's unity back through physical time.

Each soul event receives initial causal influence from its predecessor events, primarily from its immediate past soul event, but also from brain and bodily events, as well as events outside of but mediated by the body. The soul event accepts some causal determination from past events by absorbing them and their influence to begin the process of self-development in its own internal and subjective time structure. It has an intimate association with its immediate past soul event as the event that is most real to it and the event that is most causally influential on it. It not only absorbs this immediate past soul event into its very being, but is determined to be what it is in large measure by this immediate past event. Moreover, this immediate past soul event has a similar relationship to its immediate past soul event as in the diagram called "Soul." Thus, each soul event has an internal and intimate experience of its past soul events as each of these events interprets its own past. This diagram only symbolizes soul events. It would be more suggestive if it included bodily as well as other events that were influential on the coming-to-be nature of the soul event.

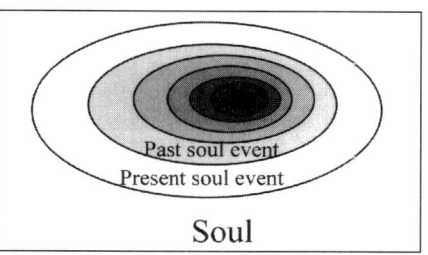

The physically nontemporal coming to be of a soul event in subjective time includes its past soul events in a bond so close they cannot be separated objectively. These past soul events, as well as other events, are welded together in a nontemporal synthesis that is the reality of the contemporary soul event—how it feels about something. Yet the soul can examine the soul. I can remember a childhood discovery that was horrible. I can remember it in a number of ways; that is, I can have various subjective feelings about the discovery that was felt with horror. I can also remember the discovery with a similar horror that was felt initially because I am examining my soul. That is, I can have an understanding about my past soul that I interpret with a certain emotional feeling, or I can experience that same feeling I had at one time, in this case horror. I have access to feelings in my soul accumulated over the years that no one else can get at, at least not exactly, in the way I can.

My soul has an intimacy and continuity that is hidden, at least in part, to others. My soul also has a unity stretching back to its beginning.

Some may ask, "Since the soul is a sequence of discrete events, could there be gaps between successive soul events?" You may have thought this when first looking at the diagram "Person." Obviously, this question could have disturbing meaning for our sense of the soul's continuity. One does not want a "gappy" soul. The answer: there are possible gaps in the soul when viewing in physical or scientific time. However, there are no gaps when viewed from the internal process of development of a soul event.

Whoa! Am I not introducing difficult views of time to explain both the event nature and continuity of the soul? As we shall discover, contemporary physics requires us to reconsider a Newtonian common sense view of time. Both relativity and quantum mechanics require a new stance. I am adapting ideas about time from current science in order to reclaim the Christian soul in its full vigor. This soul not only exists and can examine itself and have historical relationship with God; it can also understand its past self in intimate continuity with its resurrected self—even though there may be a "scientific" temporal gap between the two of millennia. I ask the reader's patience on these matters until we can discuss the issues of time in science.

Soul and Body

The soul event has some freedom to choose what it shall be, but normally it is massively and causally conditioned by the body, particularly the events of the brain. Brain events have causal sources in previous brain events, but also receive influence from previous soul events. The soul influences the body, and the body influences the soul in reciprocal manner. The soul exists because of the body, and the body cannot live without the soul. Not only is the soul privately connected with itself over time, but the soul and body are also intimately joined. The soul has its body and the body its soul, each in a mutually dependent relationship. When the body dies, the soul dies—unless both are resurrected by the power of God. The biblical doctrine of the resurrection of the body (with its attendant soul) is much more difficult to accept than a doctrine of a naturally eternal soul. In the biblical doctrine one has no natural right to life after death. One's hope rests exclusively on the power and mercy of God.

To illustrate the relationship between body and soul, consider the mundane act of speaking a sentence. In mid-sentence, a soul event accepts influence from a predecessor soul event to finish the sentence, but also receives influence from bodily events that indicate a word is being spoken. The current soul event responds to the intent of the past soul event and asserts in its own right that the next word be spoken. The brain events recognize this intent as causation on their activities, and, along with influence from previous brain events, neurons fire and brain circuits are energized to start the mouth's speaking of the next word.

Not all kinds of bodies have souls. There are substances, which are structures of events similar to the human body, but are soul-less. Rocks and vegetables are examples. They are societies of events that do not have a sequence of dominant events. A dominant event such as a human soul event is the culmination of the influences of bodily events. A sequence of dominant events, like the human soul, sums up the human body, makes (limited) choices on its own, and influences the body in terms of its goals and purposes. A rock has no overall purpose or unity of feeling. Its significant parts, which are still events, influence and act causally on each other in a pattern only to sustain their successive existence as a rock.

Souls and the Images of a Computer

We have before us two differing images of the human self and body, one including souls and soul events and the other derived from computers. The computing image allows no room for the soul image, but the soul image can, so I assert, allow for the computing image. What is a computer, if we insist that the philosophy of events is primary and the classical doctrine of hard substances moving through time and space is not?

A computer is composed of events and sequences of events we call electrons, atoms, molecules, and compounds. Electronic events are most important for computer operations. As they become electrical currents, electronic events are controlled by thoroughly predictable decision devices called "gates." The electrons as event sequences are similar in their most general structures to soul events but with one major difference. They have little freedom of choice, whereas soul events at critical times in the life of the soul can make significant decisions that affect the future of the soul. Although electronic events are almost completely determined by their past history, they do have some variability.

Contemporary quantum mechanics indicates that one cannot predict exactly what an electron will do. It is possible to design experiments where the microscopic unpredictability of 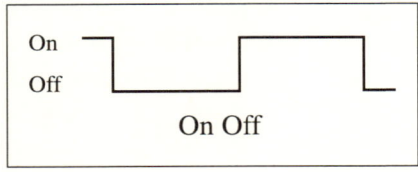 electrons can affect the large-scale operations of a machine. A computer is designed precisely to prevent any of that. Digital technology, which designs its gates so that they are either on or off, utilizes the fact that millions of electrons have an average state such that, whether signifying on or off, the aberrations of the smaller number of electrons have no effect. Computers are constructed so that any freedom possibly exercised by an electron to go against the norm will be completely discounted. If we signify *on* by the upper crest and *off* by the lower crest (say 5 volt and 0 volt stages) in the diagram called "On-Off" and then magnify the actions of the electrons at the very top of one of the crests, as in the diagram called "Electron Action," we see that a state is by no means exactly uniform. Individual and groups of electrons assume different states as indicated by the jagged lines. The average state, however, is always read as *on* and never as *off* or "not quite sure," because the different states of *on* and *off* are far apart compared to the variability of the states of the electrons. A computer is designed to give always the same output in terms of the same input. We would not be happy with our computers if they gave us different answers for the same defining conditions because of some unpredictable actions of the electrons inside it.

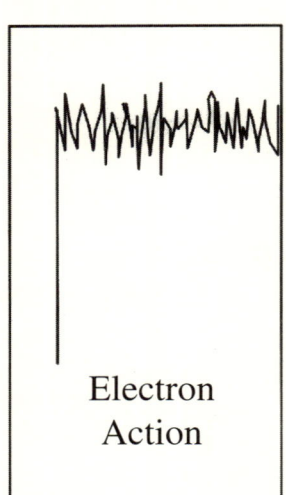

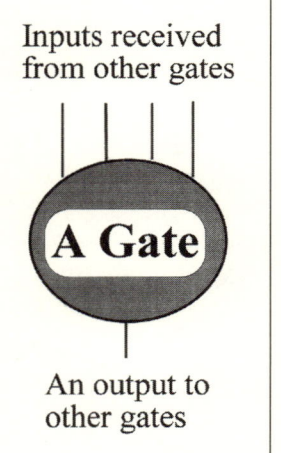

A computer gate is an electronic device that has multiple inputs and one output symbolized by the picture called "A Gate." Each input received from some other gate is either on or off (often five volts or zero volts),

and the output determined by the gate is either on or off depending on the polarities of the inputs. The total function of a computer is organized in terms of the activities of these simple gates. A neuron, the fundamental unit of the nervous system including the brain, is a nerve cell composed of dendrites, cell body, and axon (as pictured in the diagram "A Neuron"). The dendrites accept inputs from the other neurons, sometimes in many thousands, where each input, like those of a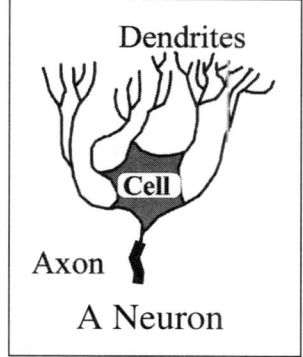
computer gate, is either on or off; that is, it either has an appropriate excitation potential, or it does not. The neuron delivers its one output through its axon in terms of the all-or-none law, which states, in simple terms, the neuron either fires or it does not.

Although the design and function of the neuron are strikingly similar to the computer gate, the neuron differs in some details; for example, different neurons vary in the electric potential difference that will trigger them, whereas computer gates are normally activated by similar differences in potential; the same neuron may vary in and be influenced by the frequency of firing, whereas computer gates are all run by the same clock. Computer gates are simpler than neurons because they have been designed to be simple for exact purposes. Neurons have evolved to their present efficiency and have some functions in addition to those of computer gates. Nevertheless, any well-defined procedure executed by the millions of neurons in the brain can be replicated by computer circuits. This is the well-grounded Church-Turing thesis. Because of the similarity of design and function of computer gates and cellular neurons, we can say at least the brain functions as a computer. We can say this, of course, within the perspective of cognitive science—but also within the perspective of the philosophy of event structures I am trying to articulate.

Although the electrons, atoms, and molecules that drive the chemical and electronic actions of neurons have as sequences of events some minimal freedom and variability, their differences from the norms that determine the all-or-none firing of neurons are inconsequential—just as the self-induced variability of electronic events do not affect computer action. The neuron structures act like computer circuits. From the same inputs, they normally give the same outputs—but not always.

The neuron is itself, so I assert, an event structure, with a sequence of dominant occasions that are influenced by its body of electrons, atoms, and especially molecules (because of its chemical nature), but also by its immediate past occasion. It can also be influenced in a significant way by the dominant occasion of the organism, which we have called a "soul event." This soul event has more freedom to choose its own nature than neuron events, and can influence the neuron events, especially those that are sensitive to very slight variations in inputs. Some neurons are poised to change slightly the conditions of their firing as influenced by the soul event. Thus the soul as a sequence of soul events can have influence on the body—cause it to move, talk, and think. And the body has massive influence on the soul supporting it from the past and determining the nature of its being in the present. It does not determine the soul completely. The soul event has some self-determining influence on what it shall be.

I indicated in the last chapter that the image of a computer as applied to brain activities answered certain puzzling questions raised by contemporary psychological experiments. Why do the centers of control in the brain seem to move around? The answer was, different controlling software circuits were activated at different times and places in the brain. We can now say from a philosophy of event structures that the dominating soul event that receives influence from the events of neuron circuits in the brain can also occupy and include different regions of the body at different times. Why does experience have meaning only in terms of whole structures, as the Gestalt psychologists remind us? The whole is not only shown by the controlling software at the time we experience sensory data, but the soul event coordinating and influenced by the software unifies the experience, which is its exact being. The brain is active to "fill in" colors and space and to show our experience in time to be continuous because the dominant soul events are active to synthesize bodily experience including that derived from the events of brain circuitry.

A computer is distinguished from almost any living organism because it has no dominant soul event and no sequence of soul events, which we now can understand to be our souls. To state the obvious, a computer has no soul. We, on the contrary, experience our own souls, at least in our nonacademic experience. It is utterly remarkable that non-souled electronic machines such as computers can replicate so many human skills, including those that employ rational decision making. These activities of the discipline of artificial intelligence are some of the most exciting work being done in contemporary science, and I heartily endorse and celebrate it. The study allows us to plumb the depths of the mechanical (a better word is procedural) activities of the human soul that are influenced by the computer-like structure of the brain. These activities, however, in no way threaten the existence of the soul. The more we follow the study of the procedural activities of the brain and try to mimic its powers, the more we become aware, by contrast, of our souls—which speak to us familiarly on almost all occasions.

Note

[1] Process thought is derived from the philosophy of Alfred North Whitehead and enriched by the creative analysis of contemporary philosopher Charles Hartshorne. There are major scientists in every discipline of science who are process-oriented, as well as theologians and philosophers.

Chapter 8
Psychology and Determinism

In chapter 6 we examined the classical doctrine of the soul and its challenge by some of the results of cognitive psychology and followed in chapter 7 with a theological and philosophical reaction to the conflict. In this chapter we present two other major parts of the discipline of contemporary psychology: behaviorist and psychoanalytic psychology, and examine their relationship to the philosophical and religious problem of determinism. These areas of psychology are considered scientific because they depend heavily on empirical data: experiments for behaviorist psychology and medical observation for psychoanalytic psychology. Each of these disciplines also conforms to our third thesis that new sciences generate philosophical orientations. Indeed, each discipline has its identity primarily in terms of its philosophical orientation. Further, each is seriously challenged, both inside and outside the scientific community, because of its philosophical orientation.

The Behaviorist Position

Although behaviorism affirms that psychology is studied under strict methodological restriction, primarily an examination of responses to stimuli by objective methods, it is characterized more by what it is against than what it is for. Begun in 1914 by J. B. Watson (1878–1958) in his book *Behavior*, the movement became dead-set against what we have called the classical soul. It asserts there is no mental stuff distinguishable from physical things as Descartes maintained. Since there is no "thinking substance," there is no substantial consciousness to study. Since there is no substantial consciousness, psychology must avoid any of the kind of introspection like that practiced by Augustine or by psychologists of the nineteenth century.

The kind of experiments appropriate for human psychology are only those similar to animal experiments—where we cannot communicate with the animal about its conscious experience. Indeed, we cannot presume the animal has consciousness. We certainly cannot examine the animal's purposes. By extension to humans, the methodology precludes our assuming a human has consciousness or purposes—even if she tells us about them. Behaviorists attempt to redefine what most of us call "purpose" to be some kind of behavior, called "goal-directedness." When a human describes her inner experience, behaviorists may label it "verbal behavior"; thinking is called "subvocal verbal behavior." These so-called "behaviors," named for purpose, inner experience, and thinking, were thought amenable to examination only through experiments. In consequence of its methodology, behaviorism has become a philosophical limitation of what psychology is about. It has made a major contribution to psychology, and learning in general, by its success in what it sought to do: describe psychology in terms of biology and by means of appropriate experiments describing human activities and reports. Unfortunately, it became overlain with (often unrecognized) philosophical assumptions, chief among them a dominant mechanism still lingering from the Newtonian age.

Our interest in behaviorism for this chapter stems from its mechanistic philosophy. It was a mechanism that, contrary to Newton's position, had no concept of soul. Since there was no room for genuine human choice or agency exercised by a soul, one had to view human activities as strictly determined. The causes are in the environment—the stimuli—and the results are human and animal behavior—the response. Although we may believe that causes affect consciousness, inner experience, a sense of purpose, and a knowledge of the soul, these latter have no agency or consequence on our behavior according to behaviorists. The firm, causal, and determined link is between stimulus in the physical environment and the physically observable response measured by the behavior of the organism.

Not only is it true that "given the stimuli, the response can be predicted," Watson also maintains that "given the response, the stimuli can be predicted."[1] In the behaviorist's dream of a completely worked out system of psychology, one could look at the environment and presumably predict exactly what a human would do. Also one could look at human behavior and determine exactly what its causes were. If true, then psychology could not only learn the causes of behavior, but in manipulating the causes could strictly control human behavior.

The central image associated with behaviorist psychology is of a direct causal link between stimuli of a human organism and its responses. In that process, consciousness (should it exist) may be affected by the stimuli but has no effect on the human's physical responses. As in the drawing "Behaviorist Filters and Other Filters," behaviorists seem to look through dark glasses and see only the causal connections between stimuli and responses, whereas most of us use a different filter and see consciousness involved in determining our action.

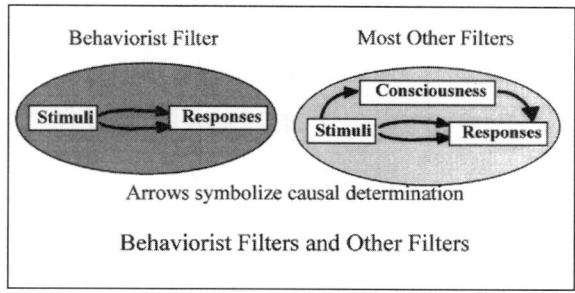

Behaviorist Filters and Other Filters

Psychoanalytic Psychology

It may seem ironic that Sigmund Freud (1856–1939), the founder of psychoanalysis, whom we shall classify with the behaviorists as a proponent of determinism, began his momentous discoveries by seeking the purpose of neurosis. Prior to Freud, abnormal human behavior—self-destructive hysteria, for example—was generally seen as pointless. It made little sense to assume that victims of such apparent madness intended it. Medical practitioners thought there must be some biological condition that caused the irrational behavior. Freud, however, maintained that the strange behavior of a neurotic could not be accurately described unless we understood his purposes. He treated aberrant behavior as goal-directed.

What could possibly be the goal of a cultured, say Christian, adult, otherwise concerned with the welfare of children, who participates in known antisocial and irrational behavior such as sexual exhibitionism towards children, thereby subjected himself to possible social disgrace and punishment as well as a feeling of sin, failure, and judgment before God? Freud would say it was not his current sexual desire that overwhelmed and motivated the man, but an intent, however misguided, to protect himself from the awfulness of specific childhood fears and anxieties. The source of this terror might not be known consciously to the person, because it was repressed, so Freud would maintain, into the powerfully motivating but nonconscious parts of the self. By recalling and reliving these experiences in the presence of a trained counselor, the fears might be understood consciously, and the power of their irrationality might be broken.

For example, a male child might love his father but fear him intensely because of the child's natural and sometimes sexual feeling for his mother. The fear could be so strong sensing (probably in error) the father's imminent desire to punish or even kill the child that he could not face it consciously. The events imagined or real that precipitated the fear as well as the fear itself so damaging to self-confidence were banished, so Freud maintained, to a subconscious part of the self. From this nonconscious realm these fears could act and impair the man's normal adult sexuality. Any intended sexual relations with an adult woman might trigger a memory of his mother and engage subconsciously the old fear of his father's wrath, whereas exhibition towards children seemed safer—even though recognized consciously as more heinous from a social and religious perspective. The man would choose without conscious knowledge the aberrant behavior to ease his subconscious fear.

I emphasize this particular explanation of sexual exhibitionism as an example, because it would not fit all cases. A proper explanation is relevant to a patient only if it could be discovered through participation between patient and counselor in a process called psychoanalysis. Freud did, however, observe—and proclaim—general patterns that might fit many cases (the one for the example above is called a "castration complex"), and from these ideas he began to develop what we can call a philosophy of the self.

Freud was not the first to discover the existence of a subconscious aspect of the self. Christian tradition felt deeply this darker part of the soul. The apostle Paul, who became painfully aware that he could not control his actions by conscious choice,[2] wrestled with this irrational side of himself until his death. What we may call "the subconscious" was described by the early theologians in their doctrine of original sin, further acknowledged by Augustine, and articulated with particular depth and force by Martin Luther. The nonconscious self, however, was obscured by the modern philosophy of Descartes, Leibniz, Newton, Locke, and Hume, among others, as well as by their theological followers.

They insisted that the world—including human nature—was essentially rational. Their model was the clarity of mathematics, which could present itself vividly in consciousness. What was not capable of being made clear and distinct, corresponding to the vividness of the ideas of Descartes or the sense experience of Locke, was considered to be an emotive expression and without descriptive value. Going against this modern tradition, Freud not only reaffirmed the existence of a subconscious part of the self but also gave it great force in determining the actions of humans. He was particularly effective in describing mechanisms by which the subconscious acted. Surprisingly, his theory and methods gave some predictive power about human behavior and explained aspects of hitherto inexplicable irrational behavior. He also claimed that many people improved under his therapy.

If Freud developed a theory that explains behavior in terms of people's choices, how can we claim that his position is deterministic, or that human behavior is set fast by forces not sensitive to human choice? Aside from the generally deterministic attitude among the physical and biological sciences, Freudianism became viewed as deterministic, not because determinism is required by Freud's philosophy, but because his perspective challenged a particular view of the nature of choice derivative from the philosophy of his day—and ours. The act of choosing was understood to be a conscious experience where one decides between rational alternatives. Against this position, Freud said that the real determination of human behavior is made in preconscious experience where the activities of rational choice have little play. Although the normally proper and religious man of our example might decide repeatedly in conscious thought never to participate in sexually exhibitionist behavior towards children again, these choices became overwhelmed by his fears held subconsciously that were hidden from his everyday consciousness. The man's unsociable activities were controlled by his subconscious.

The clue to understanding a Freudian psychological determinism is the claim that childhood experiences (rigidly) determine the subconscious. For if this is so, then Freudian determinism is similar to that of the behaviorists. The only difference is, behaviorists see through their filter that stimuli determine directly human responses, whereas Freudians see through their filter that childhood and other stimuli determine the subconscious, which in turn controls human responses. In the diagram "Freudian Filter," the arrows going directly from stimuli to responses symbolize exact physical, chemical, and biological causation.

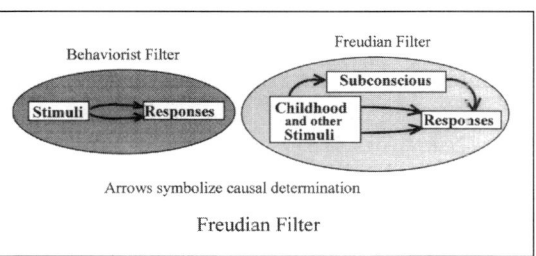

Freudian Filter

Consciousness and Freedom of Choice

In order to adapt to the developments in cognitive science, I spoke in the last chapter of considering substances, including the soul, as a sequence of events. The experience of the continuity of the soul required for any biblical perspective was interpreted to be a result of each soul event constituting itself by a process of integration from its past bodily and soul events. One feels in each subjective experience past soul events in a unity that goes back as far as memory or the subconscious can provide. In this section we distinguish the differences between conscious and subconscious experience in the process of development of each soul event in order to interpret a biblical perspective on sin that utilizes some of the insights of Freud. I suggest the secularist Freud has reminded us of aspects of human nature clearly understood by the apostle Paul, Augustine, and Luther that have been obscured in modern liberal theology. Further, I believe that the atheist Freud has unwittingly called Christians back to a more biblical understanding of the human condition.

Consciousness is normally considered to occur in the wide-awake state in which we see, hear, feel, and think clearly and vividly. Much of the time, however, we are semiconscious in some lazy daydream while awake or in some vague dream while sleeping. Other times we may be unconscious altogether.

I had heart bypass surgery in which I remember the pleasant experience of going to sleep under a mild sedative prior to the operation. An instant later, a young surgeon appeared before me in clear focal view and said, "Mr. Henry, the operation is over and was a success." I lost a day and a half for which I have no memory of consciousness. Yet I recognized immediately my condition of surgery and understood exactly what the surgeon was saying. One of the nurses told me that some people are quite frightened by this kind of experience because they interpret their soul's existence to be dependent on their being conscious. I have no doubt my soul was intact during this lapse of consciousness, even though my body was massively but beneficently assaulted during the operation.

In the figure called "Consciousness," all soul events show consciousness, indicated by white regions, except one, which symbolizes the many events of nonconsciousness during my operation. I believe that as long as humans are alive, their souls are active in their bodies. Sometimes, however, a soul is conscious; other times it is not. Consciousness is dependent upon a soul's existence, but the soul's existence is not dependent on the presence of consciousness.

Consciousness in this view is not just a froth on soul events that makes no difference. Although in the diagram "Consciousness" I grant that consciousness in the event of *Me Now* is determined exclusively by the development of the event of *Me Now*, the event of *Me Now* is influenced heavily by the event of *Me Just Past*—including its consciousness. We can accept and extend the Freudian idea that the subconscious (meaning in this case the total event structure that is not conscious) determines the nature of consciousness. We can also accept the common sense notion, not easily compatible with Freudianism, that the decisions pictured in consciousness have influence on our subsequent behavior. Our past experiences influence the event of our present subconscious that may flower into a conscious experience. This event of consciousness and its underlying subconscious

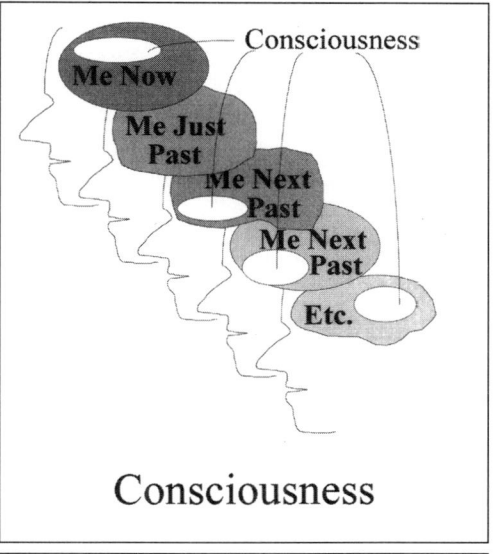

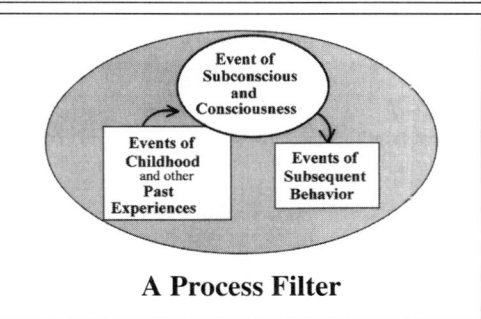

A Process Filter

can then influence the events of subsequent behavior. These conditions are pictured in the diagram "A Process Filter."

Further, we can capture in this perspective Freud's initial intent to explain abnormal and destructive behavior in terms of the purposes inherent in neurotic behavior. In addition, we can assert an aspect of freedom in human action that is necessary in order to make sense of the idea of purpose. The central point is that any event—whether human, animal, or electronic—synthesizes its past in terms of its own selection. It has options presented to it in terms of the causality of the past and then chooses among them what it shall become. No matter what behaviorists or Freudians say philosophically about freedom of choice, they all act as if they have it. Our human experience seems dominantly to assert there is an aspect of choice in our daily lives. The postulation that a becoming event exercises some initiative in deciding what it shall be among options presented to it causally, is confirmed by overwhelming experience among humans in their ordinary existence. We all think we have some say in our actions and being.

Am I claiming that humans have a natural freedom to dissipate the power of (what Freud calls) the subconscious in our actions? No, because in addition to an obvious aspect of freedom in our lives there is also causality, sometimes massive causality, that we cannot overcome by conscious choice. Who we are in the present moment is influenced by who we were in the immediately past moment. This past moment, however, is conditioned by choice, however small. The causality that influences us now is the result in large part of our past choices—going back and accumulating causality to our earliest childhood. Our past choices affect our primary nonconscious self, which in its development may or may not generate a consciousness that reflects the true self.

It is not just our individual past choices that affect us in the present. Our culture, our religion, and traumatic events precipitated by other humans influence us significantly. Freud says that our early childhood environment, particularly our relationship with our parents, determines greatly our emotional health as adults. Even our parents are influenced by their subconscious, which is determined by their choices and the previous choices of others.

The biblical position considers sin to be a condition of the soul and not some set of specific sinful acts. This condition of the soul is not rigidly determined by God, but by the choices of humans—choices that have been made recently and choices that go back to the beginning of humankind. We are responsible for our personal sins because of our choices present and past, but sin is also inherited because of the causality on us coming from those who have made choices in the past. Sin has infected all of human history and is transmitted from parents to children. "For I . . . am . . . God, punishing children for the iniquity of parents, to the third and the fourth generation" (Exod 20:5). Whether we accept Freud's position on the mechanisms of how the subconscious influences our actions, and even though we may dismiss the materialism and determinism of his philosophy out of hand, we owe him thanks for reminding us of the dark side of the soul that the Bible acknowledges and both Jewish and Christian theologians have described.

Do we not see evil in nature also? God declared that all of creation was good. It was good because God gave every creature, including the events of what we call inanimate nature, some freedom. Nature, however, has also "fallen" and shows significant destructive aspects. If we consider the philosophical position of event structures to apply to all entities human, nonhuman, and merely physical, then we also affirm that all entities of the universe are constituted in part by their own choice. We can understand how viruses may seek their own advantage as they multiply in a human host. We can understand how pit bulls may want to kill innocent human infants. We can understand how wayward asteroids, with only minute freedom in the individual molecules, but massive determination in the bulk of molecules, can impact the earth and destroy almost all living things—including the dinosaurs. We can understand how cumulative human choice could conspire to kill six million Jews or initiate an atomic conflagration that could destroy all life. We can understand how sin can infect nature as well as history through the choices of entities in nature as they reflect in part the choices of humanity. Saint Paul reminds us that nature also needs redemption and prophesies "the creation itself will be set free from its bondage to decay" (Rom 8:21).

The Experience of Causality and Freedom

It may seem strange that many scientists and philosophers act as if causality is important in their ordinary lives but deny it as appropriate for science. Bertrand Russell (mathematician, philosopher, and social reformer, 1872–1970), who supported many causes trying to influence the actions of other people, commented regarding the place of causality in science: "The law of causality . . . is a relic of a bygone age."[2] This peculiar but still dominant position among many scientists and philosophers has a history whose brief exposition can show to us what we may recognize, in contrast, as familiar causal influence in our personal lives as well as in science itself. The assumption that causal description is not properly a part of science has two sources: the mathematization of science and the trickery of consciousness.

As science has been successively made more mathematical—as with Newtonian laws, Mendelian genetics, and so on—and as the newer sciences—such as the relativity theory, quantum mechanics, and others—have made it difficult to understand science by simple images, the causal connections of science have been interpreted to be the connections of the describing mathematics. Since the "bizarre ideas" of science "can only be grasped by appeal to mathematics," which ideas are "completely beyond the power of human beings to imagine,"[4] we have to discount any ordinary understandings of causality and try to find true causality in the mathematics itself. Is there any understanding of causality in the mathematics of science? Newton's laws could be run backwards or forwards indicating in the mathematics no precedence of cause before effect. Even the second law of thermodynamics, which states that things in general must run down and gives a general direction of the arrow of time, allows local events in which time runs backwards or effects precede causes. Any other probabilistic description of causality has similar intractable problems. It is very easy to insist that mathematics describes contemporary science, but, alas, mathematics shows us nothing like our familiar sense of cause and effect. Therefore, by dismissing our ordinary experience, many scientists say there is no causality in science.

In my judgment, the real reason why science has been stripped of causality is due to the structures of consciousness itself. David Hume first noticed and wrote about the absence of causal experience in consciousness, and his position modified for current times holds powerful sway among philosophers and scientists. When we see two billiard balls collide, do we see any causality? We see a sequence of events: one billiard ball contacts another, which changes its momentum, but we do not see the causal interaction itself. When lightning strikes, we see the strike and hear the thunder. Hume would say that we understand the juxtaposition between strike and thunder, and thus import an understanding of causal relation to the two. We cannot, however, see or hear any causality between strike and thunder.

On and on, example after example, what we perceive in clear consciousness are events in relationship. Never do we have any clear presentation of causality. What is going on? In the clear rationality of consciousness we see no causality, but we all believe in it. No one of us runs his or her personal or business life without acting as if cause and effect are very important. If we act a certain way, there will definitely be consequences. We know it, and the scientists know it—even when they deny causality to science itself.

Causality is not seen or heard; it is felt. When I am in an accelerating automobile or airplane, I can feel the acceleration. It is not just a push in the back, but a very complex sensation we all can recognize even though it is not presented in the clarity of consciousness. Our sense of acceleration, though at times quite powerful, is essentially vague. It does not have the brilliance of a mathematical idea or a sighted sunset. The pure mathematical description of acceleration has none of the sense of the causality we feel when we are accelerated.

Consider the person who turns on a light and blinks his eyes. When asked why he blinked, he responds, "The light caused me to blink." We may see only the connection of light and blink, but he feels some vague connection between the two that he identifies as causation. What are the results of causation we feel only vaguely in our bodies? These causal preconditions give forth to the vivid presentations of consciousness—where there is no evidence of causal experience. Any sense of causality disappears when we attend to the bright structures of consciousness. When a light is turned on, we see clearly. We probably do not notice either the eye blink or the slight sensation in the eyes themselves. These vague sensations in the eye are feelings of the causes, among others, that bring forth our sight itself. Not all of our causal sensations vaguely felt, however, produce changes in the immediateness of consciousness. When clouds obscure our outside orientation and the interior of the plane remains the same, we still may feel the plane begin its descent to the ground. There are many varieties of gastrointestinal feelings indicative of causal actions important to us that we do not raise to levels of intense consciousness. Yet we know they are there, and they cause certain profound things to happen. We may feel a general sense of ease or disease. Only when in trouble do we normally notice the causality of our guts or our eyes—intestinal or eye pain causes our immediate and conscious focus on these important causal parts of our bodies. Otherwise they do their jobs quietly but always with a background sense of their causal importance. We are never quite as rational as we might want to seem.

It is not surprising that when both our consciousness and the mathematical characterization of science conspire to suggest causality is not a part of science, some philosophers of science may accept and champion this position. They are, however, quite wrong. We have seen the deceptiveness of consciousness in chapter 6 where it hides the gaps of spatial and temporal activity. Mathematics is an extreme abstraction that never tells the complete truth about reality. Causality is a part of every becoming actual event. Any event sums up its past in terms of the causality that affects it. Because it cannot be exactly like the sum of causation affecting it, since some of the causality is at odds with other causality, it must exercise some freedom of selection, however minor, among its causal determinants.

The experience of freedom is similar to the experience of causality. Neither shows clearly in the presentations of consciousness. Both are found in the vague but powerful feelings that attend consciousness—

vague because consciousness obscures them and powerful because they are together what create consciousness. We do not choose within events of present consciousness. We experience having chosen, which can be illuminated in part through our current consciousness. I now remember consciously having decided to ask my wife to marry me. The experience even then, however, welled up into consciousness from a nonconscious act. Also, we do not experience causality in present consciousness. Our memory shows our having been caused. I remember a compulsive act I now regret. At the time, however, I acted without consideration and only (a short time) later did I become aware of what I had done.

It is possible for us to cultivate the experiences of causality and freedom, first in our nonacademic moments and later in our application of these ideas to science itself. The assumptions that causality and freedom are both a significant part of science is just as plausible as the assumption that they are not. When articulated in a careful and systematic philosophical position, say process thought,[5] one wonders at the oddity of how causality and freedom could have ever been dismissed from science, especially since they are such an integral part of our normal human existence.

God's Causality

> We know that all things work together for good for those who love God, who are called according to his purpose. For those whom he foreknew he also predestined to be conformed to the image of his Son, in order that he might be the firstborn within a large family. And those whom he predestined he also called; and those whom he called he also justified; and those whom he justified he also glorified. (Rom 8:28-30)

The Bible says some strong things about determinism in this passage. It and a few others involving predestination have been a problem for interpreters of the Bible primarily because they approach the passage with an idea of a rigorous system in mind, either mathematical proof where things flow exactly and precisely to an inescapable conclusion or a Newtonian causal mechanism that is strictly determined. By bringing to the Bible an essentially scientific or mathematical idea, they edge closer to denying that we have some freedom of response to love. Why would God come in Christ to die for us, if we could not respond by loving God freely? Who among us would prefer a mechanical dog that could be controlled to show symbols of affection to a real one that had some feeling when it licked us?

I have no difficulty interpreting this portion of scripture quite literally in terms of a philosophical position that recognizes both aspects of human freedom and the freedom of God. Surely God has the power to work for the good of those who love God, to know more about the future than anyone (even with the mild surprises that may come from human choice), to have particular interest in specific humans, to choose that they might be conformed to the likeness of Jesus, to call them, to justify them, and finally to give them honor.

The problem is, some Christian thinkers have elevated God's reason to be more important than God's will—or God's emotions. Remember the Bible says almost nothing about God's reason, but very much about God's will and the means God will take to show God's love. If you bring a Greek or scientific rational perspective to the Bible and attribute reason to be the highest faculty of God, you may get a position such as the following.

In the beginning God created the earth according to a plan. Further, the plan was extended to include the future. Because God is so rational, God must necessarily follow the plan. I would think God would be very bored. "Ho hum, what shall we do today? What does the plan say?" Human creativity is not like this at all. Every major intellectual, scientific, or artistic creation has been accompanied by a profound emotional "ah ha" experience—the eureka of Archimedes, the conversion of Saint Paul or Saint Augustine, the mystical joy of Einstein. Do we want to deny that God has these experiences, especially in those historical choices that manifest God's surprising love, such as becoming incarnate in the womb of a virgin and suffering and dying for us? I can understand God saying, "I don't care what my plans call for. Because I love them, I am going to do what they consider unimaginable."

A reason for rejecting the idea of a strictly deterministic God, an idea that must be modeled on some pattern of mathematical rigidity, is that it gives unacceptable results when followed through logically. If God predestines everything, then God causes all manner of horrible evil. How can God be considered good if God is the author of evil? How can the gospel of Jesus Christ be the good news of redemption if God is also the cause of the sin that is redeemed? We should prefer a theology based on the Bible, or at least our common experience of some freedom of choice, rather than one dominated by ideas of rationality derived from science.

If God does not predetermine things completely but allows aspects of freedom in each event of existence, what is the nature of God's causality? How does God act? God acts, surprisingly, like every other subject. Each subject event, with its fellow subject events, exercises causality on future events. God, like other subjects, is one among many in God's causal determination of the future. Because of God's respect for the existence and choices of other entities, God does not normally overwhelm them—although God has in the past and could now if God wished.[6] God does not cure all sin immediately, because God has chosen to let the limited freedom of entities take its course through the choices they have made. This is what is meant by God's visiting the iniquities on successive generations. God does not cause the iniquities, but insists that for freedom to be freedom, it must have its consequences. Our choices and those of our forebears cause our problems. Our choices, including those in nature itself, are the root of our sin.

The biblical God does not back off from deep involvement in history. Remember that Judaism, Christianity, and Islam are the primary historical religions. Other religions emphasize the being of God or the idealized being of humans. Judaism and Christianity emphasize what God has done—at certain times and in certain places.

How, then, is God experienced in everyday activity? Like other entities, God is experienced through the vague but powerful exercise of God's causal efficacy. I seek to encourage people to cultivate generally the awareness of the real but vague causal forces of ordinary entities, because I believe they will then become more aware of God's real causal presence in their lives. God's normal activity is one of wooing, of providing options to become better, of soliciting a relationship in love with ordinary people, of challenging them for the future. God, however, has acted powerfully and decisively: at the creation (which contemporary astronomy tells us may have happened some eight to fifteen billion years ago), at the deliverance of Israel at the Red Sea, in the giving of the Law at Mount Sinai, in the Incarnation of Jesus Christ as an infant, and in the conversion of innumerable Christians over the ages. I hope the reader may see that the philosophical position being developed here not only may be more adequate for science (which we must continue to justify), but also may allow us to understand more literally God's activity in historical events described in the Bible. When God spoke to Moses in the burning bush, God was there causally active on Moses. Moses did not see God clearly in consciousness but felt aspects of God's causal power.

I have asserted that ordinary events exercise causality on us what we feel as vague forces, but these forces then manifest themselves in sight and sound having physical shape at a certain time. God, however, does not normally show God's self to our consciousness but indicates God's presence as vague causal forces. Why? These are issues of the understanding of the relationship of entities to the nature of space and time that shall be discussed shortly in terms of contemporary relativity theory and quantum mechanics. In brief, I shall maintain that space and time are established by and dependent on the relationships among entities. This is a quite different position from a Newtonian one in which space and time were preexistent and acted as receptacles for entities.

In this relativistic attitude, ordinary events are still quite bound by causal forces from previous events and show themselves in terms of conventional time and space categories. Time and space are still dependent on the nature of the entities, but are constituted by well-established relationships caused by the massive habits of past entities. We have no choice but to be spatial and temporal. God is different. God can appear, if God wishes, in a variety of modes that transcend and intersect our spatial and temporal existence. God's appearance, however, is dependent on God's reality in its relationship to other entities. This reality, despite how it may appear to consciousness, exercises continued causal influence on us that we can feel in our ordinary existence—however extraordinary it may seem.

Notes

[1] John B. Watson. "Psychology as the Behaviorist Views It," *Psychological Review* 20 (1913): 167.

[2] "For I do not do the good I want, but the evil I do not want is what I do" (Rom 7:19).

[3] Bertrand Russell, "On the Notion of Cause," *Proceedings of the Aristotelian Society* 13 (1913): 1-26.

[4] Paul Davies, *God and the New Physics* (New York: Simon and Schuster, 1983) 18.

[5] See, for example, *Science and the Modern World* and *Process and Reality* by Alfred North Whitehead.

[6] Process theologians often argue about the extent of God's power. Technically, to be a process philosopher, one acknowledges that all entities have some freedom, however minor. Nevertheless, God's power is so great and freedom, at times, so minuscule, I see no difficulty in accepting God's overwhelming power.

III.
Contemporary Science and Theology

Chapter 9
The Theory of Relativity

In this and the following two chapters I will be concerned primarily with the third historical thesis that new science comes with images and philosophical perspectives that influence perceptions about religion. Not only will I articulate some of the important images derived from science, but I shall also revise them in order to present a perspective that gives a synthesis to science and religion advantageous to Christianity. In particular, I shall continue to illustrate the philosophical nature of the event structures presented in previous chapters. I am articulating a process perspective for science *and* religion.

The Special Theory of Relativity

Newton believed in absolute space and absolute time. If there were no things, space and time would still exist. Yet Newton was well aware that we *measure* distances in terms of some standard, which itself is a physical thing, for example, lines in a gold bar. We cannot scratch absolute space in order to know where we are or where we have been. Also motions of things measure time. We cannot tag absolute time now and later to know exactly what interval of time has passed. We are dependent on the swing of a pendulum, the rotation of the earth, or vibrations of molecules for our clocks.

If absolute space and time exist, it is fair to ask what is the *true* velocity of the earth through absolute space, not its relative velocity with respect to the sun or some other star. If the sun is moving relative to absolute space and the earth is moving relative to the sun, the true velocity of the earth measured in absolute time and space would not be the same as its relative velocity. (Two cars having a relative speed difference of 20 miles per hour might be going 30 and 60, or 60 and 80 miles per hour relative to the earth.) Is there any possible physical reality that might fill or be absolute space from which we can get some reference? Surprisingly, physicists of the nineteenth century thought there might really be one.

The speculation that there is a substance that fills absolute space came about naturally. The possibility of its existence came through conjectures about another physical phenomenon—light. Light was thought to be a waveform of rapidly changing and interrelated magnetic and electric fields. As a waveform, light must have a medium, which they called the ether. It became important to establish by experiment whether the ether existed. If we could measure velocity in the ether and the ether is relatively stable in absolute space, then we could measure velocity in absolute space.

In 1881, Albert A. Michelson performed an experiment in which light from the sun was broken into two paths having the same lengths relative to the earth but different directions relative to the supposed ether. Michelson's hypothesis was that if the earth is moving through the ether, and the ether is moving relative to the earth, the ether should affect the light rays as a stream affects a boater. Going upstream, the velocity would be slower relative to the shore than going downstream. To be sure the ether was stable relative to the earth, Michelson performed the experiment at different times during the earth's orbit around the sun. The result: The experiment showed no significant differences for the round-trip times for the two light paths. Conclusion: there is no ether. Possible further conclusion: there is no absolute time and space.

This latter conclusion about absolute time and space was not decided for the scientific community until Albert Einstein proposed the Special Theory of Relativity in 1905. His theory considers inertial frames, which are frames of reference that are not accelerating. He stated two fundamental principles:

(1) The laws of physics are invariant in all inertial frames.
(2) It is a law of physics that the speed of light in empty space is the same in all inertial reference frames, independent of the speed of the source or detector of light.

These principles have many consequences that seem nonintuitive—certainly non-Newtonian—for example, the finite speed of light is the maximum speed, measured relatively, of course, for any body. Suppose an electron, called $e1$, is ejected from the sun at nine-tenths the speed of light and electron $e2$ is ejected in the opposite direction at nine-tenths the speed of light. One would think from the perspective of $e1$, that the electron $e2$ would be seen traveling away from it at 1.8 times the speed of light. Not so, according to relativity. The electron $e2$ must be traveling less than the speed of light from the inertial frame of $e1$. In short, there is no absolute perspective for time or space—no absolute time, no absolute space. Space and time are intertwined and depend on the relative velocity of one's inertial frame.

The Theory of Relativity

What familiar images are best for understanding the special theory of relativity? Can we get a single set of simple models that we can also adapt for understanding Einstein's general theory of relativity, quantum mechanics, and the "big bang" cosmology of this and the next two chapters? I wish to interpret each of these illusive and abstruse sciences in terms of the familiar Cartesian coordinate system that is part of secondary and college mathematics courses. Also I will use it to present alternative images of event structures. First, we need to remind ourselves what we know about this system. Second, we should understand how it can be modified by a shift in perspective to provide images for relativity, quantum mechanics, and examination of the earliest history of the universe.

We can symbolize the position of, say, the tip of a pencil in a room by measuring the distance of the pencil tip from two walls and the floor. We measure from some corner of the room, which we call the origin, along lines that are the intersections of the walls and floor and that we may label as axes X, Y, and Z. All this can be physically done with rulers. In a similar way we can symbolize every point in the room by ordered triples of numbers (x, y, z). Lines, planes, and volumes can be described and analyzed in terms of sets of points of this sort. We are more familiar with measurement in a flat plane, a piece of paper, for example, in terms of two perpendicular axes, which we may call the X and Y axes respectively. Any point in the plane is symbolized by an ordered pair of values, say (x, y) in the diagram "Cartesian Point," where x is the distance from the Y-axis and y is the distance from the X-axis.

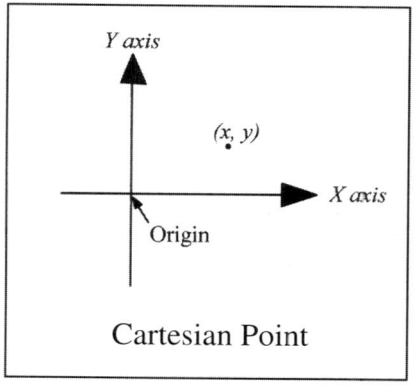

Cartesian Point

A major advantage of this method of measuring space is that we can translate spatial relationships into algebraic symbolism and then solve geometric problems by means of our algebraic knowledge. For example, the distance r of the point (x, y) from the origin can be expressed as $x^2+y^2=r^2$, because, according to the Pythagorean relationships, the square of the hypotenuse r is the sum of the squares of the other two sides x and y of the triangle formed by x, y, and r. This is illustrated in

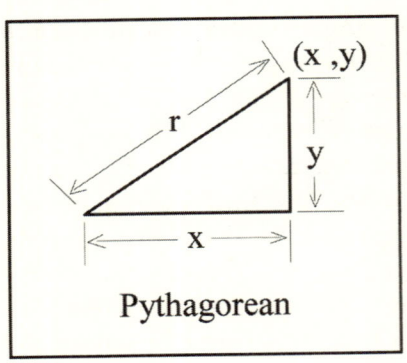

Pythagorean

the picture "Pythagorean." If we think of x and y as any points, then the equation $x^2+y^2=r^2$ gives a locus of points always a distance r from the origin, which is a circle of radius r with its center at the origin. Our algebraic knowledge about equations of this sort can give us much interesting information about circles in space. And our experience of space can also give us insight into algebra.

The mathematical experience of two millennia has led us to believe that we understand space fairly well because our human experience of it is similar. In the nineteenth century, however, the discovery of consistent non-Euclidean geometries gave us pause to reconsider that we may not understand the nature of space as well as we thought. Is there a method of examining space other than by our experience of it? In a paper entitled "On the Hypotheses Which Lie at the Foundation of Geometry" (1868), Georg Bernhard Riemann gave the clearest answer to this question.

Riemann, who developed a geometry that Einstein used later for his general theory of relativity, had an approach in this paper that did not focus on describing a single kind of three-dimensional space by ordered triples of numbers (x, y, z). Rather, he focused on the triples as the objects and asked what logical and mathematical conditions we can impose on these sets of coordinates in order to have our familiar space as well as different kinds of systems of space. Notice how different this approach is from Euclid or Newton. They defined things that were thought to be well understood—such as points, lines, planes, and so on—and then used logic to organize and explain them. Riemann suggested the objects should be ordered sets of numbers for which we supplied the logical and mathematical structure that could give us familiar properties of space. In addition, however, we could get definitions of spaces that had quite strange properties. Before the nineteenth century, it was very difficult to consider higher dimensions of space because we could not visualize them. Euclid and Newton limited themselves to the familiar three dimensions. By simply adding another coordinate, say w, we could consider ordered quadruples (x, y, z, w) and develop an abstract system of four-space. We could not see such a space, but we could define it. There are many consistent abstract systems of three, four, higher, and even infinite dimensional spaces. Although the mathematicians enjoyed the artistic explorations of these spaces, the physicists asked what are the true spatial characteristics of our world. How do we know which of these spatial systems is true, if any? The answer, especially for Einstein's new spatial categories of relativity, would become: "By carefully formulated experiments."

For this book we are not going to develop the mathematics that defines relativity and quantum mechanics. We shall take the old way of using our spatial intuition to understand the new abstract spaces rather than the new way of using the abstract spaces to clarify our intuition of space. The goal is to develop familiar images by our present intuition that gives insight to the results of the new sciences. To do this, however, we must be willing to "step down" in dimensions, to think what it must be like to experience spatially as a point, a line segment, or a flat surface, rather than our full experience of three dimensions. This is required because we shall also include a time dimension in our consideration, but our intuition cannot picture the four dimensions of time and three-dimensional space.

For the first example, let us consider ourselves to be point creatures spatially and temporally. That is, we look at the world from the perspective of a point event in space that happens instantaneously at a particular time. The point event we seek to identify with is

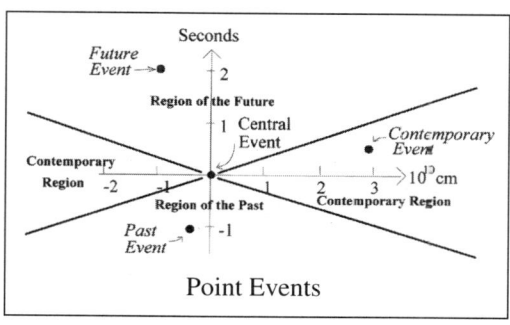

Point Events

at zero location on a line as illustrated in the picture "Point Events." As a point event on a line, we can see and receive influence from two directions, say east and west (more conventionally positive and negative). The units of the line are each 10^{10} (1 with 10 zeros) centimeters. This line is the horizontal axis. The vertical axis is temporal, with the event point at zero, which symbolizes the present or *now* point. The vertical line is in units of seconds. It can measure how far other events are in the future or in the past.

The *Future Event* will happen approximately two seconds in the future and be about 10^{10} centimeters away to the left. The *Past Event* is about a second in the past and about $10^{10}/2$ centimeters away to the left.

From our perspective looking at the graph, the *Contemporary Event* appears to be about a half-second in the future and $3 \cdot 10^{10}$ centimeters to the right. For the *Central Event*, however, *the Contemporary Event* never happens. Why?

Accepting the Special Theory of Relativity that the maximum value of the speed of light (any influence) is approximately $3 \cdot 10^{10}$ centimeters per second means it will take a full second for influence to travel $3 \cdot 10^{10}$ centimeters. The *Contemporary Event*, however, is $3 \cdot 10^{10}$ centimeters away from the *Central Event* and only a half-second ahead of the *Central Event*. No physical influence can pass from the *Contemporary Event* to the *Central Event* and vice versa. The *Central Event* can only be influenced by its past events and can only influence its future events. The *Central Event* is alone, by itself, happening in isolation from any contemporary events. This is a firm consequence of the Theory of Relativity.[1] Notice, the restrictions on the speed of light divide the environment of a point event into three regions: (1) the past from which the event can receive causal influence; (2) the future, which can be influenced by the event; and (3) the present or contemporary region in which no influence can be given or received.

I want to modify this image derived from special relativity by claiming there are no real point events. Surely we use abstract points all the time in mathematics, but that does not mean there are any such actually existing events that have no temporal or spatial dimensions. The soul events described in the last two chapters had both physical and temporal thickness. Although they did not exist indefinitely through time, they did have a brief temporal extension.

Consider an example of an electronic event pictured in the diagram "Electronic Events." (I am changing the focus from the point events above and the soul events of the last chapters to electronic events.) The image of an electron as a particle—a chunk of matter—traveling through preexistent space and time is no longer a tenable one. An electron, I believe, is better thought of as a sequence of events. The graph is the same as "Point Events," except point events have been changed to events that are spatially and

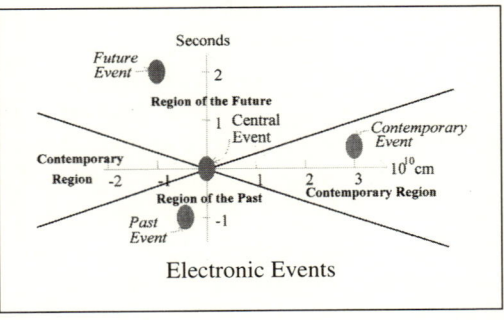

Electronic Events

temporally thick.² These events are extended in space and in time. This means the event appears to last for a brief time from the perspective of another event and appears to occupy a spatial region.

Let us make a further general philosophical claim that all events, including electronic and soul events, require a causal influence from their past for their development, but also an isolation from any contemporary events while they develop. This necessary isolation for self-development is a property, I assert, of any entity—and not a property of an objective space and time. Notice I am radically changing the perspective from viewing a contemporary region of an entity as a consequence of properties of space and time determined by relativity theory to considering the contemporary region in terms of the necessities of the event's internal development. In this manner I can define the nature of physical time and space as dependent upon the properties inherent in the fundamental structure of events and their relationship to each other rather than starting with a concept of previously existing time and space described by relativity theory. The physical time and space of physics and relativity theory are structures dependent on events and not the framework in which events reside. The structures of physical time and space are due to the longtime habits of events and can therefore change as the relationship of event structures changes. The mathematics of relativity applies equally well to this new philosophical orientation towards reality.

There appear to be some essentials established by God. I shall interpret one aspect of God's creation as God's guaranteeing of an aspect of freedom to each of God's creature events including human, atomic, and electronic ones. Every event has some period in its development when it is free of causal influence to select and sum up the causal forces already made on it. This aspect of freedom results in the contemporary region for each entity and determines certain spatial and temporal relations of the special theory of relativity.

Let us consider an electron to be a sequence of successive electronic events as pictured in the diagram "Path of Electronic Events." An electronic event is particular. The succession of electronic events—what we call the

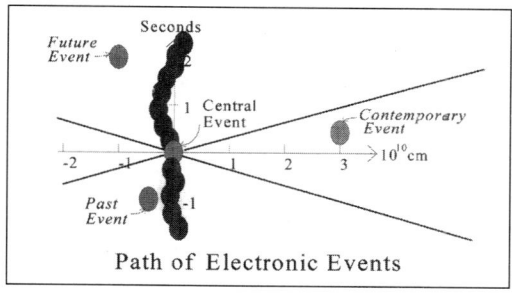

Path of Electronic Events

electron itself—forms a pattern that can have the form of a wave. This succession of electronic events can also have the impact of a particle.

The General Theory of Relativity

Einstein's special theory of relativity considers only nonaccelerated reference frames. What about the relationships between accelerated reference frames? For ten years Einstein worked on a new theory of relativity that would specify the transformation equations for any reference frames, accelerated or not. This became known as his general theory of relativity, which he published in 1916. There is some controversy about the originality of Einstein's 1905 special theory, especially in light of the contributions of his wife Mileva Maric, who was an outstanding physicist in her own right.[3] There is little question about the singular and brilliant creation by Einstein of his general theory. It ranks with Newton's *Principia* in intellectual achievement.

Like the *Principia*, however, Einstein's general theory comes replete with philosophical tendencies that have a specific impact on theology— again recalling our third historical thesis that any new science comes with a philosophical orientation. Also, as in the past, it is not the basic mathematical science that has had an impact on theology and philosophy but the images that have been naturally associated with the science, which images, so I assert, can be replaced with better ones for a more appropriate relationship between science and religion. The dominant image that attends the general theory of relativity is space—the ordinary space we live in as well as its mathematization, which takes on dimensions greater than three and includes time. Spatial images dominate temporal ones even as they embody time. These multidimensional space-times are difficult if not impossible to visualize in imagination. Only the mathematics really counts. All people, including mathematicians, use images to interpret the mathematics. We fall back on familiar images. My point is that our default or "fall back" images are not the most appropriate ones. We need to cultivate the images of time rather than those of space.

Let us attempt to present the general theory of relativity by articulating the images—but not the mathematics. Einstein noticed that the two major scientific assumptions of Newton (the law that force is equal to mass times acceleration, and the law that gravitational force is proportional to the masses of bodies and inversely proportional to the square of the difference between them) both define an idea of mass (or alternately an idea of force). If one can measure the force on and acceleration of a body, one can determine its mass. If one can measure the force on two bodies and the distance between them, one can determine the product of their respective masses. With knowledge of the mass and acceleration, one can determine the force by the law of acceleration; with knowledge of the masses and distance between them, one can determine the force by the law of gravitation. Are these masses and forces respectively equivalent? Is it always true that the mass of a body determined by the law of acceleration is exactly the same as the mass determined by the law of gravitational attraction? Careful measurements seem to indicate they are the same. Doughnut-shaped spaceships can be designed so the force of acceleration pressing a person to the outside of the ship as it rotates is the same force—in magnitude and quality—on the mass of the person as given by gravity at the surface of the earth.

Einstein has shown that since the forces and masses of gravity and acceleration are the same, and since the force on a mass can be explained by acceleration, the force of gravity can be explained also by acceleration. In general relativity theory there is no longer any need for a separate force of gravity.

Since acceleration is defined in terms of relations between space and time, the general theory of relativity describes gravity in terms of space and time, specifically in terms of the curvature of so-called space-time. Unless we go to the mathematics, we need images at this point—helpful and familiar images to make sense of this strange idea of curved space-time. Let us begin with ordinary two-space, that space of plane geometry we can see symbolized as a flat page before us. If we go north from our starting point in this space, we will never arrive back home. What does it mean to have a "curved" two-space? An ordinary example is a sphere, like the (almost) sphere of the earth, where we may picture the surface (approximately) in terms of flat maps. If we go north from our starting point in this space, we will arrive back home eventually. Such a curvature of two-space is called "closed." A surface such as a saddle would be "open," because one could never reach the starting point by always going in the same direction.

Let us relate the image of a flat surface curved into a sphere in terms of what is happening mathematically. The mathematical objects are the ordered pairs of numbers; hence we are dealing with a two-dimensional space in which any creatures existing there would have a two-dimensional experience. The ordered pairs of numbers are organized mathematically by axioms and assumptions so the properties of two-space are different from ordinary plane space. We can picture this revised two-space in the three-dimensional form of a sphere.

So far our images are familiar because we get around well in the ordinary three dimensions of space. Suppose we work with three dimensions of space, add a fourth dimension for time—whose combination we call "space-time"—and then speak of this space-time as curved. Our intuitions cannot picture this situation. The space is four-space that relates ordered quadruples (x, y, z, t) by mathematical axioms and complex constructs that attempt to define some concepts that have a familiar spatial ring. The mathematics, however, does not lead us to tangible and accurate images. We are not at home in four-space and especially in those kinds of "curvature" determined by the mathematics that violate our ordinary spatial intuition. We may be able to gain some insight into Einstein's general theory of relativity, however, by looking at analogical aspects of curvature of two-space.

In the mathematics of general relativity the curving or warping of space-time appears to cause gravity. Bodies in general and light in particular will follow the shortest allowable distance between two points (a straight line in higher dimensions of space-time), but the allowable distance is determined by the curvature of space-time. The curvature of space-time is determined by mass. We illustrate this, again analogically, by an image where we reduce the number of dimensions and consider a warp of one-space, shown in the picture "Warp" that gives us a two-dimensional trough.

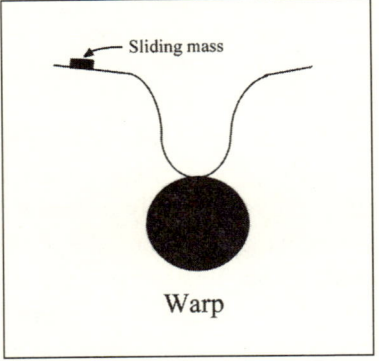

The line to the left in "Warp" contains only flat linear creatures that can go either forward or backward (I have exaggerated the thickness of the sliding black mass). This line is warped by the large circular mass at the bottom. The shortest distance between two points is on the line, not off it, but the warping of the line gives a trough in two-space, which allows us to see that the ball could "fall into the trough." In relativity images it is not "attracted by the larger mass" but only follows spatial (and temporal) considerations that are determined by the larger mass. Should not all things, even those like light waves, be determined by the limits of space-time?

A number of crucial experiments have shown that Einstein's general theory of relativity confirms data that would be anomalies in the older science. Experiments have shown that the sun "bends" light rays because of its massive "gravity." Translated, this means the sun causes a space-time warp that makes light appear to be bent as it travels in a "straight line" in higher dimensional space-time. The discrepancy in the predicted precession of the orbit of Mercury, which was considered to be a minor problem of nineteenth-century physics, is accurately predicted by the general theory of relativity. Clocks actually run slower in deep pits. There are bodies predicted by general relativity so massive that the space-time in their local vicinity curves back sufficiently so nothing can escape. These are the black holes that figure so prominently in contemporary astronomy.

In all of our analogies about space-time we have used spatial images. Even the dimension of so-called time that we added to three-space to get a form of space-time is thought of as spatial. In speaking of a physicist's attitude toward time, Paul Davies says that physicists do not consider time as something that happens. They believe that "all of past and future are simply there, and time extends in either direction from any given moment in much the same way as space stretches away from any particular place."[4] Davies goes on to say that the comparison of time to space is not just an analogy because of the binding of time to space in what physicists call space-time as described in the theory of relativity.

Here is an image held by most physicists that is currently integral to, but not necessary for, the theory of relativity: an image I call the "spatialization of time." The function of this image is similar to the images of mechanism and materialism that were once thought to be essential to Newtonianism and Darwinism. These images had a damaging effect on Christian theology and are not currently adequate for the science. Is there an image better suited for both the theory of relativity and Christianity? I think so. It is an image I call the "temporalization of space."

The time considered primary in this image is not the physical time of relativity, however, but the internal subjective time described earlier as the coming into being of an event. It is what we experience in our soul events and what we project (without consciousness) to be the subjective aspect of electrons. In this perspective the space-time of relativity is an abstraction that reflects, quite accurately, the habitual relationship among events. To repeat: Events do not happen in some objective container of space-time. Space-time is an ideal structure that tells partially how events are related to each other. If you are interested in exploring the issues of the spatialization of time and the temporalization of space, I recommend the book *Physics and the Ultimate Significance of Time*, edited by David Griffin. It is a book that resulted from a conference in which outstanding physicists, including David Bohm, made contributions, as well as philosophers and theologians.[5]

Subjective time is so different from space or spatialized physical time. The past is clearly separated from the future. We know the present, not as a point, but as a focal region of experience. We remember the past and not the future. We anticipate the future but not the past. We have a real sense of the importance of history determined by decisions in time. We know that what we decide makes a difference. There is no possibility, except in science fiction, of going back in time—as one can move backwards on a time line because it is geometrically bidirectional. I grant that the whole history of symbolizing abstract mathematics has been done primarily in terms of geometry and there are no easy temporal images that can include spatial categories, especially of complexity suitable to explain the general theory of relativity. Nevertheless, we have such intimate experience with subjective time and its correlations with objective physical time, we should have no real anguish in declaring it primary and spatial experience secondary, provided, of course, the mathematics of general relativity can be seen to fit equally well with temporal images.

This is the position I take. The images of spatialization applied to time and relativity theory are not only inaccurate, but also damaging in their relationship to religion. I maintain, with general process thought, that both space and physical time are determined by the relationships of actual events to each other and are not containers into which events fit, as held by Newtonian science. It may be some help to claim, as does Hawking, that time and space are "dynamic quantities"[6] like rubber sheets that wiggle when balls are dropped in them. Even this abstraction, like all spatializations of time, ultimately obscures and makes suspect human decision, human freedom, and the nature of history itself. It puts existence into a straightjacket where it is seen necessarily to conform to the categories of science, in particular those of relativity theory. No wonder many of those who hold to the spatialization of time tend to be determinists seeking those scientific principles that not only describe but control all things.

How much more liberating it seems to consider our experience of subjective time to be primary and the abstract characterization of both space and time to be dependent on our existence as subjective beings. As explained earlier, we have scientific, spatial, and temporal characteristics because of the well-ingrained habits of billions of years of event structures, which exercise causal influence on us to conform to the established laws of physics and other sciences. Since time and space are dependent on subjective becoming, and not vice versa, there may be experiences in our lives that transcend time and space—without transcending the natural order of things. There may be beings with whom we can communicate causally and experientially, again in the natural order, that do not manifest themselves in the narrow confines of scientific temporality and spatiality.

One of the means to explain God's transcendence used by some scientists and theologians is to claim that God is a higher order dimensional being and therefore not subject to the three spatial dimensions or even multidimensional relativity theory. In contrast, if space and time are dependent on the becoming of events, then all basic events are multidimensional. They do not fit exactly into dimensional structures but cumulatively determine them. Some of us creatures are more bound by past structures of time and space than others. Yet even we transcend space and time because space and time are constituted in terms of who we are. The difference between God and us in this matter is, we have little freedom to be other than spatial or temporal. God literally can appear to be in any way God chooses.

There must be some compromise in the images of relativity theory and quantum mechanics, to be discussed next, because at their edges they are as yet incompatible. I tend to modify images of relativity theory in terms of quantum mechanics, because I believe quantum mechanics further emphasizes the categories of space and time to be dependent upon subjective being rather than vice versa.

Notes

[1] Recent experiments, particularly those associated with Bell's theorem, indicate that information may travel faster than the speed of light. Causal influence is, however, restricted to the speed of light.

[2] Although having rest mass, an electron is so small physically as to be almost a point event. I have exaggerated the size of an electron immensely in the diagram.

[3] See, for example, *Albert Einstein, Mileva Maric: The Love Letters*, ed. Jürgen Renn and Robert Schulmann, trans. Shawn Smith (Princeton NJ: Princeton University Press, 1992).

[4]Paul Davies, *God and the New Physics* (New York: Simon & Schuster, 1983) 124.

[5]*Physics and the Ultimate Significance of Time: Bohm, Prigogine, and Process Philosophy*, ed. David Ray Griffin (Albany: State University of New York Press, 1986).

[6]Stephen W. Hawking, *A Brief History of Time: From the Big Bang to Black Holes* (New York: Bantam Books) 1990

Chapter 10
The Self-Limitation of Mathematics and Quantum Mechanics

Classical physics derived from Newtonian mechanics has led the other physical and social sciences into believing there is a mathematical description that completely explains the world in terms of smooth causality. Although the General Theory of Relativity challenges our familiar ideas about space and time, it seems to fulfill rather than threaten this prophecy about the power of science. The scientific and mathematical worlds of the twentieth century, although including relativity, are quite different from those of classical science and relativity. Crucial developments in both physics and mathematics now imply: "If you are to do legitimate physics or mathematics, you must take into account the fundamental limitations of both disciplines." These limitations are not just philosophical opinions about science. They are part of physics and mathematics itself—limitations one learns in the study of the disciplines in order to practice satisfactorily in the disciplines.

The limitations of science and mathematics are stated in terms of the laws of quantum mechanics of physics and the limitative theorems of mathematics—the latter of which applies as well to formal logic and computer science. In particular, they can be expressed in terms of Heisenberg's Indeterminacy Principle and Gödel's Incompleteness Theorem. To be understood, both of these statements of limitation should be put in their relevant context in physics and mathematics. To this end, images from quantum mechanics and mathematics are explored in this chapter.

Although part of physics and mathematics, the limitative theorems also form an aura of these disciplines that affect their philosophical interpretation. This philosophical interpretation very clearly has an impact on theology and in particular on our interpretation of the doctrine of creation, which will be examined in the next chapter when "big bang" astronomy is presented. This chapter, as did the last, will continue to be a discussion of the third historical thesis that sciences come with philosophical images and interpretations that affect theology. The images of limitation by science on science—and on theology as well—present a welcome contribution of science to the discussion of the relationship of religion and science. Properly interpreted, I believe they can allow us to understand God's action as expressed in the Bible in a more literal and intelligible manner. As in past chapters, I shall continue to explore the philosophical alternative of process thought, that position which emphasizes event structures.

Quantum Theory

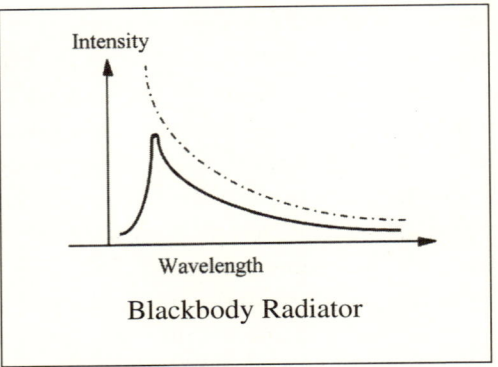

Blackbody Radiator

If you continue to heat an iron rod, it will begin to glow a dull red and finally turn bright orange or yellow before it melts. Using classical physics, which is Newtonian mechanics augmented by Maxwell's electromagnetism, it is possible to predict the intensity of various wavelengths of radiation as a function of temperature. Classical physics entails that as wavelength decreases (that is, frequency increases), the emitted intensity increases like the dashed line in the graph called "Blackbody Radiator." Experimental evidence from a special ideal emitter called a "blackbody radiator" disagrees with the projections and, like the solid line graph, shows that emitted intensity decreases as wavelength decreases for lower wavelengths. What do physicists do when experimental evidence radically challenges deductions from the major classical theory? In 1899, Max Planck tried to revise the classical theory to answer the problems posed by this so-called "ultraviolet catastrophe" and as a result set in motion the major scientific revolution of quantum theory.

Planck proposed that the individual molecular oscillators of the molecules of the emitting metal could lose (or gain) energy only in chunks he called "quanta." (The basic events described in this and previous chapters are chunks of sorts.) An oscillator could lose an integral number of quanta, but not a half quanta. The higher frequency oscillators had higher minimum values for individual quanta than the lower frequency ones. By incorporating this fundamental change into the classical theory, which then did not remain classical, Planck was able to predict the distribution of intensities from blackbody radiation obtained in the lab.

The Self-Limitation of Mathematics and Quantum Mechanics

In 1897, J. J. Thompson discovered electrons and identified them as the particles that can be knocked out of an electrically charged piece of metal by light waves. In 1905, Albert Einstein proposed a theory to explain this photoelectric effect in which he suggested light could be thought of as both a wave and a particle, which he called a "photon." Photons also have energy quanta, which Einstein calculated to be proportional to their frequency.[1] The image is of a light particle somehow carried by its wave that comes only in discrete energy values. I am attempting to change this image to think of the light particle as a succession of events and its wave to be the pattern or form of the events. In 1914, Robert A. Millikan verified Einstein's conjecture experimentally. Planck, Einstein, and Millikan received Nobel prizes for their work.

If light has energy in discrete quanta, this suggests that the energy releases of the electrons of an atom that generate light are also quantized. In 1913, Niels Bohr revolutionized the model of the atom in terms of the quantum ideas of Planck and Einstein. Then Louis de Broglie suggested that just as light waves can be considered to be particles, so electron particles can be considered to be waves.

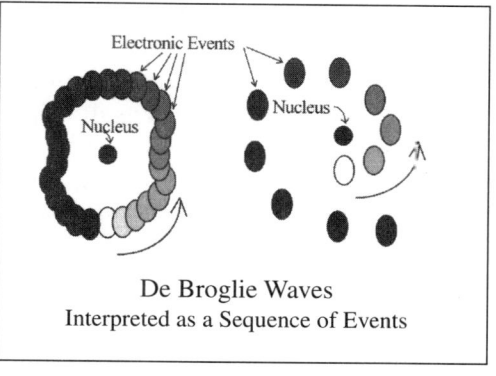

De Broglie Waves
Interpreted as a Sequence of Events

Both light and matter exhibit wave and particle properties. This idea further clarified the nature of atomic structure. The wave properties of electrons allow only certain orbits and not others. In the first picture to the left in the illustration "De Broglie Waves," electronic events begin at the bottom of the picture and go counterclockwise in a stable standing wave form around the nucleus. In the second picture an electron (a sequence of electronic events) does not have a stable waveform around the nucleus and does not establish a fixed orbit. I have pictured overlapping electronic events in the first picture so you might see a wave pattern of the electron. In the second picture I have shown electronic events as distinct and separate. Since we can interpret the electron to be the sequence of electronic events, we can say that the electron appears in one place and then another without making a spatial or temporal transition between them. Such an electron does have a wave pattern, which in the second picture does not establish a stable atomic orbit. This electron will not become a part of the structure of the atom.

We see things in terms of light waves. The shorter the wavelength (the higher the frequency), the more clearly we can see where something is. Resolution is dependent on wavelength. To "see" an electron, a very short wave length is required. A short wave length of light, however, has a higher energy, which when acting as a particle will knock the electron away from its position. How can we know where an electron is if we knock it zooming by trying to find it? It seems we cannot investigate matter at a microscopic level without changing it. You cannot see some small living things as living in an electron microscope because in seeing them you kill them.

Werner Heinsenberg proposed what has become a fundamental limiting factor of the new physics of quantum mechanics. His principle of indeterminacy says one cannot measure, predict, or know precisely both a particle's position and its momentum.[2] Neither can one know exactly the energy of a particle and the time it took to measure it. In classical mechanics it was possible (in principle) to know exactly all of the attributes of a particle. In the new mechanics, attributes are joined in pairs like position-momentum or energy-time just mentioned. Indeterminacy affects all such "conjugate" pairs; one can never know both exactly.

The theory of quantum mechanics, which was discovered and promoted initially by Erwin Schroedinger (1887–1961) in a paper published in 1926, presents mathematical functions that do not claim to predict exactly what the future will be. The mathematics only describes the probabilities of various events occurring. Schrödinger took a standard wave differential equation in classical physics, combined with it the energy/frequency and momentum/wavelength discoveries of Einstein and de Broglie, and adjusted the mathematics so that when solutions of the wave equation are combined linearly, they give solutions to the wave equation (just as when waves combine, they produce waves). A solution of the wave equation is a function, say of distance and time symbolized $Y(x,t)$, that gives a measure of the magnitude of a wave at x and t. Many wave functions in classical physics could measure something that actually wiggled in a medium. A wave function of quantum mechanics, however, contains a component with complex numbers, which resists an assignment of a physical wave image to the wave function.

Max Born, also in 1926, eschewing classical wave images for the Schroedinger equation, asserted that the value of the wave function measured the probability of finding a particle at a certain place and a certain time.[3] It is remarkable how powerful Schroedinger's analysis has been in characterizing molecules, atoms, nuclei, and subatomic particles —all subject to the Heisenberg limitations. One can derive classical Newtonian mechanics that applies to macroscopic objects from Schroedinger wave mechanics. In this contemporary physics, however, one can no longer casually hold to the strict causality and determinism of classical science. The old images of mechanism must give way. What kind of images and attendant philosophy should take their place?

Although I am suggesting that event structures from process thought give adequate images for quantum mechanics, the physics community remains divided, or at least tentative, about the philosophical foundations of its new dominant discipline. Our third historical thesis that new science brings with it philosophical images still holds. Einstein, Bohr, de Broglie, Schroedinger, Heisenberg, and others—with considerable contention—became dramatically engaged in discussing the nature of reality entailed by quantum mechanics. The reason for the current distancing of many physicists from *any* philosophically realist position is that the mathematics and experiments of quantum mechanics show a pervasive and pernicious clash of images from classical physics. These incompatible images of waves and particles, although having an elegant mathematical reconciliation, present no easy philosophical interpretation.

Waves spread out, whereas particles occupy a small region. Waves break up, their parts going in many directions; a particle goes in a single direction. Waves interpenetrate, adding and subtracting to and from each other. Two crests may reinforce to create a larger resultant wave, or a crest and trough may cancel. As the waves emerge from interpenetration, they go back to their original forms. Particles, however, do not interpenetrate. They crash together

To see some of the problems of this clash of images when the electron is considered to be both a wave and a particle, let us look at a classical double-slit experiment. I am following the form of these experiments as presented by Richard Feynman.[4] In the diagram "Water Waves" (p. 160), circular waves encounter a baffle with two openings. New waves come from the holes, combine, and create another wave whose heights at the next barrier are represented by the wavy line. (If you mentally turn this line up vertically, you can see the heights of the wave as measured at the barrier.) The resulting wave looks as it does because the combining waves add to and subtract from each other as they meet. This interference pattern caused by interpenetrating waves is a clear mark that one is dealing with waves and not (classical) particles.

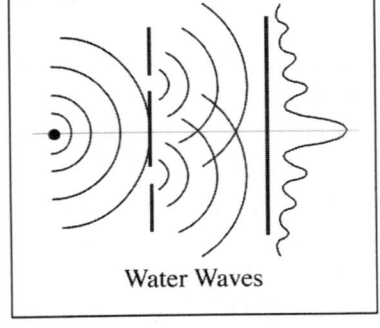
Water Waves

Consider a similar experiment, except this time we shall use electrons instead of water waves. In the diagram called "Electron Waves," an electron generator spews electrons in

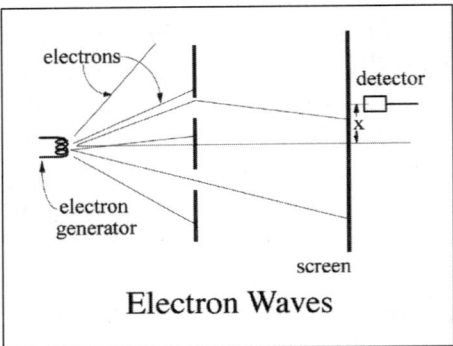
Electron Waves

all directions. The electrons have the same energy, but we control how many are generated. (On your television set the brightness control determines the number of electrons, whereas the high voltage control sets the energy of the individual electrons.) The electrons strike a barrier with two holes, and some of them get through. We measure where and how many of these electrons strike a screen by a detector that we can move up and down a distance x.

What kind of pattern do these electrons generate? To the surprise of all, the pattern is similar to one generated by waves, in particular, pattern A in the figure called "Patterns." If we close the bottom opening and only allow electrons through the top opening, we get pattern B. Closing the top slit with the bottom open, we get pattern C. Since electrons show no wave properties through each opening singly, if we open both, we should expect to get pattern D. Why do we get the interference pattern at A? What are electrons like in order to give us these strange properties? How can electrons as particles have wave properties?

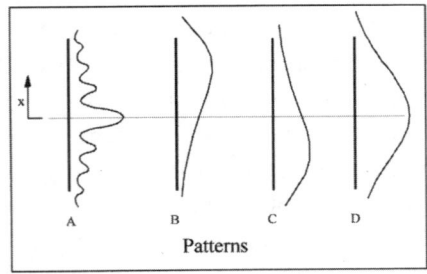
Patterns

Some have suggested that the only logical answer is, an electron must go though both openings. Maybe an electron is like a cloud that partially goes through each hole. Physical experiment shows this image is not correct. If we put a strong light source on the barrier, as shown in the figure called

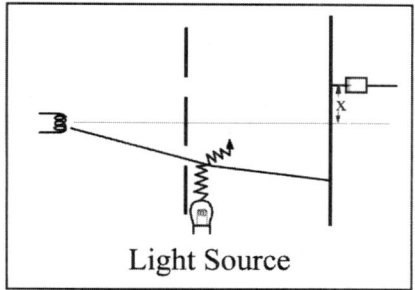
Light Source

"Light Source," we can tell which opening the electron comes through, because it scatters light in a distinct fashion. This experiment tells us that a single electron acting like a particle comes through one opening or the other, never both. Other experiments confirm this fact by showing that the full charge of an electron comes through a slit, never a partial charge. Also an electron always acts like a particle when it is detected—that is a requirement of the detector.

Adding a light source to detect which opening an electron comes through adds a further bizarre feature to the double-slit experiment. Summarized: if we know through which slit an electron passes, it does not show wave interference properties. For example, electrons determined to come through the upper slit have the distribution of pattern B, which was the pattern for an open upper slit and a closed lower one. These electrons, which we know to come through the upper slit, now have pattern B even when the lower slit is open. If we reduce the intensity of the detecting light source so we do not catch all the electrons coming through one or the other slits, these elusive electrons do interact and have the wave interference pattern A. As a result of these experiments and his theory of quantum mechanics developed on "paths," Feynman expresses Heisenberg's uncertainty principle in a different way: "Any determination of the alternative taken by a process capable of following more than one alternative destroys the interference between alternatives."[5]

How do we understand the image of an electron in these circumstances? Perhaps an undetected electron going through one opening has some mysterious connection with another electron going through an alternative opening. That seems unlikely, because we can control the flow of electrons so only one electron comes through the double-slit barrier at a time. It cannot communicate with another electron in the opposite opening in this case because there is none. These individual electrons, unchallenged through which slit they passed, coming blip,

blip, blip, to the screen, still give the typical interference pattern that is based on the electron's wave properties. How does an individual electron, acting like a particle as it comes undetected through a particular hole, know that it must act like a wave because the other hole is open? How can a particle at times be a wave and a wave at times be a particle?

The answer to this last question is, "It cannot." To assert that a particle is a wave seems to be a hard contradiction. We need an image of some kind of quantum stuff that can take on particle properties and wave properties. What could that be? I suggest that an electron, as well as a soul, consists of a sequence of events.

In this interpretation each electronic event occupies a distinct spatio-temporal region and in itself does not move. Consider an electronic event to be located at the entrance of the upper slit as shown in the diagram "At Slit." This event is fixed in its temporal and spatial relationship to the past events of the barrier and has a low-level feeling of their spatial and temporal locations including the absence of events in the barrier's slits. This existent electronic event and other events of the relevant experimental situation (as well as those everywhere) exercise a causal influence on an emerging electronic event, which has a number of choices for its exemplification. Some of these are illustrated in "At Slit." Where shall this event occur, and what considerations influence the spatial and temporal location of its appearance?

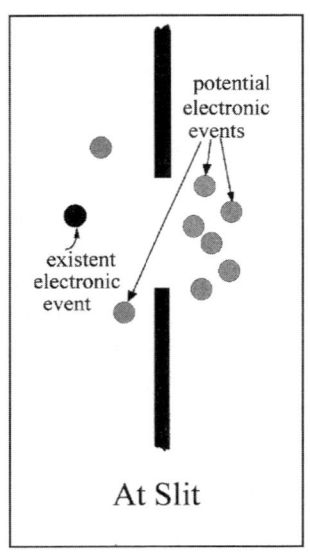

At Slit

As emerging, this event feels and absorbs (the technical word from process thought is "prehends") the events of its past including the given electronic event as well as all of the events of the double slit experimental situation. It may also prehend electromagnetic events (should they exist) generated by a strong light source on the other side of the barrier designed to detect its existence. There are many forces on this emerging electronic event that determine what, where, and when it shall be. Although these forces have a massive power, they do not establish the event uniquely. There are potential forms for the emerging event, determined by its general past but especially by its immediately past electronic events and the events of the experimental situation. These forms give options for the spatio-temporal location and being of the emerging entity. I maintain that the emerging electronic event has some minimal "choice" of the possibilities of its being and location. These choices are perceived as randomness from the outside. If the lower slit is open, then these choices are different than if it is closed. If electromagnetic events are generated to detect an electronic event, they will modify also the emerging entity's options.

I have not drawn paths between the actual electronic event and the future potential events because there is no movement of events themselves, nor do we know where the future potential events will be. It is better to consider a path between multiple past electronic events. We may think of this as the path of the electron understood as a temporal sequence of stationary electronic events. The diagram "Electron Path" illustrates such a path from a time of the last electronic event shown. In this case the electron as a path of events was also detected by electromagnetic radiation. Because we can think of paths portraying the historic route of electronic events, we may also consider potential electronic paths. The quantum mechanics developed from Schroedinger equations can tell us of the potential temporal and spatial location of an electronic event. Feynman has developed his understanding of quantum mechanics from potential paths.

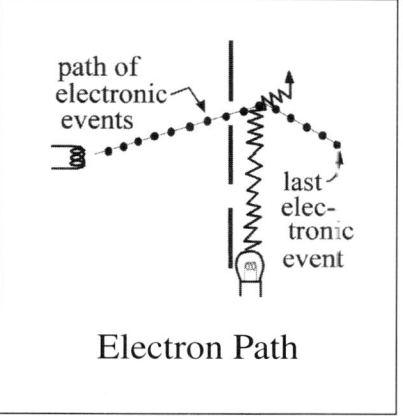

Electron Path

In our philosophical understanding of quantum mechanics, as well as of the soul, there are no fields (and hence waves in fields) that exist independently of events. There may be waves of events that are seen (or inferred) by some human experiential event or measured by some experimental device. These waves are intelligible correlations of events—forms of their relationships—that are part of both the perceiving event and the perceived events. In this sense, fields as the medium of waves are powerful methods of understanding the relationship of events, as in relativity theory. Nevertheless, in the position I am asserting, events are ontologically primary. Forms are presented as potentials from events of the past to an emerging entity, for which it has some choice of instantiation.

Limitative Theorems

The most important of all contemporary limitative theorems was proposed by Kurt Gödel in 1931. Working with *Principia Mathematica* of Russell and Whitehead, which sought to secure all mathematics from a few logical assumptions, Gödel proved the following (restated) result. There is no set of consistent axioms, finite or infinite, from which all the true theorems of arithmetic can be derived.[6] For example, suppose we have axioms and find a theorem, which does not follow from them. Add the theorem to the axioms, and then it will be derivable from them. Gödel's Incompleteness Theorem says there still remain theorems true in arithmetic that cannot be derived from the augmented axioms. Furthermore, no matter how much you augment the axiom system, there still remain true but nonderivable theorems from the axioms.

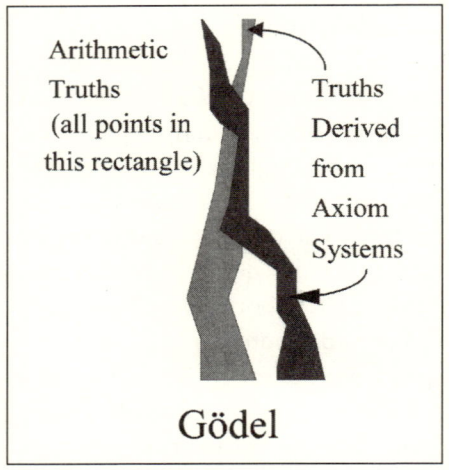

In viewing the diagram called "Gödel," think of all points in the rectangle as arithmetic truths and those points in the two different, but overlapping, gray areas as theorems respectively derived from different sets of axioms. If you add the different axioms to each other, you will get the area of the combined gray areas. Gödel's Incompleteness theorem says you can never get an axiom system whose theorems will symbolically cover the whole area. Our picture misleads in emphasis. The white area of true but unprovable theorems from the axioms should be vastly larger. There is probably much more unknown truth than known truth. Gödel's theorem is not an isolated one. Other limitative theorems affect profoundly the study of logic and of computer science.[7]

What does Gödel's theorem tell us about science? It reveals that no rational system or well-defined procedure can ever present all truth, for then it would have to generate all truths of arithmetic. Also by extension it can show that no exact scientific description can ever describe fully any particular thing or any historical event. There is always more to be known than can be shown by any precise procedure or system. As Pascal said in the seventeenth century, "The last proceeding of reason is to recognize that there is an infinity of things which are beyond it."[8] For example, can physicists ever claim that when we know the primary physical laws operating in the first instants of origination of the universe, we can then predict the remaining events? Can biologists ever claim that when we know precisely how cells work, we can know fully about multicellular organisms? Can cognitive scientists claim that when we know how the brain works, we can predict exactly what it will do? Of course not.

What do the limitative theorems tell us about philosophy? They tell us we should adopt some philosophical position that recognizes the relativity of human knowledge. Newtonian philosophy, as well as traditional metaphysics starting with the Greeks and lasting until this century, was motivated by the dream of getting an accurate, complete, and objective systematic knowledge. We know now that this dream can never be fulfilled. The philosophical position asserted in these pages is not traditional metaphysics or science in this sense. I maintain that all knowledge is limited to the perspectives of occasion events of their immediate past. Our soul events may receive from that past the inherited wisdom of others, but it is still relative to our perspectives. It must be confirmed by our relationship to the world and to God.

What do the limitative theorems tell us about religion? They tell us what we should already know, that there is no rational theology or philosophy by which we understand the full truth about God or any other matter. They tell us what the Bible so adeptly shows, that the revelation contained there is not complete except in relation to the person of Jesus Christ, and then only for our encounter with God and not scientific matters. The Bible is far more interested in our being saved by God's grace than in imparting scientific or philosophical knowledge. The early church lashed out at the Gnostic heresy that claimed one could be redeemed only by gnosis—knowledge—of special truths. We are not redeemed by what we know, but by God's action. The Christian church does accept and assert God's revelation, but again primarily in terms of the person of Jesus and the community of Christians's reaction to him. Theology and science are responses to our encounter with reality, with our world, and with God as a part of our world. Some theology and science are better than other theology and science, because they are more indicative of the truth of our encounter. The better science and theology are not only more commensurate with our experience of the world but also, I believe, with biblical Christianity.

What do the limitative theorems tell us about the Bible? They clarify the notion of biblical truth, and in the process the notions of biblical inerrancy. In a Newtonian perspective, many thought we possessed one scientific system that could describe exact truth. Facts could be tested in terms of the variables of mass, distance, and time and declared conforming or nonconforming to the theory. We believed we needed only to extend or modify the system appropriately to understand anomalous facts. In that context, because Christians accepted the Bible as superior to any science, they began to view the Bible also as a system of truth. The Bible became for them inerrant in the sense that they believed Newtonian science to be inerrant. The limitative theorems tell us we cannot have it both ways. If the Bible is a systematic structure and inerrant, it cannot be general. If the Bible is not a systematic structure, then inerrancy in the scientific sense has no meaning. I prefer to see the Bible, not as a system, but as a window to the primary events of God's causal and historical encounter with humankind—that still continues.

Randomness and Freedom Revisited

I have posited metaphysically the fundamental status of being as an event. General events are similar to the kinds described above and in previous chapters as soul events and electronic events. I have also said that substances, those familiar things of ordinary experience, are collections of events—but not just any collection of events. A substance—an electron, soul, or rock—is a collection of events that cohere in a certain way and have continuity of properties.

How does my current soul event, the totality of experience I now feel, establish connection with a previous soul event? It experiences the being of the past event and absorbs it into its being. These experiences of the past events, which we may call "feelings of past events," act as causes in the development of the current event's being. Any event has feelings of past events, but some past events have stronger causal action on it than others. An electronic event is most influenced by its immediate predecessor electronic event, but also by other electronic events, events in an atom's nucleus and molecules near it. A human soul event is most influenced by its experience of its predecessor soul event, but also by a vast variety of other brain and body events. Both soul and electronic events experience, for example, the spatio-temporal location of past predecessor events, and also feel, among other feelings, the spatio-temporal possibilities of their own existence. These spatio-temporal

The Self-Limitation of Mathematics and Quantum Mechanics

possibilities are quite limited. I cannot fly, but I can push my typing chair away from the table in a number of directions. An electronic event has limited possibilities for its occupying a particular spatio-temporal region that it feels from its environment of past local events. These possibilities can be stipulated by the wave functions of quantum mechanics.

John Polkinghorne, an Anglican priest who was a quantum physicist for most of his professional life, compares an actuary of an insurance company with a physicist to illustrate the difference between ordinary understanding of causality and causality interpreted by the dominant philosophical position of quantum mechanics. An actuary is unable to say when a particular person will die, and a physicist is unable to say when a particular unstable nucleus will decay, but both can give a good probability of these events over a specified time. The important difference between the two, Polkinghorne asserts, is there are real causes why the person dies, even if the actuary does not know them. "There are asserted to be no causes for individual events in the quantum world."[9] Why should we accept this awkward distinction between causality of human events and causality of quantum events, when we can postulate similar kinds of causal conditions for both?

As an example, consider the diagram of electronic events in the picture "Atomic Paths." These events are similar to ones pictured earlier, which in their pattern show a wave structure. In addition, the leftmost diagram has dotted lines inside and outside the dominant wave pattern that

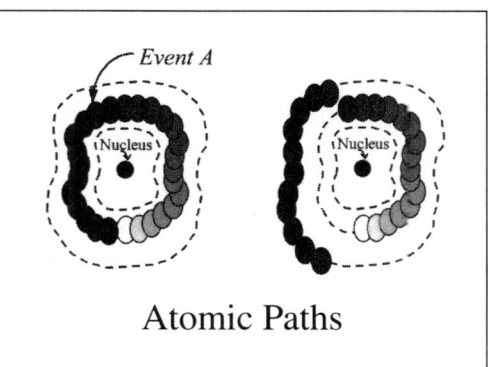

Atomic Paths

symbolize potential locations of electrons. These "paths" show the discrete possibilities of electronic events. Event A as it comes into being has a number of possibilities presented to it. Three of these are illustrated. The first is to develop itself in the wave pattern established by its predecessors, as illustrated in the leftmost diagram. The second and third options are to go inside or outside to the paths indicated. Event A feels the causality of its predecessor electronic events as well as causal forces of events inside and outside the atom. These causal forces may not dominate in one way or the other but leave some option, some freedom of choice, to the emerging electronic event itself. The rightmost diagram illustrates its decision to enter the outer orbit where its successor events are maintained, among other forces, by its causality on these events. Quantum mechanics cannot predict the actions of an individual electron, but it does extremely well in predicting the actions of millions of them. I maintain that an electron may have some freedom about which potential options it will follow. This freedom is the source of randomness.

The death at a particular time of an individual human, unpredictable by an actuary, also has specific causes—where each cause is explainable in terms of high and low level choices of events in event structures. The person can choose to commit suicide and follow through on this high level choice to causally bring about this result. Cancer cells following their low level intent to maximize their numbers may overwhelm this person's supporting bodily functions.

The reader probably feels awkward about my language of an electron's feeling and choosing, because we normally associate such emotions with consciousness, which an electron does not have. Alfred North Whitehead, whose philosophy I follow in this case, uses a neutral word "prehension" to describe human and electronic connection between current events and past ones. He also uses feeling, the word I employ, in the same sense. Electronic events have a nonconscious kind of subjectivity that allows them to make some very minimal choices based upon their prehensions or feelings of past events. How do we know this? We do not. We also cannot be assured that an electron is a hard chunk or soft cloud of featureless material. We choose between philosophical options in order to get intelligibility and meaning in science, mathematics—and theology.

I am attempting to reformulate a philosophy of science for the benefit of Christians, because I think the old materialism of Newtonian, Darwinian, and contemporary science is bankrupt. Neither am I enamored by some of the contemporary philosophical interpretations of quantum mechanics. To accept the old style philosophy of science forces many Christians into a biblical fundamentalism where they are even more captured by a discredited Newtonianism. That, in my judgment, is not what the Bible intends. To accept the dominant position on quantum mechanics makes the real existence of electronic events, and their associated electronic societies, difficult to accept. I prefer to think of electronic and soul events, and consequently electrons and souls, actually to exist. Understanding both electronic reality and soul experiences primarily as events gives, in my judgment, an integrated understanding of reality that is more compatible with Christianity than the alternatives.

In the process thought of Whitehead, which I repeat from previous descriptions, electronic and soul events have an internal development. Speaking in temporal language (although the development of an event is not in physical time), we say that both electronic and soul events "begin" their development with feelings of past events, especially those immediate predecessor soul or electronic events that influence them most. Then these feelings are integrated in various stages by the entity into a consummate "final" feeling, which is the ultimate fixed being of the entity. The entity loses its subjectivity as it fades into the past, but acts causally on subsequent entities to transfer some of its own subjective feeling to them. A human event differs from an electronic event because at a "later" stage in the human event's development, consciousness may occur. Consciousness is an addition to basic causal human feeling, not its background or source. All events, like an electronic event, are subjective. Only a small percentage of events have consciousness.

How an electron chooses what it shall be within its potential options based upon its causal past is a mystery. How we choose as humans, which most of us believe we do, is also a mystery. I do not pretend to explain the mystery of freedom of choice. I accept it, and believe that all events have some, perhaps very minimal, aspect of it. The electron is almost completely causally determined; we less so. Is not this philosophical position preferable to one that declares microscopic being has no subjectivity, is strictly material, from which we have to justify how materialism either becomes subjective, or never becomes subjective at all, violating dominant human experience?

Images of Reason

In this section I have presented two of the major limitative theorems of science: one in physics and one in mathematics. Heisenberg's indeterminacy principle focuses on small atomic particles and says that one cannot know both the position and momentum of an individual particle. I have interpreted this principle as allowing electronic events (whose historic route is an electron) to have some minimal freedom to become actual in accordance with their given potentials. Gödel's Incompleteness Theorem is about axiomatic systems or theories of explanation. It states that one can never get the complete properties of arithmetic from any axiomatic system. There is no well-defined procedure from which all the true theorems of arithmetic can be generated. By extension, Gödel's theorem entails that no theory can completely describe any event, much less all of them.

Yet quantum mechanics, in which the indeterminacy principle is embedded, and mathematics, which must take account of Gödel's theorem, are extremely powerful explanatory systems. Quantum mechanics describes accurately atomic and molecular phenomena—in the aggregate. Mathematics is the primary means of expression of all of science, and it is inordinately successful in this venture. In examining science, and especially considering the relationship between science and religion, one should be sensitive to the power of explanation of quantum mechanics and mathematics as well as to their limitations. I do not think this is hard to do. Many of our best philosophers of science, however, forget this balance just at the point where they are putting forth powerful images about the relationship of science and religion. These images, coming often at the end of their books, affect the discussion of science and religion without their having proper authority or justification. I shall give some examples by previewing central results of the next chapter.

Assuming the powerful descriptive powers of general relativity as couched in the descriptive medium of mathematics, Stephen Hawking and Roger Penrose proved in 1970 that the universe began in an explosion from an infinitely small volume—a "singularity" where time begins and all known laws of nature fail. This "big bang" origin of the universe has been confirmed by recent stunning experiments, the latest and most spectacular of which were the results of the COBE satellite in 1992. I shall outline this experimental data in the next chapter. Hawking has since modified his position to claim there are no such singularities given by his initial proof. What the mathematics really indicates is that the beginning of the universe occurred (still) in a very small volume in which quantum mechanics holds sway and in particular a quantum theory of gravity. My point is, the powerfully descriptive mathematical theory of relativity points to an origin of the universe in which quantum mechanics is dominant, a quantum mechanics that insists on certain aspects of indeterminacy, which in our interpretation means no less than some aspects of freedom for the events involved. The power and precision of mathematics and physics have led to a conclusion that accepts indeterminacy and freedom.

Yet Hawking claims that we can get "a complete description of the universe"[10]—including and especially the origin of the universe—in the big bang. When such a description is formulated, Hawking maintains, we shall learn "why . . . we and the universe exist," and can thereby "know the mind of God."[11] These emotional sentiments are made in his conclusion when he wants to make a final point, and unfortunately to reinforce an image dominant among scientists.

How can we have a complete description of the universe when its very beginning is fraught in uncertainty about the position and momentum of the particles, whatever kind they are? Far more significant, how can we claim to have a complete theory of the universe, that is of everything, when it is impossible to have a complete theory of arithmetic? Theories are just abstractions about reality. Good theories describe at best only partial aspects of what really is. Suppose we finally get the exact truth about the big bang? This only means that what the theory says is true, but the theory, no matter how good or comprehensive, can only describe the big bang partially. To think, or even assume in the form of an image, that theory can describe the origin of the universe completely, is an error of significant magnitude. This is an error made by many expositors of science.

Consider also concluding remarks of James S. Trefil in his book *The Moment of Creation*. After so carefully and professionally presenting big bang physics, he lofts an image without justification or analysis, an image that may remain with the reader long after she has forgotten the physics.

> Within a few years . . . we will find a universe that is ultimate in simplicity and beauty. All of the apparent complexity we see will be understood in terms of an underlying system in which particles of one type interact with each other through one kind of force.[12]

The image here, as with that of Hawking, is that the universe is sufficiently simple to be captured in completeness by our mathematical ideas, and in particular by a single mathematical system. This image is radically misleading. There can be no single mathematical system that captures the complete truth of lowly arithmetic, much less the universe.

The universe cannot be completely described by reason. I am not saying that some things are completely hidden from reason, only that reason can know (possibly everything) only partially. I believe science has some very helpful things to say about God, the human soul, and other aspects of the Christian religion. Science, however, will never be able to speak the whole truth about God, the human soul, or the electron. Even the electron has some secrets.

Abstract reason is not a fundamental or universal part of the universe. Adaptability may be fundamental, but not reason. I have spoken of the freedom of electrons. All entities, including electronic events, adapt to current circumstances in terms of their past. Very few kinds of entities have reasoning ability. Abstract reason, the kind championed for theories of physics, is a dependent phenomenon. Like consciousness, described earlier, it is a result of experience of the past and contingent on it.

Notes

[1] Using a constant determined by Planck, Einstein predicted that the energy E of a photon was Planck's constant h times the frequency v. In symbols, $E=hv$.

[2] Mathematically, the uncertainty in the position times the uncertainty of the momentum is always greater than Planck's constant h divided by 2π. In symbols, $\Delta x \Delta m \geq h/2\pi$.

[3] Since the probability $P(x,t)$ had to be a real number, it was found by multiplying $Y(x,t)$ by its complex conjugate, symbolized $Y^*(x,t)$.

[4] R. P. Feynman and A. R. Hibbs, *Quantum Mechanics and Path Integrals* (New York: McGraw-Hill Book Company, 1965) 2–11.

[5] Ibid., 9.

[6] Can we not derive all true theorems of arithmetic from the true theorems of arithmetic taken as axioms? Of course. This, however, is a trivial statement giving no information about arithmetic or axiomatics. We must limit our axioms to any logical statement that can be decided to be an axiom by some preestablished well-defined procedure. With this definition in place, we can show that Gödel's theorem also says that there is no well-defined procedure whatsoever from which all the true statements of arithmetic can be generated.

[7] I am thinking specifically of Church's theorem, which states there is no procedure that in all cases can tell us whether an argument is valid or not, and Turing's Halting Problem, which states (in an informal translation) there is no procedure that can tell us in all cases whether a computer given an arbitrary program will halt or not.

[8] Blaise Pascal, *Pensées; The Provincial Letters. Pensées* trans. W. F. Trotter. *The Provincial Letters* trans. Thomas M'Crie (New York: The Modern Library, 1941) 93.

[9] John Polkinghorne, *One World: The Interaction of Science and Theology* (London: SPCK, 1986) 10.

¹⁰Stephen Hawking, *A Brief History of Time* (New York: Bantam Books, 1988) 13.

¹¹Ibid., 175.

¹²James S. Trefil, *The Moment of Creation: Big Bang Physics from Before the First Millisecond to the Present Universe* (New York: Charles Scribner's Sons, 1983) 220.

Chapter 11
Creation: The Big Bang

I call this chapter "Creation: The Big Bang" because of what I observe to be a cheerful rush by many theologians and church officials to interpret the doctrine of creation in terms of new scientific developments, those commonly discussed under the descriptive name of the "big bang." The historical situation has similarities to that occurring in the English church after Newton's *Principia* brought such joy to theologians. They not only understood Newton's science to solve the problems of the (newly affirmed) solar system but also to provide a way to formulate clear proofs of God's existence by means of arguments from design. Newton was seen to be a champion of Christianity and the Bible.

Today current astronomy, buttressed by relativity theory and to a lesser extent quantum mechanics, declares that the universe as well as time and space had a beginning some eight to twenty billion years ago. At this beginning the whole universe was a "singularity," which means in some accounts that it was contained in an infinitely small volume and in other accounts that it engaged primary quantum gravity conditions throughout because it was so compact. This incredibly small and dense universe exploded in a "big bang" and has been expanding ever since.

The nature of the beginning described by science has a familiar echo with the creation account of the first chapter of Genesis while challenging those fundamentalists who claim that God created the world in a literal six days (approximately) 6,000 years ago. Some evangelicals have asserted on the theologically conservative Trinity Broadcasting Network no less that the scientific big bang theory clarifies what the Bible says in contrast to the account and early creation date espoused by the six-day creationists. The Catholic Church has accepted the contemporary scientific explanation of the beginning of the universe as confirmation of divine creation and, in 1951, officially announced the compatibility of big bang science with the Bible. Stephen Hawking reports that in his audience with the pope in 1981, he was told that he could study the universe *after* the big bang but should leave consideration of the big bang itself alone because "it was the moment of Creation and therefore the work of God."[1]

This happy accommodation of religion accepting good science is an example of our first historical thesis that Christianity normally has a friendly view towards science when it is convinced that the science is fit and proper for religious interpretation. We made the case in chapter 5 that the hostility of much of so-called creation science to evolution was the result of their advocates accepting an old science, namely the classical science that developed out of Newton's work, and then hallowing it, that is, seeing it to be a part of the Bible. Many of these same people apply Newtonian presuppositions to creation and accept the literal six-day account—even though Newton believed that the biblical day was an extended period of time.[2] This tendency to use an old sanctified science to challenge a new one is, of course, our second historical thesis.

It is our third historical thesis, which claims that any new science comes ready-made with images and a philosophical interpretation, that gives both an opportunity and challenge to contemporary theologians. The opportunity arises because the science surrounding big bang astronomy is still so new that philosophical interpretations coming from science are not as yet firmly established. One can engage the science with images and philosophical positions that are more compatible with a biblical perspective without having to undo "what most scientists believe." The danger is that there are a number of images and philosophical interpretations proposed by scientists that are antagonistic towards any theistic interpretation of the big bang. These are interpretations that are readily accepted by scientists and others who are already committed nontheists. We need to understand these images, evaluate them and, if necessary, discount them.

I am amazed at the brilliance shown by some physicists and astronomers to uphold, often by the flimsiest of reasons, the image of a secular beginning. Chief among these is the admittedly excellent and, to many, balanced argument that the initiation of the universe was an accident![3] In my experience, I have never known people to come to a belief in God through argument, theory, or physical evidence. We should not expect big bang science to convert anyone. For those, however, who know and respect the doctrine of God's creation of the universe, the results of big bang cosmology are instructive and utterly fascinating.

We also need to exercise some caution in accepting big bang cosmology too quickly and too literally into the heart of Christianity, because as in the past we may be led to do bad theology and be inclined to resist new science when it appears. It continues, however, to be such a pleasure to read the science journals and to see surprising developments that aid in understanding and confirming what may be a sound approach to a biblical doctrine of creation.

Creation: The Big Bang

As in previous chapters, I shall present what I consider the science of big bang astronomy and then analyze its interpretation in terms of images and philosophy. The following two parts of this chapter are an analysis of the images of big bang science and then their secular interpretation in what is called the "anthropic principle." The next chapter considers a Christian doctrine of creation.

I recommend two excellent books written by astronomers and designed to be read by laypersons: *The Creator and the Cosmos*,[4] by an evangelical Christian Hugh Ross; and *A Brief History of Time*,[5] by a nontheist Stephen Hawking, regarded by many scientists as the most brilliant theoretical physicist since Einsten. Hawking had a great impact on scientific laypeople, occupying for more than 100 weeks a position on the *New York Times* bestseller list and being made the subject of a popular program on Public Broadcasting System (PBS).

Images of Big Bang Science

Newtonian science finally confirmed with theory and observations that we live in a solar system in which the sun is the center and the planets, including the earth, rotate around it. The stars are not on a single sphere a great distance away as Aristarchus imagined, but at varying distances as seen from the earth. The milky way has its seeming flow of continuous white substance, because it is composed of billions of stars, far more than the number of people on earth (more than 100 billion stars compared to about 5 billion people). In this count, each person could be matched with more than twenty stars. Our sun is a star. The stars vary in size. Some are larger than our sun; others smaller. If the stars were parceled out to people on earth, you could have your twenty suns, some possibly with inhabited planets.

Looking from earth, the density of stars in the Milky Way indicates that the stars are arranged in a spiral similar to the flat spiral of planets around the sun, except that the stars number in the billions and the planets are only nine. In addition to the billions of stars in the spiral, our galaxy includes a halo of old stars through which the disk of stars would shine brightly to any outside observer. The nucleus of the galaxy is composed of stars more densely packed. A massive black hole from which nothing, even light, can escape is thought to exist at the center of the nucleus. It holds the galaxy together by its immense gravity, like the sun hangs on to its planets.

Observable stars are of all colors and of many kinds, extending in size from the enormous red giants to the incredibly dense white dwarfs. In addition to the spherical bright objects we call stars, we can also observe objects in our universe that are not spherical but disk-like and look suspiciously similar to the shape of that spiral of stars we know as our galaxy. These objects were discovered only in the 1920s to be vastly further away than the stars we observe and are themselves galaxies like our own consisting of billions of stars. Some galaxies are not spirals but appear like roundish, fuzzy ellipticals. There are at least 100 billion of these distant galaxies so that if they were counted out among people, each person could have at least twenty galaxies, each with its approximately 100 billion stars. The universe is a very big place. The sun and the earth are very small in this comparison. Humankind seems quite insignificant.

The grandeur of the universe has inspired an image of a universe, which is believed to be infinite in size and eternal in age. Neither position is new. Aristarchus measured the size of the universe (chapter 1) as the ratio of a sphere to its center, which at least tells us that he considered the universe to be unthinkably large. You may remember as a child asking the question "What is beyond space?" and coming up with the answer "More space," and after that even "More space," and so on. It is not hard to ask the question "What is beyond the stars we see?" and keep answering it "More and more stars." In letters to Richard Bentley,[6] Newton, who did not like a collapsing universe, argued that if the universe had a finite number of stars, it would fall into itself because of gravity. He allowed, however, that if there were an infinite number of stars evenly and exactly distributed, then the gravitational force on each star would be balanced, and the universe as a whole would be stable. Newton did not observe such an even distribution of the stars and concluded that only God could establish and maintain a stable universe—finite or infinite.

We know today that there can be no finite or infinite static model of the universe with gravity always attractive. Unless there is some massive force pushing outwards like an initial explosion, the universe will eventually collapse on itself. Newton knew this but depended on God to keep the universe stable. Nevertheless, the image of a static, infinite, and eternal universe—often without God—became very popular. The breakdown of this image among scientists at the hands of big bang astronomy has caused many of them anguish, and has precipitated at times what I consider to be ad hoc theories to maintain and repair the image. This activity of trying to save the image has afflicted some of the most competent scientists.[7]

Aristotle argued and thought he had proved the world to be eternal —that it had no beginning and will have no end. Christian theologians, particularly Augustine and Aquinas, grappled with this idea. Although the nature and meaning of an infinitely physically extended universe has been a controversial point in Christian theology, theologians have consistently challenged the proposal that the universe had no temporal beginning. The message of the doctrine of creation has been too clear and strong in the Bible as well as in Christian tradition.

During the nineteenth and early twentieth centuries there were two main models of the universe: a secular one and a religious one. The secular one, which was orthodoxy to much standard astronomy, saw the universe as infinite and eternal. The religious one, accepting the Christian doctrine of creation, posited a large but finite universe that began in time or, as Augustine would maintain, in which time and the universe began simultaneously. No one either in science or for Christianity had seriously considered and systematically proclaimed an expanding universe. There was some observation of minor movement of the stars in what we now know to be our galaxy, but this movement did not indicate to anyone a general expansion of the whole universe.

The first significant hint for an expanding universe was given in the early 1920s by American astronomer Edwin Hubble, who was seeking to demonstrate that ours is not the only galaxy. In his early work Hubble showed that some few objects, thought to be galaxies, were much further away than the observable stars in our galaxy. He did this by observing the relative brightness of standard stars in our galaxy and similar stars in other galaxy candidates. Part of his study involved the routine examination of light coming from the stars in these newly discovered galaxies. Any hot body gives off a characteristic radiation dependent on its temperature. The chemical elements in the atmosphere of a star absorb particular frequencies of its radiation, leaving spectral lines. By examining the light and other radiation from stars, one can get information about their temperatures and chemical composition. This information seemed routine. One could recognize the presence of familiar elements in the stars of the galaxies by the telltale pattern of their spectra.

Surprisingly, the pattern of spectral lines of the identifiable elements was shifted to the red side of the spectrum in almost all of the galaxies examined, which meant the galaxies are moving away from us because of a Doppler effect. (We may see an example of the Doppler effect when the pitch of a car horn drops as it passes us and speeds away). If the galaxies are all moving away from our galaxy, the universe is expanding. Furthermore, in a paper published in 1929, Hubble reported that the magnitude of the red shift of a galaxy is proportional to its distance from us. The galaxies most distant from us are moving away from us the fastest.

A helpful image for understanding the expanding universe is to think first about a large rubber band with black spots symbolizing galaxies (see "Rubber Band with Black Spots"). Choose some spot as our galaxy. To achieve the Hubble conditions, one must stretch the rubber band so that each galaxy is increasing from ours and the ones farthest away from us are increasing fastest. This is not so hard if you realize that an increasing circular band satisfies the conditions. Paste the band on the outside of a balloon and blow up the balloon. The spots on the rubber band grow distant from each other in the manner required.

Rubber Band With Black Spots

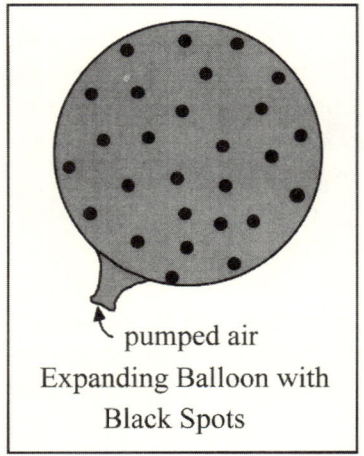

pumped air
Expanding Balloon with Black Spots

It would be simpler to paint spots on the balloon not just in a circular pattern but all over it (see "Expanding Balloon with Black Spots"). Notice that we increased dimensions from an expanding circle to an expanding sphere or, put another way, from a warped line to a warped surface. In each case, circle or sphere, every galaxy is moving away from the others. A galaxy further away is moving away faster. Notice that no galaxy has a privileged position (an important part of relativity theory). We no longer have to choose a spot to be our galaxy. The universe looks (almost) the same from any galaxy. The Hubble conditions in this image are satisfied from any place in the universe.

Understanding that there is an expanding balloon does not necessarily tell us its early history. One could have let the air out and then pumped it back in. Accepting that the galaxies of the universe are rushing away from each other does not tell us how the universe began. Science does not live on experimental results alone. To make sense of Hubble's work requires correlating it with contemporary theory, in particular general relativity.

When Einstein developed his general theory of relativity, he was so intent on maintaining a static universe that he fudged. He introduced a nonobservable anti-gravity force that he thought should keep the universe from collapsing from its own attractive force of gravity. Without this anti-gravity force, which Einstein eventually abandoned, one can argue from the general theory of relativity that not only is the universe expanding as Hubble found out, but that it had a beginning. In 1970, Penrose and Hawking proved that the general theory of relativity predicts a big bang origin of the universe from an infinitely small volume. Furthermore, contemporary astronomy predicts that we should be able to observe this ancient and primordial explosion at the origin of the universe by means of the radiation generated at its beginning. What is the nature of this radiation, and where should we look for it?

Let us think about directions in our two models, the expanding rubber band and the expanding balloon. From the perspective of a galaxy-spot on the band, there are only two directions as on a line. Call them east and west. From a perspective of a galaxy-spot on the balloon, there are the full directions of a plane: north, south, east, and west, and directions in between. On the balloon we have to accept ourselves and our galaxy to be completely flat because of the nature of the image. We understand how the Hubble conditions can hold in our simulated flat world by appealing to a curved flat surface, namely, an increasing sphere in higher dimensions.

From our position in the flat world on the surface of the balloon, let us accept the conclusion of the mathematical description of big bang theory that there was an enormous explosion that started it. We cannot point to "where" it started (at the center of the balloon) because we are in two physical dimensions. Only if we allow ourselves to participate in three dimensions can we "see" where the beginning is. In our two-dimensional status let us accept, as predicted, that some of the radiation from the big bang is flowing through the universe. If we acknowledge that there is no privileged position in the universe and that the universe looks the same from any direction, where should this radiation come from? It should come from all directions in the plane (but not, of course, from the center of the sphere because we are now considered to be perfectly flat).

In our three physical dimensions we can understand that the big bang began at the center of a warped higher dimension of space-time from the mathematics, but we cannot picture it or point to it. If asked, however, from what directions the predicted residual radiation would come, we must respond, as in the flat case, "all directions," which now means all directions in three dimensions. Not only that, but the radiation should have the same intensity in all directions, because, according to big bang theory, now confirmed by relativity theory, the universe is supposed to appear the same in all directions.

In 1948, George Gamow and his research team estimated what the temperature conditions of the early universe should be and the rate of its expansion—if indeed it is expanding as Hubble's evidence indicated —in order to produce the kinds of elements and their abundance that we observe today. In 1965, Bob Dicke and Jim Peebles, following on the work of Gamow, argued that we should be able to "see" the big bang from radiation still traveling across space. (Because of the finite speed of light, when we look at a star, we see it as it was and look back into the past.) What we see from the big bang is not light, but radiation so changed because of the expanding universe that it appears as microwave radiation. Gamow's research team had predicted that this radiation should be about 5° Centigrade above absolute zero (-273° Centigrade) and should come evenly from all directions.

Arno Penzias and Robert Wilson, who were testing new varieties of sensitive microwave detectors, had already observed this radiation. They initially thought their instruments were defective, because they showed a low-grade radiation coming from no direction in particular, and concluded that it was from noise generated from inside their instruments. Penzias and Wilson were given the Nobel Prize in 1978 for their inadvertent discovery. In 1990, a special cosmic background explorer satellite (COBE) was launched to confirm and strengthen these results. It showed no irregularities in the distribution and temperature of the predicted radiation greater than one part in 10,000.

There was a problem, however, with these results. If the radiation were perfectly smooth, it would be counter evidence that galaxies had formed from the big bang. The formation of galaxies would require in the current theory that there be variations in the radiation field of about one part in 100,000, far beyond the sensitivity of the first COBE satellite. The second COBE exploration found these variations in the

Creation: The Big Bang

right places. The announcement of the results in 1992 was a stunning confirmation that our universe had an origin in an enormous explosion.

The evidence continues to pour in that the expansion of the galaxies will go on. Physicists and astronomers, theists and nontheists alike, generally agree that the mass of the universe by current estimates is not sufficient to cause the expansion of the galaxies to halt and return together to form a "big crunch." Were there to be a big crunch, we could understand how the universe might be infinitely old: big bang, big crunch, big bang, big crunch, and forever. There is further significant evidence, should there be enough hidden matter to cause the universe to collapse, that we are in the first of the big bang stages. Further big bangs would wear down, and there could not be the distribution of elements we observe in our universe, much less life. In short, science confirms the initial set of events of our universe that looks to Jews and Christians, as well as to those who follow Islam, like what their scriptures teach as Creation.

Big Bang Design? The Anthropic Principle

It is not just that the big bang as described by science indicates a beginning to our universe compatible with the creation accounts described in the Bible. The forces, relationships, and constants established in the first few seconds of the big bang seem to show a purpose for the cosmos—the ultimate evolution of life and humanity. This is information from science, not just scripture. That scientific information causes secular physicists to consider possibilities of divine goals in the initial beginnings of the cosmos is quite significant. Here are a few of the recent scientific discoveries about universal constants, which are not as yet derivable from relativity or quantum theory but must be assumed to be initial conditions of the early universe. They are the first five of Hugh Ross's careful and documented list of twenty-five (!) similar characteristics, with the wording slightly revised.[8] The values of the constants must lie in very narrow ranges. For example, the ratio of electromagnetic force constant to the gravitational force constant (number 5 below) cannot differ by more than one part in 10^{40} (1 with 40 zeros after it). That this ratio would happen by accident is like picking out just the right penny in a pile of ten million, trillion, trillion, trillion pennies. The point is that unless these constants were determined within bounds of extreme precision, there could be no life at all. Some of the constants are:

(1) Strong nuclear force constant: If it were larger, there would be no hydrogen. The nuclei essential for life would be unstable. If it were smaller, there would be no elements other than hydrogen.

(2) Weak nuclear force constant: If it were larger, too much hydrogen would be converted to helium in the big bang; hence star burning would make too much heavy element material. There would be no expulsion of heavy elements from the stars. If it were smaller, too little helium would be produced from the big bang; hence there would be too little heavy element material made by star burning. There would be no expulsion of heavy elements from the stars.

(3) Gravitational force constant: If it were larger, stars would be too hot and would burn up too quickly and too unevenly. If it were smaller, stars would remain so cool that nuclear fusion would never ignite. There would be no heavy element production.

(4) Electromagnetic force constant: If it were larger, insufficient chemical bonding would occur. Elements more massive than boron would be too unstable for fission. If it were smaller, there would be insufficient chemical bonding.

(5) Ratio of electromagnetic force constant to gravitational force constant: If the ratio were larger, no stars less than 1.4 solar masses would exist, hence short stellar life spans and uneven stellar luminosities. If the ratio were smaller, no stars more than 0.8 solar masses, hence no heavy element production.

Assuming God's initial hand in the creation as evidenced by the finely tuned constants of the universe, many have wondered why God took so long to create life and particularly human beings. If that was God's goal, why did God not do it more efficiently? Bertrand Russell once remarked, "Are we really so splendid as to justify such a long prolog?"[9] One answer is that due to the consequences of the constants, ostensibly chosen by God at the initiation of the universe, it takes about twelve billion years to get the right mixture of heavy elements necessary for life. Successive generations of giant stars have to come and go. Perhaps God enjoyed the extended prolog of creativity necessary for life to emerge. Perhaps God considers great value to exist in this extensive prehuman and prelife period. Perhaps God wanted to see what freedom given to a nonliving creation would produce—while insisting that it develop within the bounds that would ultimately allow life to form.

Creation: The Big Bang

What may seem to Christians as evidence for God's initial creation of the universe cannot be so interpreted by secular scientists and philosophers, for that would require a reorientation of their philosophical and religious perspective. In their position, they must provide answers to the questions of apparently purposive big bang science in terms of science alone—a science dependent primarily on mathematical theory and observation.

The central idea is called the anthropic principle, introduced to modern thought by Brandon Carter—and now much discussed by philosophers and scientists. It has a weak and a strong form. The weak form as stated by Carter: "Our presence in the universe is necessarily privileged to the extent of being compatible with our existence as observers."[10] This is somewhat like people who speak and understand only ordinary English, saying, "What we expect to hear must be restricted by the English tradition that informs our language speaking ability." If we speak only English, we are not surprised that written or spoken information comes to us only in English. Everything else is gibberish. Hawking says that the weak form of the anthropic principle is "like a rich person living in a wealthy neighborhood not seeing any poverty."[11] This person is not surprised to see those affluent conditions (especially those of his parents) that have established his condition as rich. The weak anthropic principle restated: If we are human observers, we should not be surprised to observe a world that produces human observers—even at the earliest beginnings. I find the weak form of the anthropic principle to be very weak, almost vacuous. It has none of the intelligibility or power of the image of a person designing and creating a watch, which can be extended by analogy to a God who can design and create a cosmos.

To Carter, the more questionable form is the strong anthropic principle: "The Universe . . . must be such as to admit the creation of observers within it at a certain stage."[12] The strong anthropic principle immediately calls for the question, Why? Why should the initial constants of the universe be such as to admit human life? We are then right back to the mystery of apparent design of the universe raised by the scientific findings about the big bang. Those who believe in a creator God for reasons other than those of science find big bang science fascinating. It becomes science that enlivens and informs a traditional Christian doctrine of creation. This is our first historical thesis that Christianity normally accepts, and this time apparently gladly accepts, good science.

Notes

[1] Stephen Hawking, *A Brief History of Time: From the Big Bang to Black Holes* (New York: Bantam Books, 1990) 116.

[2] Isaac Newton, from a letter to Thomas Burnet, *Newton's Philosophy of Nature*, ed. H. S. Thayer (New York: Hafner, 1953) 60–62.

[3] P. C. W. Davies, *The Accidental Universe* (Cambridge: Cambridge University Press, 1982).

[4] Hugh Ross, *The Creator and the Cosmos* (Colorado Springs CO: Navpress, 1993).

[5] Hawking.

[6] Newton, *Newton's Philosophy of Nature*, 50-58.

[7] The most famous of the attempts to establish an infinite and "steady state" universe is due to Hermann Bondi, Thomas Gold, and Fred Hoyle. The universe is considered static, not because the galaxies are not moving, but because the steady state model has it look roughly the same in all times and in all places. In order to achieve this condition, the model requires the natural creation of new matter. The predictions of this theory have now been falsified and the theory abandoned. Even Einstein introduced a force in his general theory of relativity to balance the force of gravity so the universe would not be seen to expand.

[8] Adapted from Hugh Ross, *The Creator and the Cosmos* (Colorado Springs CO: Navpress, 1993) 111–14. Used by permission of NavPress/Pinon Press.

[9] Bertrand Russell, *Religion and Science* (New York: Oxford University Press, 1961) 221.

[10] Brandon Carter, "Large number coincidences and the anthropic principle in cosmology," *Confrontation of Cosmological Theories with Observation*, ed. M. S. Longair (Reidel: Dordrecht, 1974) 293.

[11] Hawking, 124.

[12] Carter, 294.

Chapter 12
A Christian Doctrine of Creation

It can be difficult to classify oneself among the parties of Christian division. Coming from a Protestant background and driven by my new-birth experience to investigate Catholic sensitivities, I now find myself as much at home in the eucharistic service commonly called "the mass" as I do participating in an evangelical revival that invites a decision for Christ. I am thrilled at a conversion of one previously uncommitted to Christianity who then submits to baptism by immersion. I am also awed by infant baptism, which following ancient Catholic tradition has long been called a "new birth."

After I began attending mass regularly, one of my evangelical friends asked me if I ever witnessed change-of-life new-birth experiences in, as he said, the "high church" environment. My reply was, "Yes, more often than you would expect, but they call it by a different name." Following Jesus' statement "No one can enter the kingdom of God without being born of water and Spirit" (John 3:5), Catholic tradition emphasizes new birth as being born of water, and Protestant tradition emphasizes new birth as being born of spirit. It was a remarkably integrative experience for me to realize that Catholics also consider (what evangelicals would call) an emphasis on spiritual new birth to be a normative and sought-for development after baptism. Catholic theology calls this a "second conversion," which is "the movement of a 'contrite heart,' drawn and moved by grace to respond to the merciful love of God who loved us first."[1] This view of an underlying unity of the church on the issues of baptism and new birth, however named, presented to me a vision of a cheerful integrity in the church universal, Catholic and Protestant.

I mention this personal experience of relating two separated Christian traditions because I believe the philosophical perspective now being articulated as process thought, developed so far to relate science and religion, can also be used to integrate Christian theological topics previously separated because of bad philosophy. I would like to believe this integrative philosophical position can give a further cheerful integrity to the general theological venture—and thereby better locate the center of the Christian religion. In this chapter I shall present what I believe to be that theological core—a Christian doctrine of creation. By this means, I shall illustrate not only big bang science, but also the ideas of God's incarnation in Christ, resurrection of the body, inspiration of the scriptures, and what divine healing means. These are all aspects of God's creativity, which I believe to have been intellectually obscured by a dominant but erroneous idea about the nature of a substance—as something that exists by itself through space and time.

If one believes that primary substances once here stay around and last in space and through time, the choices about the nature of God's making heaven and earth are few. They are: God made the earth out of God's own existence. God made it out of some preexistent material. Or God spoke the words "Let there be" and made heaven and earth out of nothing. If God made the world out of God's own existence, then the world in some sense is divine. That position is called "pantheism," which most Christians have rejected as not biblical. If God made the world out of some preexistent material, then a question arises about God's relationship to this material. Was it eternally existent with God, or did God make it also? An eternally preexistent material is not normally considered a proper biblical doctrine. If God made the material, then we are back to the question of whether God made it out of nothing or out of God's divine existence. With these choices, Christians have normally said that the correct doctrine is, "in the beginning" God made the heavens and the earth out of nothing.

If God made the heavens and the earth out of nothing, and under the assumption that the substances of the components of the heavens and the earth last through time, do they need divine maintenance to uphold them and cause them to continue to exist? The traditional Christian answer is Yes. All things are supported by God's sustaining (as distinguished from God's creative) power. If one changes perspective to event structures, where the basic things in the world are events that do not exist through space and time and have relationships we have explained in previous chapters, then God's creativity can be understood to be the same kind of creativity in the beginning of time as in the present. God's creative power is the same as God's sustaining power—except different in degree. Furthermore, the separate doctrines of Incarnation, resurrection of the dead, healing, and inspiration of the Bible can all be interpreted in terms of this more general doctrine of God's creative causality. In this case, the doctrine of creation out of nothing has to be revised, because its very meaning is dependent on a traditional understanding of substance. I shall begin first with a theological analysis of the initial creation that is illuminated by big bang science. Notice I am attempting to bring an account of event structures

A Christian Doctrine of Creation

that was developed in order to make science intelligible to an interpretation of religion. First, let us be sure what the Bible, and particularly the New Testament, says about the initial creation.

Biblical Understanding of Creation

Most interpretations of God's creative act at the initiation of the cosmos begin with the account in the first verse of Genesis, "In the beginning . . . God created the heavens and the earth." For a Christian doctrine of creation, however, I think it appropriate to begin with New Testament teaching through which we may interpret the Old Testament including the Genesis description.

The Gospel of John speaks of Jesus as the Word and claims he was preexistent with God before creation and participated with God in creation. "In the beginning was the Word, and the Word was with God, and the Word was God. He was in the beginning with God. All things came into being through him, and without him not one thing came into being" (1:1–3). Jesus seems to confirm an understanding of his own preexistent status by referring to the "glory, which you have given me because you (God) loved me before the foundation of the world" (17:24).

When one sees the Greek words *logos* and *arche* (discussed in chapter 2) for Word and beginning, one may suspect Greek philosophical influence on the Gospel. Most biblical scholars, however, claim that the primary literary influence for John's statements came from a tradition in the Old Testament. Consider the similarity of the following verses from Proverbs about wisdom.

> The LORD created me at the beginning of his work, the first of his acts of long ago. Ages ago I was set up, at the first, before the beginning of the earth. When there were no depths I was brought forth, when there were no springs abounding with water. Before the mountains had been shaped, before the hills, I was brought forth—when he had not yet made earth and fields, or the world's first bits of soil. When he established the heavens, I was there, when he drew a circle on the face of the deep, when he made firm the skies above, when he established the fountains of the deep, when he assigned to the sea its limit, so that the waters might not transgress his command, when he marked out the foundations of the earth, then I was beside him, like a master worker; and I was daily his delight, rejoicing before him always. (8:22–30)

The major point of interest is that the Gospel of John, confirmed by other New Testament passages as well as the passage from Proverbs, indicates God and Jesus existed prior to the creation of the world and were separate but unified. Classical theology includes also the Holy Spirit in a trinitarian formulation. Could this be at best an unintelligible spiritual mystery and at worst a contradiction? Not if we look at the meaning of societies in event structures. Remember we described a human as a unification of bodily events in a dominant occasion, which also brought into itself and unified previous dominant occasions. From a subjective point of view, the soul of a person is unified historically because of its integration in the current dominant occasion. From an objective point of view, the soul is a sequence of events.

In my judgment, the best of careful and philosophical presentation of a process view of the Trinity has been done by Joseph Bracken in his book *Society and Spirit: A Trinitarian Cosmology*.[2] Bracken understands the "Father," "Son" and "Holy Spirit" to be each personal societies unified in tight communion as the society "God." I anticipate that the reader may feel as awkward with this beginning description of the societal nature of God as I do. We are attempting to describe what cannot be described accurately or fully by human philosophy or analogy. I want only to point out that, in my opinion, a process philosophical description of event structures gives us far more flexibility in discussing the societal nature of God than any traditional substance orientation. I believe we can discuss possibilities of trinitarian unity and diversity with more meaning than in the old philosophy even though we may never hope to "get it exactly right."[3]

One of the difficulties in attempting to talk about the societal relationship between God, Jesus, and the Holy Spirit before the creation of the world is that our language requires us to use temporal terms. Yet contemporary science claims that what we know as scientific time and space began at the big bang. There is no getting behind the big bang in terms of ordinary temporal or spatial description. The New Testament also hints that time had a beginning. Paul speaks in a number of places about God's actions "before the ages (or time) began" (2 Tim 1:9; Titus 1:2). In the previous quotation from the Gospel of John, Jesus speaks of God's actions "before the foundation (or creation) of the world." Do we not necessarily presuppose temporal categories in speaking of God's actions before time began?

The answer is Yes and No. Yes, such speech does presuppose temporal categories, but, No, it does not presuppose the temporal categories of space and time described by the physicists. What could we mean by a kind of time that is not part of physics? We have claimed that a more appropriate understanding of temporal and spatial categories for relativity and quantum mechanics is one that recognizes time and space are determined by the relationship of events and not vice versa. Yet each event has an "internal" or "subjective" time, a process that is non-temporal when viewed by means of clocks. Any actual entity receives causality from past events and synthesizes them into its own being.

This is a different kind of time where the past is rigidly separated from the future by a contemporary present. These structures of past, present, and future determined by the development of each event in its relationship to other events decide what we call "physical" or "scientific" time. This physical time, which is a special relationship between events, was born at the big bang. The more fundamental kind of time, of which we have some hints in our intimate experience, precedes the big bang and allows us to speak of the possibility of God's actions during this period.

How did God act to create the cosmos? What are some interpretations of creation in terms of event structures? Let us accept God to be societal and preexistent of creation eternally. We do not know the nature of God's communal nature or whether there were beings in addition to a bare Trinity. The Bible, however, does give us some hints. There were a number of angelic announcements in the Old and New Testaments, especially about the birth of Jesus (I write at Christmas time). There may have been a rich community of angelic beings in addition to a societal God. These beings, and God—certainly Jesus (as confirmed by his resurrected status)—had spiritual bodies, but bodies no less.

The existence of bodies entails a world of separated events from God even though they may have a different temporal and spatial structure from what we observe in our created time. We remember the story of God's creation in the words of Genesis "A wind from God (or the Spirit of God) swept over the face of the waters" (1:2) before God said, "Let there be." Genesis hints that there was an initial chaos of events before God created our world. Any world preceding creation would have been entirely different from the world we know, at least in terms of spatial and temporal categories. We have hints of it, not from discoveries within physical time and space, but in terms of God's action, which we may feel subjectively in a more fundamental subjective time.

Creation was not, as I maintain, a bringing into being of substances that exist on their own in some more fundamental structure of time and space. Physical time and space were not created before the things in it. Creation was a result of God's causality bringing forth events that had some freedom to choose their basic nature among limited options. The relationship of these events determined the nature of physical space and time. Some of the options given to newly created entities, for example, those determining the basic physical constants, appear to have been very narrow. Nevertheless, while wearing process philosophy glasses, this is the kind of creation we observe before our eyes today—one that involves a causal cooperation, as well as possible animosity, between created events and God.

Each soul event is caused to become itself by past bodily events and previous soul events—as well as by God's causality. In this case, God's causality is self-limiting because of God's creation of conditions at the big bang that allow freedom and causality among entities of the created world. God helps maintain the emerging entities by God's causality and the causality of the previous temporal world in which past decisions have a present effect. The causality of God is of two kinds, a direct efficient causation in which God "nudges" a developing entity with various degrees of power, and a presentation to a developing entity with some of the limited options it may have for its freedom of choice.

The version of process thought maintained in this book puts a different light on the "creation out of nothing" doctrine, which I have argued is not strictly biblical but derived from Greek philosophy. Nevertheless, I claim the doctrine for our position—properly reinterpreted. God creates the world, in our example the initiation of the "big bang," causally from God's societal existence, not out of God's (traditionally understood) substantial existence. God *makes* the world, not *is* the world. In this sense God's initiation of the physical world is creation out of nothing, for God does not use any other substance, including God's self, to make the world. The striking thing in our process-oriented position is that the initiation of any mundane event also comes out of its immediate causal past, now including the vast array of worldly events, particular predecessor electronic events, and God, in a manner similar to the created universe coming out of God's past. In this sense, the most ordinary electronic event is "creation out of nothing," for it, too, is caused to begin to be by its settled past including God.

In the initial creation symbolized by the big bang, there was little if any preexistent world to exercise causality or, put another way, to limit God's freedom. The societal God set in motion through an awesome creative act the beginning of the universe, which was a set of events.

A Christian Doctrine of Creation

These events, though caused by God, were also presented with options that established the constants of the universe. The events, like all events, had some limited freedom. Once there, these events, as events do today, exercised causality with God for the evolution of the universe. The most amazing thing to me about the big bang is not its power, but that God took an enormous gamble in giving away some of God's freedom to a burgeoning cosmos. In so many ways we are still what we choose, as well as what options we are given by the choices of the cosmos as past. Not all of the range of our choices is determined by the created order. Some come uniquely from God. This is part of the message of the Gospel, the good news of Jesus Christ.

The Incarnation

The Incarnation, God's becoming human, or as John says, "the Word became flesh and lived among us" (John 1:14), is also a creative act of God. Preposterous as it may seem, the traditional story is that God entered the womb of a virgin and was born as an ordinary baby, lived as a fully human man, and suffered an ignominious death on the cross. If true, this act of God is a further and even more radical self-limitation of God's freedom than at the creation—a subjecting of the Godhead not only to the physical forces of the cosmos but also to the accumulated political forces that were the result of evil choices of humans. As Saint Paul says in Philippians,

> Christ Jesus, who, though he was in the form of God, did not regard equality with God as something to be exploited, but emptied himself, taking the form of a slave, being born in human likeness. And being found in human form, he humbled himself and became obedient to the point of death—even death on a cross. (2:5-8)

The awesomeness of the initial creation of the universe pales in comparison to the Christmas story. We may think of the big bang origin of the universe as an indescribable singularity point. It is also appropriate to think of the Incarnation as a singularity point in which God entered the cosmos God had created and subjected God's self as a defenseless embryo, later to become a boy and a man, to its structures.

The miracle of God's activity in the Virgin Birth, like the zero point of the big bang, is not subject to scientific scrutiny. Both, however, are found to be immediately interpretable in terms of natural law, which is a habitual pattern of events within the potentials of divine selection.

Scientists seek a naturalistic explanation of the big bang as far back to the zero point as possible. After the miracle of God's insemination of Mary, the development of the baby Jesus in the womb of his mother is surprisingly and completely normal. Miracles fit well and are taken over immediately by the normal structures of the world. Mary had a normal pregnancy and delivery. It is possible to talk about the miracle of the Virgin Birth itself, like the singularity of the big bang, by means of event structures. God exercised God's causality along with the causality of the body of Mary, as well as that produced by her consensual choice, to produce the event structure of a fertilized egg, which then took its normal and natural course. Remember, natural here means, not images of substances existing through space and time, but event structures that receive causality from the past choices of physical events, human activities, and God.

To speak of God as entering human history is even more difficult than understanding the miracle of the Virgin Birth. It is of comparable difficulty as talking about the societal nature of God before the big bang—fraught with the hazards of trying to describe what cannot be described. Nevertheless, a call to theology must necessarily engage some aspects of this central event of the Christian message.

One way to think about the Incarnation is not to consider how God became man in Jesus, but to begin with the church's experience of Jesus and ask what it means for Jesus to be divine. Jesus was obviously human and subject to the same general scientific and philosophical structures as are we all. Yet the experience of the community of believers who form the church is that in an encounter with the person of Jesus, one experiences a quality of divine causality and grace more than and different from other humans. We see Jesus subject to the event structures that affect us, and yet we see Jesus as a unique channel for the richness of God's very nature. This experience has caused the church to speculate on how God can exercise God's holiness and divinity, as well as God's compassion and love, through Jesus. These experiences ratified by the choice of books to form the New Testament, confirmed by church councils, and articulated by the theologians of the early church have coalesced to declare that Jesus the Word "was with God and was God."[4] It is in this spirit that process theologians look first at the person of Jesus, and then attempt to describe his divine transcendence in terms of event structures.

A Christian Doctrine of Creation

Inspiration of the Bible

To illustrate what the Bible is, and what it is not, let us go directly to Peter's confession that Jesus is the Messiah (Christ), contained in Matthew, Mark and Luke, but not in John. Read carefully these primary sources about the event, translated so that the English is different if the original Greek is different, but the same if the Greek is the same. For example, "You are the Messiah" in Matthew and Mark derives from the Greek σὺ εἶ ὁ χριστός, whereas Luke's statement "The Messiah of God" is translated from τὸν χριστὸν τοῦ θεοῦ, which as you can see are two different Greek statements.

Matthew 16:15-16	Mark 8:29	Luke 9:20
line 1 He said to them,	line 1 He asked them,	line 1 He said to them,
line 2 But who do you say that I am?	line 2 But who do you say that I am?	line 2 But who do you say that I am?
line 3 Simon Peter answered,	line 3 Peter answered him,	line 3 Peter answered,
line 4 You are the Messiah,	line 4 You are the Messiah.	line 4 The Messiah of God.
line 5 the Son of the living God		

Notice the third line is different in all three Gospels, the second line is the same in each Gospel, and the fourth line is the same in Matthew and Mark and different in Luke. The fifth line where Matthew identifies Christ as "the Son of the living God" is found in neither Mark nor Luke.

All biblical scholars, Jewish, Christian, and nonreligious, seek to get a manuscript as close to the original authors as possible. Surprisingly, after massive effort, there is general agreement that whatever standard translated version we may use (including the passages above) is generally accurate but may or may not reflect some scholarly refinements still held with mild controversy that have occurred in the last two centuries. In short, good scholarship has confirmed the basic integrity of the received text.

The major religious reason for seeking an accurate original is to get as clear as possible the message of God's revelation in Scripture. The closer we get to the original authors, the less we accept of possible human corruption of the text. Let us assume that the biblical text is strictly reliable and that God inspires each (Greek) word in the Gospels. What, then, do we make of lines 4 and 5 that give the words of Peter's central confession, which has a different expression in each of the three Gospels (and none in the Gospel of John)? We really have only two choices: Peter's confession occurred on three separate occasions in which he used different words each time; or the event occurred only once, and we have three different perspectives with three different language structures about it. If we choose the former, then we must accept that most events of Jesus' life, death, and resurrection also happened in duplicate, triplicate, or quadruplicate—because these events are registered throughout the Gospels in a manner similar to the presentation of Peter's confession. I believe Jesus died only once for our sins, not four times.[5] Should we not also think that Peter's confession happened only once? Do we not have a richer perspective on Peter's confession because the three differing accounts were not harmonized into a single text?

I hope this analysis and example illustrates what the Bible is not. It is not a book given by God in which each word is divinely and rigidly prescribed. As mentioned earlier, this narrow understanding of scripture is one held commonly in Islam about the Qur'an.[6] The Qur'an is believed to have an exact formulation on gold tablets in heaven. If such literal inspiration is not the case for the Bible, how do we understand its character as holy and divinely inspired?

We understand the inspiration of the Bible in the same way as we understand the creativity of God in the big bang creation event, the Incarnation event, the Virgin birth, and subsequently our discussion of the resurrection of the dead and divine healing. God cooperates with the freedom of the disciples and early Christians to produce the written documents of the New Testament. Like the restrictions on the big bang to insure appropriate physical constants, God acted to insure that the limits placed on the authors of the New Testament were such as to insure the quality of a document that is fitting to its subject matter—God's incarnation and redemption of the world through Jesus.

Contemporary biblical students—secular, Jewish, and Christian—generally see the beginnings of the Gospels to be in oral traditions. The disciples and other friends of Jesus saw him, heard him, emotionally reacted to him, and remembered well. What they remembered, retold, and heard from others was what was most important religiously to them. They remembered from their own perspectives. I would think that at this point the Holy Spirit could and did interact with these early "historians" to assist in the selection of the most relevant of oral materials with the intention of showing the love of God. As the oral materials were written down, the process of "editorship" of the Holy Spirit continued, without ever dominating the human writers who were communicating human emotions. With the final completion of the New Testament, the Christian church had a document that had been with Jesus through the memories of its oral traditions, that had been inspired by the Holy Spirit, and that had been refined by religious usage. As such, it is the document that most clearly illumines God's love of humanity through Jesus Christ.

Healing

During my undergraduate years as a physics major at Duke University, I developed friends among students at the theology school, some of whom were pastors. One of them was reporting an interesting controversy in his church: whether God had healed an elderly woman through prayer. Although the pastor believed she had been healed, others in the congregation were quite skeptical. Somewhat perplexed, I said, "Why don't you ask her?" My friend replied sheepishly that he had not and could not, because she had already died from another ailment.

A year later, on brief shore leave from the U. S. Navy, I saw Lazarus's tomb, the place where some traditions state Jesus raised him from the dead. On leaving, our Catholic Arab guide asked me if I had seen Lazarus's other tomb. Already shaken from discovering there were two tombs claimed for Jesus' resurrection, I asked whether this was some "Protestant" tomb in a nearby location. No, he said laughingly, this tomb is on the French Riviera. "You do know Lazarus died again." I have since enjoyed that Lazarus, who was raised from the dead, may have gone to the beach for the rest of his life (as a missionary so said our guide), and then died as we all must.

Healing of the body and soul is a prominent part of New Testament Christianity—then and now. In the Bible and Christian history, bodily healing is temporary, followed by death, whereas healing of the soul, called "salvation" is a long-term matter (to put it mildly). As John Newton would declare in his famous hymn, "When we've been there ten thousand years, bright shining as the sun, We've no less days to sing God's praise, than when we first begun."[7]

In the philosophical posture I am proposing for science and religion, there is a vital explanation of what it means for God to heal someone's body—over an extended or a very short period of time. Since all substances, including those of the human body, involve sequences of events, and since God can act both as causative agent on, and as one who sets a range of potentials for, coming-to-be events, God can influence these events in the direction of physical health—including even the example of decisive physical healing found in the resurrection of Lazarus's body. Although God does not act alone in these matters: the other players may include the bodily cells, disease agents, genetic factors, and particularly those events and intent of the person being healed, or in Lazarus's case, those praying or grieving for him; God can effect whatever degree of power and causation God chooses for acts of healing. In any case, a healing, like all miracles, would not be visible to everyone, but only to those who have an appropriate perspective to see it. (Remember our analysis of the healing of the man born blind in chapter 3.)

Why would God want to raise Lazarus from the dead, when in a few years, he would die again, possibly in great pain? Obviously Jesus loved Lazarus, wept in grief over his death, and wished to see him alive. The reason Jesus gave for Lazarus's temporary bodily resurrection was a sign of the resurrection to eternal life that could be effected through Jesus himself. "I am the resurrection and the life. Those who believe in me, even though they die, will live" (John 11:25). Although having Lazarus back was important to Mary and Martha, his resurrection to only a few years of human life served a more valuable purpose—to allow anyone who may have had an interest to see the redemptive power for both body and soul available in Jesus.

Physical healings are not the only, or even the most important, signs of God's power. More significant are the signals of God's grace given by those who are not healed. How many of us have known a child stricken with an incurable disease who has shown extraordinary love, generosity, and power through the ordeal. I have been far more influenced by those who suffer without healing than by the character of some others who claim they have been healed. Saint Paul prayed that a certain (now unknown) ailment be lifted from him but heard as an answer from God, "My grace is sufficient for you, for power is made perfect in weakness" (2 Cor 12:9). The ultimate sufferer, Jesus himself, was never healed of physical or emotional pain during the time of his passion. God almighty who entered fully as Jesus into our time and space

A Christian Doctrine of Creation

accepted the full weight of physical and emotional suffering with none of the drugs of healing—easily delivered by his own power. He participated without buffer in the sin of our world, caused by choices made in the physical, biological, and especially political realms in his day, but also going back to the dawn of time. That is the ultimate sign of God's love for us. The acquiring by Jesus at his resurrection of a new resurrected body, which retained "those glorious scars"[8] of his old one, only confirms his love for us shown by his passion.

Resurrection of the Body

The death of a person entails the death of his or her body. The body can no longer sustain the soul. The soul can no longer guide and support the body. The organs fail, the cells die, and the molecules and atoms that had supported the cells become "dust and ashes." There is almost a total destruction of the personal society that at one time was the person. Death is real. It is a complete annihilation of the person—body and soul.

God, however, remembers the forms that symbolize the molecules, the cells, the organs, and the person. Although these forms are abstract and cannot determine completely the real personal society that had once existed, they are sufficient to identify and distinguish the person from any other. These forms serve to maintain God's extensive recollection of the person. God can also reproduce for God's experience the intimate feelings of a person during his or her lifetime.

The resurrection of the body—yet another singularity point—is similar to God's creation of the big bang in the following respect. The complete destruction of the person at death removes all of those elements of the person's soul and body from their future causal influence. At the beginning of the cosmos there were relatively few if any events to act causally on the big bang other than the societal God (and other associated beings). God's freedom to create was not limited by the causal freedom of a created order; indeed God's extensive power was required to effect those initial events that became the big bang. For the resurrection of the body, God has to act, as Saint Paul says, to create a new spiritual body (1 Cor 15:44). This creation is based on God's remembrance of the person, but is essentially something quite new.[9] Consider the following resurrection appearance of Jesus.

> When it was evening on that day, the first day of the week, and the doors of the house where the disciples had met were locked . . . , Jesus came and stood among them. (John 20:19)

> They were startled and terrified, and thought that they were seeing a ghost. He said to them, ". . . Look at my hands and my feet; see that it is I myself. Touch me and see; for a ghost does not have flesh and bones as you see that I have." (Luke 24:37–39)

The disciples were well aware that ordinary bodies do not pass through locked doors, and thus thought Jesus to be a ghost. Jesus was insistent that he occupied a body, one that was different from but more real than the walls. He also asked for and ate a piece of broiled fish in their presence (Luke 24:42–43).

We have spoken of the Creation and the Incarnation as singularity points—those creative miracles of God that can be approached only partially by science or philosophy. There is even greater mystery in understanding the literal death of Jesus, especially if he is considered to be the incarnate God. There may be only minor advantages in shifting a focus from substance metaphysics to event structures for such a mystery. I believe, however, that a process perspective allows us more readily to accept the actual death of Jesus, as indicated in the Bible, and accordingly to face our deaths, rather than a philosophy that promotes an eternal soul. The biblical doctrine of death is a tough one. The biblical doctrine of resurrection puts all of the responsibility on God.

Notes

[1] *Catechism of the Catholic Church* (Ligouri MO: Liguori Publications, 1994) 359.

[2] Joseph A. Bracken, S. J., *Society and Spirit: A Trinitarian Cosmology* (Selinsgrove NJ: Susquehanna University Press, 1991).

[3] The reader also may want to consult my technical philosophical work, in particular chapter 6, "God and Religion." Granville C. Henry, *Forms of Concrescence: Alfred North Whitehead's Philosophy and Computer Programming Structures* (Cranbury NJ: Associated University Presses, 1993).

[4] John 1:1

[5] His death is recorded slightly differently in each of the four Gospels.

[6] In my recent class for undergraduates on science and religion, there were different types of Christians, some agnostics, some who professed Judaism, and two Islamic brothers, who read the Qur'an in the original language as well as knew much history and philosophy of Islam. Students often stayed after class

to talk to each other about issues. One afternoon when evangelical students were trying to convince the Islamic students of the divinity of Christ using the authority of the Bible, the Islamic students replied: "Your New Testament was written down and canonized at least a century after the events. The Koran was divinely dictated word by word to the illiterate Prophet, who memorized it, and was written down within months. Which scripture should have more authority?"

[7]John Newton, "Amazing Grace."

[8]Charles Wesley hymn, "Lo He Comes with Clouds Descending."

[9]For further discussion of resurrection and process thought, see Granville C. Henry, "Does Process Thought Allow Personal Immortality?" *Religious Studies* 31 (Fall 1995): 311–21.

Chapter 13
Faith and Reason

In previous chapters I showed that general images of an old science were accepted by theology, made holy, and then seen erroneously by many Christians to have originated in the Bible by revelation. Early and medieval theology accepted the scientific geocentric position of the universe and found many examples of biblical confirmation. The Hebrew God, transformed and made rational, all-powerful, and all-knowing by Greek philosophy, became orthodox theology. And millions of Christians saw this God as the Immutable One revealed, so they thought, in the Bible.

The official theology of many English Christians adopted Newtonian principles and believed that the God of the Bible was the same distant God found by arguments from design. Miracles became their justification of the divinity of Christ. Their heirs in America used Newtonian science to justify a "young earth" scientific theory supporting a particular and literal "seven-day" interpretation of Genesis. Some, like Morris, saw the first and second laws of thermodynamics to be taught in the Bible and used the dual authority of Bible and classical science to oppose evolution. Many liberal theologians who championed a cultural evolutionary theory following ideas of Darwinian progress saw it as an explanation of the Kingdom of God proclaimed by Jesus. They took great pains to declare their message a biblical one.

Each of these positions has been effectively confronted by new science or by technology dependent upon science—or resisted successfully on theological grounds alone. I point out again that it is not the basic Christian religion or the Bible that has been sorely challenged by science, but rather philosophical or theological interpretations of biblical religion that have come from nonbiblical sources. The reawakened Aristarchan astronomy asserted by Copernicus set off a tremendous theological conflict that has only been officially rectified in this decade.[1] The limitative theorems derived mainly from contemporary mathematics challenge the old orthodoxy about our knowledge of God as strictly omnipotent (all powerful), omniscient (all knowing), and immutable (nonchanging), which characteristics were initially clarified and motivated by classical mathematics and Greek philosophy. The general academic regard for scientific evolution has threatened the Newtonian position held by many fundamentalists that allows no acceptance of evolution. The technological results of contemporary science that have been shown in the form of nuclear conflagrations and the systematic torture and killing of millions of Jews and Russians have all but ended the liberal Christian dream of the kingdom of God in which sin was presumed reduced by natural progressive processes.

The historical conclusion from these theses seems apparent. Every time Christian theology takes to its bosom some powerful perspective derived from science, it finds its message compromised, especially when science changes. Theology cannot take much consolation that science has the same problem. Every time science believes that a current theory is rigidly true, whether it be an Archimedian earth-centered universe, a strict Newtonianism, or an early Darwinism without Mendelian clarification, it must face the dislocation that accepted anomalies bring to the science—especially when a new scientific system is proposed.

In the last two chapters we celebrated the scientific facts and theories associated with the big bang interpretation of astronomy, which seems to offer a startling illumination of the biblical doctrine of creation. I have not hesitated to accept this contemporary science as an exposition of Christian theology. I admit fully my tendency, shared with astronomer Hugh Ross and others, to give science a hallowed authority to speak about the meaning of Holy Scriptures. I see big bang science in the Bible and authorized by the Bible. Yet, I realize how vulnerable this position may be.

All it will take for this synthesis of big bang science and a biblical understanding of creation to unravel is (1) a discovery of sufficient hidden matter in the universe that will cause its eventual collapse due to gravity,[2] (2) a theoretical understanding that the singularity postulated for the beginning of the big bang is similar to the ordinary events observable in the nature of black holes already existing in the universe, and (3) such black hole singularities can be unstable and may eventually explode starting the process over again with possibly new laws of nature and new space-time structures. From a scientific point of view, our universe could then be viewed as an oscillating one that has existed forever.

In terms of the current evidence and theoretical development, I do not believe these three conditions will ever be achieved. Yet, for at least a millennium, Christians accepted the best of science coming from Archimedes and Ptolemy about the earth-centered universe. We have observed the pain and dislocation that occurred religiously when the new scientific sun-centered universe challenged the old scientific view of an earth-centered one. For more than two hundred years many Christians accepted a Newtonian science for their religion. We have outlined how this perspective lay the groundwork for a damaging conflict with evolution. Now relativity theory and quantum mechanics have replaced Newtonian science. Are we not setting up Christian theology for another major fall by aligning it too closely with contemporary science? What justification can we give for accepting big bang astronomy, evolution, relativity, and quantum mechanics into a contemporary theology after our observation of the history of the relationship of science and religion in the past? We need to examine some general postures on the relationship of faith to reason. What are our options regarding believing and knowing? How can we appropriately balance the emphases of Christianity and those of science?

Positions on Faith and Reason

Saint Paul says contrasting things about faith and reason. He asserts that we are "justified by faith" (Rom 3:28)—Martin Luther added the word alone—but God's "eternal power and divine nature, invisible though they are, have been understood and seen through the things he has made" (Rom 1:20). Paul claims that we can know of God's existence by reason, but that we can know God personally only by faith. He further asserts that when we know of God's existence by reason and then do not choose to know God by faith, our thinking becomes futile and our senseless minds are further darkened (Rom 1:21).

In chapter 2 I outlined how Greek mathematics conditioned a philosophic position that understood God as a divine foundation, which was made known by its logical structure. Because Christian theologians believed in the personal Hebrew God who acted in history, they rejected this Greek spiritualist position. Yet in their attempt to use logic to explore the Hebrew God, they precipitated the problem of faith and reason. How far can argument lead us to know the personal and acting God? How does faith interact with reason? Answers to these questions affect our attitude towards the relationship between science and religion.

In a short and elegant presentation, Etienne Gilson (1884–1978), French Catholic philosopher of superb talents, outlined four positions on faith and reason developed during the Middle Ages.[3] I take satisfaction that medieval theologians isolated these options on faith and reason so applicable to the issues of science and religion today. Also I assume considerable liberty in articulating Gilson's analysis for contemporary relations between science and religion.

Gilson's four positions, or families of theologians following particular leaders, are those of Tertullian (160–220), Augustine (354–430), Aquinas (1224–1274), and the Islamic scholar, Ibn Rochd, better known by his Latinized title, Averroës (1126–1198). Tertullian claimed that faith and reason should be strictly separated. He saw that reason harms faith. The hearts of people are so darkened, they cannot get at any relevant truth about God through reason. Only faith gives access to the mysteries of salvation. Augustine said that faith and reason can be combined, but only after one has an appropriate relationship with God through faith. After conversion, the darkened minds to which Paul referred are cleared, and reason—even about God—can be accurate. Aquinas agreed with Augustine that conversion is necessary in order to use reason effectively. In this context, however, what we know (the results of reason and demonstration) is different from what we believe (what we accept on authority or from experience). Therefore, reason can be separated from faith, since they are different activities, and reason can be used to confirm the beliefs of faith. Although deeply pious, Averroës believed that all the best of religion could be expressed through reason. The knowledge of religion is included within philosophy and science.

As Christians viewing the dilemma of incorporating science into theology, we may have some considerable sympathy for the Tertullian position that religion ought to be strictly separated from science. In this perspective science can only contaminate religion and lead it astray. Is it possible to separate religion from science? I say Yes, but only to a degree.

There are no doubts that Tertullian had religious experience of God independent of Greek philosophy. In spite of his protestations against philosophy, however, he was one of the greatest (and thereby worst) logic choppers of all time. He used reason, which was not derived from the Bible but from Greek mathematics, as a weapon to discredit Greek philosophy. If philosophy, which Saint Paul called "empty deceit" (Col 2:8) and can be translated alternatively as "hollow and deceptive," deters someone in their Christian quest, then Tertullian's position may be helpful. If, however, one is also interested in the science of logic and then is told logic is evil, when all the while logic is being used to proclaim this very position, then the position is destructive.

To be told that I ought to "follow the Bible" and not accept or even be interested in evolution, when the justification of this admonition aligns with Newtonian science—and not the Bible—is hypocritical. I identify with Morris, whose position I presented in chapter 5, as representative of a modern-day family of Tertullians. Morris pretends to claim that the Bible alone teaches us truly about history and the physical world. He speaks to and for Christians who want to be able to depend on the Bible for religious reasons and who care little about the issues of philosophy or science. He seeks to support the natural images they have derived from the Bible, especially those from the creation accounts in Genesis, as literally true, even though some of these images come from a background science. Like Tertullian, who used Greek logic to attack Greek philosophy, Morris uses classical science to attack contemporary evolution. The quality of the attacks on both of them is virulent—at best unappreciative and at worst dishonest.

I have no quarrel with those Christians who accept the scriptures at face value, even when their images of the Bible are conditioned by classical science. The Bible is well able to communicate its primary message in various cultural settings. I am concerned when scholars or scientists seek to lead the faithful about science and religion and speak from a very narrow or outdated perspective on science—especially when they exclude and attack those aspects of science that may be fruitful for interpreting scripture. When Morris wrote his primary work in 1963, relativity theory, quantum mechanics, and the limitative theorems of mathematics were well developed. I wish he had been more interested in and appreciative of contemporary science, for then I believe he also would have been more loyal to and respectful of the Bible.

Averroës saw no incompatibility between revelation and reason. Each of them promoted the same truth but appealed to different types of people. Religion is necessary in order to communicate (philosophical) truth to those whose imagination dominates their reason, that is, those who care little about philosophical or scientific arguments. Others who can follow rational discussion insist only that there be no contradictions between science and religion. They want to be able to believe their religion without serious challenge. In addition, there are those few who believe only what can be demonstrated philosophically and mathematically—we would say they are those who believe only what can be demonstrated scientifically. For Averroës, it is they, and only they, who know the truth. All others merely follow their imagination.

Averroës thought he had truly included religion within his philosophy. He taught, for example, that when theologians claimed God created the world, they really meant God upheld an eternally existing world.[4] This philosophical sleight of hand is not practiced by contemporary Averroëists, among whom I consider Stephen Hawking and Paul

Davies (chapters 11 and 12). Both of these men seek to argue strictly from scientific principles to religious truth. They seldom claim more than their arguments demand. They also never reach much, if any, religious content. Their religious claims are primarily negative. Their faith has none of the robustness of ordinary Christians.

I side with Augustine or Aquinas, rather than Tertullian, because like Averroës, they had no fear of reason. They loved the challenge. They believed there is one truth, God's truth, much of which is not given by revelation in the Bible but by appropriately conditioned reason. I prefer Augustine and Aquinas to Averroës because they believed there is a revelation, which is more fundamental than reason. In particular, I accept Augustine's assertion that we believe in order to understand.

On the surface Augustine's position is perplexing. How could belief in the statement "The Virgin Birth happened" give any explanatory information about the complicated biological aspects of conception and birth, which more appropriately should come from science? I interpret this example to be unfair to Augustine's position. He meant something quite different. Belief is a form of participation or involvement. We participate in order to understand.

How did we learn to skate—by having someone tell us about it, or by skating? Why do we now understand skating? Is not the answer—because we skate? Very few of us have ever read any instructions or literature about skating. We know, however, quite well what it means to skate. I cannot really understand the rules of basketball, written and unwritten, unless I play the game. We evidence our "belief" in skating by skating and our "belief" in basketball by playing. Someone who does not believe in basketball would not play the game and probably would not want others to play it. Someone who does believe in basketball probably enjoys it and wants others to join in the fun.

Some students try to learn mathematics by memorizing facts and rules, even problems, and it becomes a horror to them. Because a teacher says something is true does not in itself cause one to know it is true. I cannot understand, for example, that the internal angles of any triangle always add up to 180 degrees, unless I participate in the proof of the proposition. The secret about mathematics is that there is more than a little ecstasy in the participation of it, but sheer boredom and frustration in its mere surface memorization. One has to believe in mathematics, that is, participate in it, in order to enjoy it. Otherwise, it can become a major burden. Think of the many long years of involvement in mathematical studies necessary for Stephen Hawking and Paul Davies to understand physics and astronomy well enough to be creative at it.

Even ordinary instruction and learning in science requires participation. Would not it be easier and more efficient for books to describe laboratory experiments and have students learn about them rather than do them? Why do scientists insist that laboratories should be an integral part of any good science teaching? Do they really believe one cannot learn about chemistry without involved participation in the activities of laboratory experimentation?

Just as knowledge of science and mathematics requires participation in laboratories and proofs, Augustine would point out that knowledge of Christianity, or of any religion, requires participation in that religion. We can learn surface knowledge about science without participating in the experiments that illuminate it, just as we can learn something about Buddhism without practicing it. I take very seriously my Buddhist friend's comments that I can never really understand Buddhism unless I practice it for at least a few years.

The reason I can affirm that contemporary astronomy illuminates and confirms a biblical understanding of creation without fear of the consequences to my faith if science changes is that I am more grounded in the participation of Christianity than I am in the participation of science. I accept that the propositional assertions of my faith should be challenged by the best of science, and when so challenged will probably be modified. This possibility does not alarm me, because the propositions of the Christian religion are not ultimately what are important. They are the result of a deeper participation that has its own authority and that itself, along with science, tends to modify any conventionally held doctrine. In fact, I believe this deeper participation is at the same level and has the same authority for science. Participation at this level may allow each of us to say *I believe in order to understand—both science and religion*. I shall articulate this revised Augustinian position for the rest of the chapter, first in terms of the philosopher and poet Martin Buber and then in terms of a brief summary of process philosophy.

I and Thou

During the first half of this century major theologians attempted to formulate a theology that separates religion not only from science but also from philosophy. It was a position that sought a return to biblical perspectives and is called, at least by critics, "Neo-orthodoxy" (the new orthodoxy). Some names are: the theologian Karl Barth, the New Testament scholar Rudolf Bultmann, and the religious philosopher Langdon Gilkey. The basic idea is that God is always behind (under, the ground of, creator of) the laws that rule the scientific universe, but is never subject to them. God so transcends us—some call God the "Wholly Other"—that we cannot talk accurately about God, certainly not in formal, scientific, or logical language. As described in previous chapters, I prefer a conceptuality that allows an explanation of an objectified God who is involved with us in the world. The Bible is correct when it describes God's actions as historical.

I disagree with Neo-orthodoxy primarily because their doctrine of an aloof and nonobjectifiable God is influenced by their understanding of the nature of—classical science. Most of the theologians in this movement so completely gave up on traditional science as having any benefit for theology, they failed to consider seriously contemporary scientific developments. For them, God must radically transcend the world that science studies. In contrast, one of them, the Jewish scholar Martin Buber, who had no intent to deal with science, proposed a theological outlook that seems to me ideally suited for relating contemporary science to religion. His position as expressed poetically gives insight and depth to the perspective of process thought I have articulated in previous chapters as well as provides a clear example of an Augustinian position regarding faith and reason.

Buber's major work *I and Thou*,[5] written as poetry and not metaphysical prose, is pointedly anti-substantialist, by which I mean Buber also opposed understanding the nature of being as substance existing in space and through time. Upon first reading, many see *I and Thou* as espousing a kind of psychological religion. Buber distinguishes between a deep personal experience called I-Thou, for example, an intimate encounter with a family member, and more objectifying, nonpersonal experience, called I-It, which is an experience, say, of an idea or a doctrine. I-Thou is primary. I-Thou is the true, renewing, life-giving encounter. I-It is secondary, a reaction to I-Thou in the form of scientific theories and theological doctrines, which seek to describe the world objectively. Buber, however, marshaled devastating emotional criticism against "psychologism," which presupposed some substantial thing existing over time within a person that did the experiencing. He set himself against an eternal soul as well as against any philosophical system that was presumed to be both true and complete.

For Buber, whatever we are substantially is conditioned by our relation to the world, either the modes of I-Thou or I-It. Process thought finds the being of any actual entity determined by its relation to its past as well as how it chooses to select among causal forces of the past. It claims that all entities have some subjectivity; therefore, any contact among entities is a Thou contact, however minimal. Buber was also skeptical of any emphasis on a spiritualism or mysticism that sought to find the Thou of God away from the world in some transcendent realm. Biblical religion requires that God, who revealed God's self historically in the world, be found in the world. To be saved, one must go at the world, not away from it. One finds God through historical encounters, like the Hebrews at Sinai, but refreshed in terms of current Thou relations. In Christian terms, one must first feel Jesus' suffering for us on the real wood of the cross in Jerusalem before we understand or appreciate his resurrected and transcendent state. My interpretation of process thought allows sensitive expression of mystical experience but finds the source of mysticism from encounter with God who is with us in the world.

I-Thou encounter has highest priority for Christians. One can meet God in the world without being philosophical or scientific. Indeed, following Augustine, one must believe (participate in meeting) in order to understand ideas appropriately. It is the I-Thou relation that determines the It structures of science or theology. I-Thou encounter provides the authority for distinguishing between competing theological or scientific theories. Every major innovator in science has expressed in private literature some sentiment of personal awe at the world he or she is describing. I-Thou relation provides authority for belief in both science and the Bible. What one understands scientifically or philosophically, however, is not the heart of Revelation, but something we are called to formulate—like artists who paint pictures, carve sculpture, write poetry, play music, or sing songs. Accordingly, scientific and theological creations can never achieve the importance of God's action for us, or of our engagement with the world. The most beautiful of scientific theories becomes stale if it is not refreshed by encounter with the Thou of the real world.

In this posture of Buberian relation, process perspective, or Augustinian belief, we revel in the basic experience of God and the world. We seek abstract ideas, metaphysical systems, and artistic images to understand and celebrate our experience of the real world—including God. These abstractions are means to add richness to our experience.

Their truth, which means their integrity in describing the world, is very important to our esthetic appreciation of them. Like any artists, we take what we can get. Those ideas that enliven our experience or, as Buber might say, call forth the Thou, are more important to us than some others.

Accordingly, I have no hesitation to accept big bang science to explain and enrich a biblical doctrine of creation. I prefer a quantum mechanical emphasis rather than the classical one of relativity because of its compatibility with the idea of God's bequeathing some freedom to the cosmos. I seek a modification of some of the images of this science, such as changing the spatialization of time to the temporalization of space as described earlier. Current astronomy is a very dynamic discipline. When big bang science changes, I have confidence that there may be some wrenching modifications but also some encouraging surprises to allow a continuing use of science to interpret theology—provided we are nimble enough to champion the appropriate images for science and theology. Process thought is also an abstraction, an It structure. It has value, as does big bang science, only as it fulfills our scientific and religious experience. Therefore, it is dependent upon our encounters with the world and God and should be replaced if it loses its esthetic and religious function.

Although theoretical science and philosophy are mere I-It structures, I believe God takes interest and pleasure in our academic and artistic creativity. I think God enjoyed and resonated emotionally with Bach and his music just as God would in a qualitatively different but equally important act of spontaneous, personal charity. God probably takes esthetic satisfaction in the theory of evolution, with a chuckle about its major limitations and, at times, presumptuous demeanor of its advocates. God must enjoy what is to us the new astronomy, which God established at creation, but we are now just discovering. God, however, is no academic snob. According to the gospel, God much prefers the simple folk who have no pretension of importance, especially about their ideas, to the ones who become pompous over their science —physical or theological.

I am saying in the language of Buber that the It, which is dependent on Thou encounter with the world, is also important to God. God wants to share the It-structures. God is greedy for involvement with us and our ideas. As Buber maintains, the scientific idea (theological doctrine, artistic form) becomes stale and unrewarding when it is isolated from encounter with the world and the Thou that waits just on the other side of our pretension.

Because we may believe in order to understand, seek the Thou to formulate the It, we should have no fear of science or philosophy. This does not mean we may not be critical about some aspects of science, the materialism of Darwinism, for example, or be simply wrong in our position. We may accept, however, that all truth is God's truth, and that no good science will ever detract from God's actions and gifts. Some aspect of science, philosophy, or theology may provide provocation to our beliefs—which only means the adventure of science and religion continues. We have an exciting challenge.

Process Philosophy and Christianity

Process philosophy accepts with Augustine and Buber that participation is prior to knowledge. Experience is more fundamental than ideas. As described in previous chapters, the initial development of an event begins with experience of past entities including God. The very being of an actual entity is self-initiated from its immersion in its immediate past. The coming-to-be entity accepts and includes its past occasions into itself by assimilating them, and they, in turn, influence it. The predecessor entity events have already achieved their own completion but now, as past, exercise determination on coming-to-be entities. As an entity assumes being, it creatively synthesizes its feelings from past causal events, now intimate to it, and then achieves a fixed character. It then passes into objectivity, causally influencing subsequent events.

There is great variety in the quality of self-subjectivity among kinds of entities. I feel presumptuous attempting to describe the experience of an electronic event, but I judge that the electron does not see, hear, taste or think. It does, however, feel, which is my term for its accepting causality from the past, and has a minimal subjectivity, which is my way of saying it actively synthesizes its past into its very being. Its final state, however, is not much different from its electronic predecessors, except perhaps its place in time and space where its minimal creativity makes its exact potential determination unknown and establishes the random properties that are associated with large numbers of electronic events.

In contrast, a human soul event has a far richer experience than an electronic event. It too accepts causal influence subconsciously from past events, including its predecessor soul and bodily events. It can also, among others, feel past societies of events and then project them into a visual or auditory experience that seems contemporary as well as feel past ideas, again subconsciously, from other entities, and then array them in a vibrant understanding with a flavor controlled by itself. In short, the human soul can develop consciousness with all its marvels. Consciousness, however, always occurs in a late stage of development out of more basic, but vague, feelings. Consciousness is derivative from these feelings. It is not some substance existing through time that is the foundation or background expression of these feelings. As stated above, but now somewhat expanded, vague experience is more fundamental than conscious ideas. The Thou is more fundamental than the It.

One of the liberating aspects of religion, Christian and other, provided it is not too dependent on the clarity of theological thought, is that it can condition one to be more sensitive to the obscure perceptions of ordinary causal events. We may see at a glance the brilliant sun, but we feel its powerful influence on us and on all other things that influence us—in a vague and awesome way. We can feel the influence our cat may have on us and may visually see it in a vibrant and complex context (without causality) that is related to the welter of powerful but visually obscure feelings of love, warmth, and dependency we may have for the cat.

In the philosophical posture of process thought, vague feelings are closer to concrete reality, the Thou of Buber, than the clear and distinct presentations of consciousness, which is a later synthetic addition to fundamental causal feelings. No modern person will want to deemphasize the thrills of intense consciousness. Contemporary preoccupation with the rationality of consciousness, however, leads to a loss of meaning, a divorce from understanding true causal interactions, which come through the rough and tumble world of vague perceptions. It is in the vague causal perceptions that we experience God, who is as concrete and real as any other event.

The Christian religion is primarily about causal experience, human and divine. The claim that God became human in Jesus Christ, lived, loved, suffered, was murdered—and rose again—is an assertion that God feels strongly enough to make common cause with and for us, and finally to seal our redemption through Jesus' passion and resurrection. Christian conversion and growth occur when humans begin to understand how God feels about them, literally when they feel God's feelings, and not how they feel about themselves feeling God. Biblically and in Christian history, the experience of God's love is couched in some human community. Humans feel, and are influenced by, the feelings of other people. They can feel the anger, frustration, and evil intent, as well as cheerfulness, forgiveness, and love.

A fetus's experience of its mother can be used as analogy of the creature-God relationship. The developing human does not see its mother objectively even in the latest stages of pregnancy, because the mother surrounds and encloses her. The mother does not see the unborn baby for similar reasons (except perhaps indirectly in a sonogram). Yet both are bound in a strong, primary, causal, caring relationship. The mother is not distant from the baby nor the baby from the mother. Their relationships are concrete, upfront, direct, not secondary, rational, visual. The mother influences the baby, and the baby influences the mother.

After birth and the subsequent development of the bodily apparatus of sight, the baby can see its mother. Yet the basic causal forces are still dominant, not the secondary conscious ones. The infant feels the mother causally and then projects the delights of sight within its consciousness. God's relationship with God's creatures is normally causal, concrete, and particular, manifesting itself in the vague but primary feelings of direct encounter. Because of the dependence of the structures of consciousness on causal feelings, and the control God has over the relativity of time and space, God may appear literally in whatever mode God chooses, whether it be in a "still small voice," out of the storm, or in the physical person of the suffering, dying, and resurrected Jesus.

Because we can feel the feelings of people, we can feel their feelings of religion. It is possible to know something of what Moses felt before the burning bush or the disciples before the risen Christ, because we can feel the feelings of feelings that go back to these seminal events. A church is a community that values, conserves, and transmits the feelings of its defining historical events—Moses; the prophets; the life and encounters of the teaching, suffering, and risen Christ; the lives of the saints and reformers. Christians naturally gravitate to some church community where they can experience the history and participate in it.

Christianity, however, is not just a religion of reverence for the past. No matter how valuable Eucharist (the Lord's supper of bread and wine) is as a remembrance of Jesus' passion—"Do this in remembrance of me"—it is the Lord's real presence that is essential. Jesus' real presence, which is concrete and causal, is perceived vaguely. So also is God's presence felt in the Old Testament encounters and in the early church's experience. I do not mean to assert that God cannot appear in the visual or auditory field of consciousness. God did so in the person of Jesus in his life and resurrection. God did so in the burning bush before Moses and on Mount Sinai. In each of these occasions, however, the visual or auditory presence was of a human person, a burning bush, and a great storm with God speaking in a voice "like thunder." Behind, underneath, and associated with these unusual events was an experience of God's enormous, but restrained, power. It is the remembrance of these events, the feelings of interpreted feelings in a long chain going back to the original events that are the foundations of Judaism and Christianity.

Science and Religion, a Summary

The source of science is the real world that exists objectively on its own independently of our observation. We are a part of this world and experience it. Science is understood in terms of its abstract, normally mathematical, structure, which we create. Because this abstract structure is necessarily a partial description of the real world by virtue of the limitative theorems, theoretical science changes because of our refined experience of the world. We discover new things about the world that challenge old theory and precipitate new theory.

The source of religion is God, who exists objectively and independently of our observation. The religions of Judaism and Christianity claim that God reveals God's self to humans and that humans experience God. A deposit of this revelation and human experience is contained in the Bible, which does not have a mathematical or theoretical structure. It has a historical, narrative, and mythological nature. Like scientific theory, classical theology, which is an attempt to describe God by abstract logical structure, is also created by human invention. Although it seeks loyalty to the biblical revelation, it is necessarily only a partial description of any divine reality because of the limitative theorems. Theology changes as religious experience becomes richer or different.

Because the experiences of God and nature seem so different, to compare science and religion by academic analysis, we must contrast the theory of science with the theology of religion. In this comparison, we discover a mutual influence going both ways based on images and philosophy. In particular, the images of science have influenced theology historically and conditioned a number of important doctrines, for example, those of an eternal soul, of an unchanging God, which do not seem to be biblical. Images from recent science allow theological interpretations to appear more biblical.

Images from science, mathematics, and religion can lead to more refined and articulated philosophical systems whose goal is to have a general description of some attributes that apply to all things. Some of the problems of science are philosophical, for example, the mind-body problem of cognitive science or the proper interpretation of quantum mechanics. Some of the problems of theology are also philosophical such as the existence of evil in world where God is considered to be wholly good and all powerful. Theology becomes particularly problematic when it veers from its sources of religious experience in the Bible. A bold question: Is there a systematic philosophical perspective that can solve problems in science and theology and relate them in an integrated manner? Can this philosophical outlook make science more intelligible and theology more biblical?

In this book I have attempted to show how the images of science have affected theology historically. In addition, I have attempted to present a philosophical overview, called "process thought," that relates contemporary science and biblical religion. This philosophy, because it is abstract and systematic, is subject to the limitative theorems and is necessarily incomplete. It struggles to be adequate to religious experience and scientific fact without contradiction. It can only be a suggestion for both science and religion. I see its main purpose as positioning us to see religion and science in a more rewarding way, giving us insight into both religious and scientific experience. My main hope, however, is that it challenge young scientists to think philosophically about science and religion so that they can provide a more adequate reconciliation between science and Christianity.

Notes

[1] The Catholic Church gave full exoneration to Galileo and admitted that it was in error in 1992.

[2] For a process perspective, a creation after a massive collapse of the universe (called the "big crunch") could be considered as thoroughly biblical. After a big crunch there may be left only a chaos of events, by which God can then cause, as described in chapter 12, a new universe. Genesis 1 indicates a preexistent chaos from which God created our world.

[3] Etienne Gilson, *Reason and Revelation in the Middle Ages* (New York: Charles Scribner's Sons, 1938).

[4] Gilson, 45-46.

[5] Martin Buber, *I and Thou*, tr. Walter Kaufmann (New York: Charles Scribner's Sons, 1970).

Epilogue
Two Emotionally Derived Positions

Any lasting appeal of the philosophical position of this book will depend, not on how cogent my analysis is, but on how well I have marshaled effective and emotive arguments. In this epilogue, I would like to speak personally on two contrasting attitudes whose emotional consequences are important to me. These are attitudes that might popularly be called scientific and religious, but are in fact expressions of emotional dispositions held at different times of my life now modified and overlapping in my contemporary experience.

Who can forget the beginning discovery of scientific knowledge as a young person? That the world can be understood in terms of elegant principle, which tames raucous fact, rather than the impress of human emotion couched in the conflicting wills of aggressive people, is often no less than, as the Pythagoreans claimed, a form of ecstasy. This sense of power over, but humility towards, the world, which does not release its secrets easily, appears to have much more integrity than the conflicting and confusing teaching of religion, especially when it is presented with threats, special pleading, and sometimes more than a little fraud. Scientific insight seems cleaner, more invigorating, than the petty, anthropomorphic God who is not quite powerful enough to do what we, and surely God, know to be good, or not good enough to do well what God's supposed power is capable. God's purpose, as presented by popular advocates, seems no larger than to satisfy certain psychological needs of troubled people.

To bring a tortured, dying, Palestinian peasant into the matter with an assertion that he "makes it all right" with God, justified by a convenient claim that he rose from the dead, destroys any rational clarity. The ones who claim conversion by, or special insight into, God's will are not often ones you would trust with your wallet, much less your soul. One becomes suspicious that their kind of God could ever create the universe, or subject the current one to God's will, because this surprising and fascinating world seems to show much more creativity in itself than the proclaimed God of religion.

Who would want everything to have a purpose, anyway? The world of which we are a small part has done well on its own to produce the dinosaurs, the birds, rational thought, and the music of Mozart. The rational clarity of science has at its heart a virile, random, adventure but without a sentimental, maudlin purpose. To overlay purpose on the world, especially one that is so clearly human wish fulfilling, is at best suspect.

Fascination with the facts and logical structure of the world, no matter how intense, must ultimately focus on the nature and mysteries of humankind, because that is what we are. There are personal problems and relationships to deal with that ultimately put integrity and its failure to the forefront. As humans we must respond to love, hatred, forgiveness, contempt, humor, and sadness as well as triumph, sex, disease, birth, and death. It is not that we lose interest in science, but personal issues take precedence during the times they are dominant. We are human and must respond as humans. No psychology lesson, and certainly not the teachings of physics, chemistry, or biology, can replace immediate human decision and emotion. In the breach we must act as humans, not as some scientific rational creatures.

Practice in human response increases our sensitivity to the world of animals, and from there to the general animate and finally inanimate world. Then, to our profound surprise, we may begin to acknowledge feelings of engagement with the world we have known vaguely all of our lives, sometimes poignantly as children. We may feel a gentle, but at times emotionally judgmental, *personal presence* that is right there with the random, the familiar, the evil, and the holy. This vague presence, tapping here with humor and support, there with judgment, and always with fascination and mystery, finally presents an integrity and substance so profound that we fall away in utter shame, only to be jogged with a wink and a communication like "I really don't find your sins all that interesting, and there is something about you I like."

A few such experiences can leave us feeling as if we are losing our grasp, but no matter, the quest, strangely like some we have known in science, must go on. And then, surprise on surprise, upon reexamination of our old discarded religion through friends, the Bible, church, music, literature, or prayer, we begin to suspect that our vague feelings of a friendly, judging, but fascinating presence point to a fact that he (or she) has already taken profound action historically. There is no more awesome human experience than to awaken to the realization that the presence who with subtlety woos us is the very same one who was born of a teenage woman in Bethlehem, took on our flesh, lived, suffered and—we all know the story. It is so odd, and remains ever amazing, that it is true!

Science then takes on a different flavor not just because we see God's purpose in it, but also because we perceive that God is interested in protecting the integrity of the world and its random character—from too sentimental or too rational Christians. Our old conviction of maintaining the autonomy of the world from overlays of imposed emotional purpose seems to have found an ally in God who appears to require the limited freedom of subatomic particles as well as that of humans as a condition for God's own enjoyment. The freedom inherent in the world, however, not only creates stunning and wonderful biological creatures as well as human experiences of exquisite character, but also profound and heinous evil. The evolution of cancer cells proceeding in part from their own freedom and self-interest becomes a scourge of humanity. The cumulative choices of humans that become causal can infect the deepest structures of human and societal existence producing incalculable misery. The malevolence of some spiritual beings seem to act on us in ways for which we have little resistance.

The problems of good and evil and their dynamics that affect our personal and societal lives engage both religion and science. Science can say a great deal about the physical and biological domains, for example, those conditions necessary for a potential cure for cancer. It cannot speak well about the religious arena in which individual purpose and complex emotions are paramount. This world—our most real world—where God, humans, and the other created order are involved in relation must be learned and dealt with by human religious experience. This experience may also show those rational structures of science that give intelligible meaning to the objective world. For that we are very grateful, for science allows us to value our common world, one we share in esthetic appreciation with God.

Bibliographical Essay

The following is a selection of books and articles whose content I judge to have significantly influenced me and the position of this book. In a typical manner, I examined some of the works only after learning about their authors and what they wrote. For example, I knew of Augustine's conversion before I read his *Confessions*. I struggled with plane geometry before encountering Euclid's *Elements*. I was a classroom student of physics before examining Newton's *Principia*. I understood Turing machines before looking up Turing's article. I became intrigued with Zen before participating in Jōshū's sayings. I made a decision for Christianity before studying the Bible. Nevertheless, in each case the original sources cited are those that have exercised a fundamental and continuing authority on my thinking.

The books are referred to generically because some of them have multiple presentations and translations. Specific citations are listed in the Bibliography, which includes other sources that have contributed ideas to, or background for, this book.

Religion

The *Bible* in its original languages and translations. I learned years ago not to try to defend the Bible, for I believe it has its own divine conservator and is in no need of my support. I welcome anyone who wants to study it critically, for insights on the Bible from whatever source have value.

Augustine's *Confessions*. The very personal account of the Christian conversion of a brilliant man who used his powerful intellect to influence all subsequent philosophy, religion—and science.

John Wesley's *Journal*, especially Volume 1 of the Standard Edition. An intimate account of a sensitive, intelligent, and well-trained priest of the Church of England, who, after a failed missionary venture to the new colony of Georgia, became converted to a form of Christianity that began the great evangelical revival of the eighteenth and nineteenth centuries in England and America.

C. S. Lewis's *Mere Christianity* and *Miracles*. Lewis was an articulate and sophisticated champion of simple or mere Christianity. Although I now disagree with his philosophical position on miracles, his work initially gave me the means to accept both hard-core physics and the historical and miraculous actions of God.

Zen, in particular *Radical Zen–The Sayings of Jōshū*, translated with a commentary by Yoel Hoffmann. This book delivers the jolt that most Westerners need in order to appreciate the historical reality of the Hebrew and Christian religions.

Science

Euclid's *Elements*. The summary and consolidation of Greek mathematics prior to Archimedes. The *Elements*'s axiomatic method and logic derivative from it had profound influence on subsequent science and theology.

Newton's *Principia*. The first truly systematic explanation of physical phenomena that initiated modern physical science and set conditions for a different understanding of God and miracles.

Darwin's *Origin of Species*. An esthetic thesis about how species develop that has tremendous general power of explanation. It need not entail materialism and can indicate how God acts in nature compatible with a biblical emphasis.

The works of Sigmund Freud and Carl Jung, especially Freud's *Future of an Illusion*, which shows how Christianity may be an illusion (yet true), and Jung's *Psychology and Alchemy*, which shows how human psychological archetypes conditioned an ancient science, and by extension contemporary science.

Kurt Gödel's Incompleteness Theorems found in his article "Über formal unentscheidbare Sätze der *Principia Mathematica* und verwandter Systeme I" ("On Formally Undecidable Propositions of *Principia Mathematica* And Related Systems I"). Although there are many secondary explanations of Gödel's theorems, there is no substitute for his original work, which set in motion the contemporary study of limitative theorems.

Alan Turing's article "On computable numbers, with an application to the *Entscheidungs-problem.*" Before computers were ever developed, Turing began the discipline of computer science by establishing the scope and limits of computers in this elegant and simply stated paper.

I learned those aspects of relativity theory that have influenced my thought primarily from textbooks and secondary sources. Only recently did I discover Einstein's lucid and compact description of both the special and general theories of relativity in his book designed for the nonspecialist called simply *Relativity: The Special and General Theory.* This is the book that the beginning student should read.

My knowledge of quantum mechanics came primarily from physics classes. There are a number of good books written by the originators of quantum theory, namely those by Bohr, De Broglie, Heisenberg, Dirac, Bohm, Von Neumann, and Feynman. The book I recommend for those not willing to engage the technical details is by Nick Herbert called *Quantum Reality, Beyond the New Physics: An Excursion into Metaphysics and the Meaning of Reality.*

Philosophy

Historical fragments from the Presocratic philosophers. Like many, I began my study of philosophy with Plato and Aristotle, who seemed relatively tame and almost modern. Only when I began studying philosophers who preceded Socrates did I experience the shock and wonder of the beginnings of philosophy in Greece and how starkly different this philosophy was from the beginnings of Christianity. I recommend the classic by Kirk and Raven called *The Presocratic Philosophers.*

Martin Buber's *I and Thou*. A book more poetry than philosophy that analyzes with precise intellectual insight and emotional accuracy the relationship between God, humanity, and the world.

Process and Reality in which Alfred North Whitehead establishes a new vision of what it means for reality to be concrete. It is a highly technical, very powerful, and unusually difficult book that allows incorporation of Buber's relational philosophy. *Process and Reality* is the recurring source of my positions on process thought.

Articles by Charles Hartshorne, especially in the collection *Creative Synthesis and Philosophic Method*. Hartshorne, in his tenth decade, is a master philosopher who continues to make good sense of Whitehead's philosophy as it is relevant to contemporary philosophical and scientific issues.

Bibliography

Altizer, Thomas J. J., and William Hamilton. *Radical Theology and the Death of God.* Indianapolis: The Bobbs-Merrill Co., 1966.

Archimedes. *The Sand-Reckoner.* From *The Works of Archimedes.* Edited by T. L. Heath. New York: Dover Publications, Inc., 1897.

Augustine. *City of God*, Book XVI, Chapter IX. *Basic Writings of Saint Augustine.* Edited by Whitney J. Oates. New York: Random House, 1948.

———. *The Confessions of Saint Augustine.* Translated by Edward B. Pusey. New York: Pocket Books, 1951.

Barbour, Ian G. *Religion in an Age of Science, The Gifford Lectures 1989–1991.* Vol. 1. San Francisco: HarperSan Francisco, 1990.

———. *Issues in Science and Religion.* Englewood Cliffs NJ: Prentice-Hall, Inc. 1966.

Barr, Avron, and Edward A. Feigenbaum, eds. *The Handbook of Artificial Intelligence.* Vol. 1. Los Altos CA: William Kaufmann, 1981.

Basinger, David. *Divine Power in Process Theism, A Philosophical Critique.* Albany: State University of New York Press, 1988.

Benacerraf, Paul, and Hilary Putnam, eds. *Philosophy of Mathematics.* Englewood Cliffs NJ: Prentice-Hall, 1964.

Beth, Evert W. *The Foundations of Mathematics: A Study in the Philosophy of Science.* New York: Harper, 1966.

Birch, Charles, and John B. Cobb, Jr. *The Liberation of Life: From the Cell to the Community.* Cambridge: Cambridge University Press, 1981.

Blakemore, Colin. *Mechanics of the Mind.* Cambridge: Cambridge University Press, 1977.

Bloesch, Donald G. *Essentials of Evangelical Theology.* Vols. 1 and 2. San Francisco: Harper & Row, 1982.

Boardman, William W., Jr., Robert F. Koontz, and Henry M. Morris. *Science and Creation.* San Diego: Creation-Science Research Center, 1973.

Bohm, David. *Quantum Theory.* Englewood Cliffs NJ: Prentice-Hall, Inc., 1951.

———. *Wholeness and the Implicate Order.* London: Routledge & Kegan Paul, 1981.

Boyer, Carl B. *A History of Mathematics.* New York: John Wiley & Sons, 1968.

Bracken, Joseph A., S. J. *Society and Spirit: A Trinitarian Cosmology.* Selinsgrove: Susquehanna NJ University Press, 1991.

Brainerd, Walter S., and Lawrence H. Landweber. *Theory of Computation.* New York: John Wiley & Sons, 1974.

Brams, Steven J. *Biblical Games: A Strategic Analysis of Stories in the Old Testament.* Cambridge: The MIT Press, 1980.

Bronowski, J. *Science and Human Values.* New York: Harper Torchbooks, 1965.

———. *The Identity of Man.* Garden City NY: The Natural History Press, 1971.

Bronzino, Joseph D., and Ralph A. Morelli. *Expert Systems: Basic Concepts.* Stony Brook NY: NLA Monograph Series, 1989.

Brooke, John Hedley. *Science and Religion: Some Historical Perspectives.* Cambridge: Cambridge University Press, 1991.

Buber, Martin. *I and Thou.* Translated by Walter Kaufmann. New York: Charles Scribner's Sons, 1970.

Bunge, Mario. *Causality: The Place of the Causal Principle in Modern Science.* Cleveland OH: Meridian, 1963.

Burton, Ernest DeWitt, and Edgar Johnson Goodspeed. *A Harmony of the Synoptic Gospels for Historical and Critical Study.* New York: Charles Scribner's Sons, 1917, 1929.

Burtt, Edwin Arthur. *The Metaphysical Foundations of Modern Physical Science, A Historical and Critical Essay.* London: Routledge & Kegan Paul Ltd., 1924.

Butterfield, Herbert. *The Origins of Modern Science, 1300–1800.* Rev. ed. New York: The Free Press, 1957.

Cantor, Georg. *Contributions to the Founding of the Theory of Transfinite Numbers.* Translated by Philip E. B. Jourdain. New York: Dover, 1915.

Carter, Brandon. "Large number coincidences and the anthropic principle in cosmology," *Confrontation of Cosmological Theories with Observation.* M. S. Longair, ed. Dordrecht: Reidel, 1974.

Cassirer, Ernst. *An Essay on Man: An Introduction to a Philosophy of Human Culture.* New Haven CT: Yale University Press, 1944.

———. *Language and Myth.* Translated by Susanne K. Langer. New York: Dover, 1946.

———. *Substance and Function and Einstein's Theory of Relativity.* New York: Dover, 1953.

———. *The Philosophy of the Enlightenment.* Translated by Fritz Koelln and James Pettegrove. Boston: Beacon Press, 1951.

———. *The Problem of Knowledge: Philosophy, Science, and History since Hegel.* Translated by William Woglom and Charles Hendel. New Haven CT: Yale University Press, 1950.

Cobb, John B., Jr. *A Christian Natural Theology.* Philadelphia: The Westminster Press, 1965.

———. *Process Theology: An Introductory Exposition*. Philadelphia: The Westminster Press, 1976.
———. *The Structure of Christian Existence*. Philadelphia: The Westminster Press, 1962.
———. and David Ray Griffin, eds. *Mind in Nature: Essays on the Interface of Science and Philosophy*. Washington DC: University Press of America, 1977.
Code, Murray. *Order and Organism: Steps to a Whiteheadian Philosophy of Mathematics and the Natural Sciences*. Albany: State University of New York Press, 1985.
Collingwood, R. G. *The Idea of Nature*. New York: Oxford University Press, 1960.
Coombs, M. J.,ed., *Developments in Expert Systems*. London: Academic Press, 1984.
Corballis, Michael C. *The Lopsided Ape: Evolution of the Generative Mind*. New York: Oxford University Press, 1991.
Crossley, J. N. *What Is Mathematical Logic?* London: Oxford University Press, 1972.
Crown, Gary D., Maureen H. Fenrick, and Robert J. Valenza. *Abstract Algebra*. New York: Marcel Dekker, 1986.
Daly, Herman E and John B. Cobb, Jr. *For the Common Good: Redirecting the Economy Toward Community, the Environment, and a Sustainable Future*. Boston: Beacon Press, 1994.
Dantzig, Tobias. *Number: The Language of Science*. Garden City NY: Doubleday, 1954.
Darwin, Charles. *The Illustrated Origin of Species*. New York: Hill and Wang, 1979.
Davies, P. C. W. *The Accidental Universe*. Cambridge: Cambridge University Press, 1982.
———. *God and the New Physics*. New York: Simon and Schuster, 1983.
Davis, Stephen T. *The Debate about the Bible: Inerrancy Versus Infallibility*. Philadelphia: The Westminster Press, 1977.
———. *Risen Indeed: Making Sense of the Resurrection*. Grand Rapids: Wm. B. Eerdmans Publishing Co., 1993.
De Broglie, Louis. *Matter and Light: The New Physics*. New York: Dover, 1939.
———. *Physics and Microphysics*. New York: Pantheon Books, 1955.
Dedekind, Richard. *Essays of the Theory of Numbers*. New York: Dover, 1963.
Dennett, Daniel C. *Consciousness Explained*. Boston: Little, Brown and Co., 1991.
DeYoung, Donald B. *Astronomy and the Bible: Questions and Answers*. Grand Rapids: Baker Book House, 1988.

Dillenberger, John. *Protestant Thought and Natural Science, A Historical Interpretation*. Garden City NY: Doubleday & Co., 1960.

Dirac, P. A. M. *Directions in Physics*. Edited by H. Hora and J. R. Shepanski. New York: John Wiley & Sons, 1978.

———. *The Principles of Quantum Mechanics*. Oxford: Clarendon Press, 1958.

Drees, Willem B. *Beyond the Big Bang, Quantum Cosmologies and God*. La Salle IL: Open Court, 1990.

Dreyfus, Hubert L. *What Computers Can't Do, The Limits of Artificial Intelligence*. Rev. ed. New York: Harper Colophon Books, 1979.

Dubish, Roy. *The Nature of Number: An Approach to Basic Ideas of Modern Mathematics*. New York: The Roland Press, 1952.

Dykstra, Clifford E. *Introduction to Quantum Chemistry*. Englewood Cliffs NJ: Prentice Hall, 1994.

Einstein, Albert. *Albert Einstein, Mileva Maric: The Love Letters*. Edited by Jürgen Renn and Robert Schulmann. Translated by Shawn Smith. Princeton NJ: Princeton University Press, 1992.

———. *Relativity: The Special and General Theory*. New York: Crown Publishers, 1931.

———. *The Human Side: New Glimpses from His Archives*. Selected and Edited by Helen Dukas and Banesh Hoffmann. Princeton: Princeton University Press, 1979.

———. *The World As I See It*. Translated by Alan Harris. New York: Philosophical Library, 1949.

Eisberg, Robert and Robert Resnick. *Quantum Physics of Atoms, Molecules, Solids, Nuclei, and Particles*. 2d ed. New York: John Wiley & Sons, 1985.

Escher, M. C., *The Graphic Work of M. C. Escher*. London: Pan/Ballantine, 1961.

Euclid. *The Thirteen Books of Euclid's Elements*. 2d ed. 3 vols. Translated by Sir Thomas L. Heath. New York: Dover Publications, Inc., 1956.

Eves, Howard. *An Introduction to the History of Mathematics*. 3d ed. New York: Holt, Rinehart, and Winston, 1969.

Farrer, Austin. *Finite and Infinite: A Philosophical Essay*. Westminster: Dacre Press, 1959.

Feigenbaum, Edward A. and Pamela McCorduck. *The Fifth Generation, Artificial Intelligence and Japan's Computer Challenge to the World*. Reading MA: Addison-Wesley Publishing Co., 1983.

Ferré, Frederick. *Language, Logic, and God*. New York: Harper & Brothers, 1961.

Feuerbach, Ludwig. *The Essence of Christianity*. Translated by George Eliot. New York: Harper Torchbooks, 1957.

Feynman, R. P. and A. R. Hibbs. *Quantum Mechanics and Path Integrals.* New York: McGraw-Hill Book Co., 1965.
———. *The Theory of Fundamental Processes.* New York: W. A. Benjamin, Inc., 1961.
Ford, Lewis S. *The Emergence of Whitehead's Metaphysics, 1925–1929.* Albany: State University of New York Press, 1984.
Frege, Gottlob. *The Foundations of Arithmetic.* Translated by J. L. Austin. New York: Harper, 1950.
Freud, Sigmund. *The Future of an Illusion.* Translated by James Strachey. New York: W. W. Norton & Co., 1961.
Galileo Galilei. *Dialogues Concerning Two New Sciences.* Translated by Henry Crew and Alfonse De Salvio. New York: Dover, 1914.
Gillispie, Charles Coulston. *The Edge of Objectivity: An Essay in the History of Scientific Ideas.* Princeton NJ: Princeton University Press, 1960
Gilson, Etienne. *Reason and Revelation in the Middle Ages.* New York: Charles Scribner's Sons, 1938.
Gleick, James. *Chaos: Making a New Science.* New York: Viking, 1987.
Gleitman, Henry. *Psychology.* 3d ed. New York: W. W. Norton, 1991.
Gödel, Kurt. *On Formally Undecidable Propositions of Principia Mathematica And Related Systems.* Translated by B. Meltzer. Edinburg: Oliver & Boyd, 1962.
Gogarten, Friedrich. *Demythologizing and History.* London: SCM Press, 1955.
Gore, Al. *Earth in the Balance, Ecology and the Human Spirit.* New York: A Plume Book, 1993.
Gould, Stephen J. *Ever Since Darwin, Reflections in Natural History.* New York: W. W. Norton & Co., 1979.
Green, John C. *Darwin and the Modern World View.* New York: Mentor, 1963.
Griffin, David Ray, ed. *Physics and the Ultimate Significance of Time: Bohm, Prigogine, and Process Philosophy.* Albany: State University of New York Press, 1986.
———. *Evil Revisited: Responses and Reconsiderations.* Albany: State University of New York Press, 1991.
Halmos, Paul R. *Algebraic Logic.* New York: Chelsea, 1962.
———. *Naive Set Theory.* Princeton: D. Van Nostrand, 1960.
Harmon, Paul and David King. *Expert Systems, Artificial Intelligence in Business.* New York: John Wiley & Sons, Inc., 1985.
Hartshorne, Charles. *A Natural Theology for Our Time.* La Salle IL: Open Court, 1967.
———. *Creative Synthesis and Philosophic Method.* Lanham MD: University Press of America, 1983.

———. *Insights & Oversights of Great Thinkers, An Evaluation of Western Philosophy*. Albany: State University of New York Press, 1983.

———. *Omnipotence and Other Theological Mistakes*. Albany: State University of New York Press, 1984.

Hawking, Stephen W. *A Brief History of Time: From the Big Bang to Black Holes*. New York: Bantam Books, 1990.

Heath, Thomas L. *The Thirteen Books of Euclid's Elements*. 2d ed. 3 vols. New York: Dover, 1956.

———. *The Works of Archimedes*. New York: Dover, 1912.

Heidegger, Martin. *Being and Time*. Translated by John Macquarrie and Edward Robinson. New York: Harper & Brothers, 1962.

Heim, Karl. *Christian Faith and Natural Science*. New York: Harper Torchbooks, 1953.

———. *The World: Its Creation and Consummation*. Translated by Robert Smith. Philadelphia: Muhlenberg Press, 1962.

Heisenberg, Werner. *Physics and Philosophy, The Revolution in Modern Science*. New York: Harper Torchbook, 1958.

Henry, Granville C. *Forms of Concrescence: Alfred North Whitehead's Philosophy and Computer Programming Structures*. Lewisburg NJ: Bucknell University Press, 1993.

———. *Logos: Mathematics and Christian Theology*. Lewisburg NJ: Bucknell University Press, 1976.

Herbert, Nick. *Quantum Reality, Beyond the New Physics: An Excursion into Metaphysics and the Meaning of Reality*. New York: Doubleday, 1985.

Hick, John. *Faith and Knowledge, A Modern Introduction to the Problem of Religious Knowledge*. Ithaca NY: Cornell University Press, 1957.

Hilbert D., and W. Ackermann. *Principles of Mathematical Logic*. New York: Chelsea, 1950.

Hintakka, Jaakko, ed. *The Philosophy of Mathematics*. London: Oxford University Press, 1969.

Hoffmann, Yoel, trans. *Radical Zen, The Sayings of Joshu.*, Brookline MA: Autumn Press, 1978.

Hofstadter, Douglas R. *Gödel, Escher, Bach: an Eternal Golden Braid*. New York: Basic Books, Inc., 1979.

———. and Daniel C. Dennett. *The Mind's I: Fantasies and Reflections on Self and Soul*. New York: Basic Books, Inc., 1981.

Hughston, L. P. and K. P. Tod. *An Introduction to General Relativity*. Cambridge: Cambridge University Press, 1992.

Husserl, Edmund. *Cartesian Meditations*. Translated by Dorian Cairns. The Hague: Martinus Nijhoff, 1960.

———. *Formal and Transcendental Logic*. Translated by Dorian Cairns. The Hague: Martinus Nijhoff, 1969.

———. *Ideas*. Translated by W. R. B. Gibson. New York: Collier Books, 1962.

———. *Philosophie der Arithmetik: Psychologische and Logische Untersuchungen*. Halle, Belgium: C. E. M. Pfeffer, 1891.

Jammer, Max. *Concepts of Mass in Classical and Modern Physics*. Cambridge MA: Harvard University Press, 1961.

———. *The Philosophy of Quantum Mechanics*. New York: John Wiley & Sons, 1974.

Johnson, Phillip E. *Darwin on Trial*. Downers Grove IL: Intervarsity Press, 1991.

Jung, C. G. *Psychology and Alchemy*. Princeton NJ: Princeton University Press, 1968.

Kierkegaard, Sǐren. *Purity of Heart Is to Will One Thing: Spiritual Preparation for the Office of Confession*. Translated by Douglas V. Steere. New York: Harper Torchbooks, 1956.

Kirk, G. S. and J. E. Raven. *The Presocratic Philosophers*. Cambridge: University Press, 1957. 351.

Klaaren, Eugene M. *Religious Origins of Modern Science*. Grand Rapids: Wm. B. Eerdmans Publishing Co., 1977.

Kline, Morris. *Mathematical Thought from Ancient to Modern Times*. New York: Oxford University Press, 1972.

———. *Mathematics in Western Culture*. New York: Oxford University Press, 1953.

Körner, Stephan. *The Philosophy of Mathematics: An Introduction*. New York: Harper Torchbooks, 1960.

Kowalski, Robert. *Logic for Problem Solving*. New York: North-Holland, 1979.

Kramer, Edna E. *The Main Stream of Mathematics*. New York: Fawcett, 1951.

Kuhn, Thomas S. *The Structure of Scientific Revolutions*. Chicago: The University of Chicago Press, 1962.

Langer, Susanne K., *Philosophy in a New Key*. New York: Mentor Books, 1948.

Lewis, C. S. *Mere Christianity*. New York: The Macmillan Co., 1960.

———. *Miracles: A Preliminary Study*. New York: The Macmillan Co., 1948.

———. *The Problem of Pain*. New York: The Macmillan Co., 1948.

Locke, John. *An Essay Concerning Human Understanding*. Vols. 1 and 2. New York: Dover Publications, 1959.

Luther, Martin. *Table Talks*, 15397.

Mac Lane, Saunders. *Mathematics: Form and Function*. New York: Springer-Verlag, 1986.

Macquarrie, John. *Twentieth-Century Religious Thought: The Frontiers of Philosophy and Theology,* 1900–1960. New York: Harper & Row, 1963.

Malinowski, Bronislaw. *Magic, Science, and Religion, And Other Essays.* Garden City NY: Doubleday Anchor Books, 1948.

Mandelbrot, Benoit B. *The Fractal Geometry of Nature.* San Francisco: W. H. Freeman, 1977.

Mendelson, Elliott. *Introduction to Mathematical Logic.* Princeton: D. Van Nostrand, 1964.

Minsky, Marvin. *The Society of Mind.* New York: Simon & Schuster, 1985.

Morris, Henry M. *The Twilight of Evolution.* Grand Rapids: Baker Book House, 1963.

Nagel, Ernest and Newman, James R. *Gödel's Proof.* New York: New York University Press, 1958.

Neugebauer, O. *The Exact Sciences in Antiquity.* 2d ed. New York: Harper Torchbooks, 1962.

Neville, Robert C. *Reconstruction of Thinking.* Albany: State University of New York Press, 1981.

Nevison, Christopher H. *Turing Machines and What Can Be Computed: A Historical Perspective.* Stony Brook NY: NLA Monograph Series, 1992.

Newton, Isaac. *Mathematical Principles.* Translated by Andrew Motte in 1729. Revised by Florian Cajori. From *Sir Isaac Newton's Mathematical Principles of Natural Philosophy and His System of the World.* Berkeley: University of California Press, 1966.

———. *Newton's Philosophy of Nature.* Edited by H. S. Thayer. New York: Hafner, 1953.

Novikov, Igor. *Black Holes and the Universe.* Cambridge: Cambridge University Press, 1992.

Otto, Rudolf. *The Idea of the Holy: An inquiry into the non-rational factor in the idea of the divine and its relation to the rational.* Translated by John W. Harvey. New York: Oxford University Press, 1958.

Pascal, Blaise. *Pensées; The Provincial Letters. Pensées* translated by W. F. Trotter. *The Provincial Letters* translated by Thomas M'Crie. New York: The Modern Library.

Paulos, John Allen. *Mathematics and Humor.* Chicago: The University of Chicago Press, 1980.

Pietsch, Paul. *Shufflebrain.* Boston: Houghton Mifflin Co., 1981.

Plato. *Phaedo.* Translated by H. N. Fowler. Loeb Classical Library. Cambridge MA: Harvard University Press, 1958.

Polkinghorne, John C. *The Quantum World.* Princeton NJ: Princeton University Press, 1989.

———. *One World: The Interaction of Science and Theology.* London: SPCK, 1986.

———. *Reason and Reality: The Relationship between Science and Theology.* London: SPCK, 1991.

Poole, Michael. *A Guide to Science and Belief.* Oxford: A Lion Manual, 1990.

Popkin, Richard H. *The History of Scepticism From Erasmus to Descartes.* New York: Harper Torchbooks, 1964.

Popper, Karl R. *Quantum Theory and the Schism in Physics.* Edited by W. W. Bartley, III. Totowa NJ: Rowman and Littlefield, 1982.

———. *The Logic of Scientific Discovery.* New York: Harper Torchbooks, 1959.

Prigogine, Ilya and Isabelle Stengers. *Order Out of Chaos, Man's New Dialogue with Nature.* Toronto: Bantam Books, 1984.

Radner, Daisie and Michael Radner. *Science and Unreason.* Belmont CA Wadsworth, 1982.

Raphael, Bertram. *The Thinking Computer, Mind Inside Matter.* San Francisco: W. H. Freeman and Co., 1976.

Restak, Richard M. *The Brain, The Last Frontier.* Garden City NY: Doubleday & Co., Inc., 1979.

Riegle, David D. *Creation or Evolution: The Fallacies of the Evolutionary Theory Explained for Junior High Students.* Grand Rapids: Zondervan Publishing House, 1971.

Robinson, James M. *A New Quest of the Historical Jesus.* Naperville IL: Alec R. Allenson, Inc., 1959.

Robinson, J. A. *Logic: Form and Function, The Mechanization of Deductive Reasoning.* New York: North-Holland, 1979.

Rogers, Carl R. *Client-Centered Therapy, Its Current Practice, Implications, and Theory.* Boston: Houghton Mifflin Co., 1951.

Rolston, Holmes, III. *Science and Religion: A Critical Survey.* New York: Random House, 1987.

Ross, Hugh. *Creation and Time: A Biblical and Scientific Perspective on the Creation-Date Controversy.* Colorado Springs CO: Navpress Publishing Group, 1994.

———. *The Creator and the Cosmos.* Colorado Springs CO: Navpress, 1993.

———. *The Fingerprint of God.* Orange CA: Promise Publishing Co., 1991.

Rubenstein, Moshe F. and Kenneth Pfeiffer. *Concepts in Problem Solving.* Englewood Cliffs NJ: Prentice-Hall, 1980

Ruse, Michael Editor. *Philosophy of Biology.* New York: Macmillan, 1989.

Russell, Bertrand, "On the Notion of Cause." *Proceedings of the Aristotelian Society* 13 (1913) 1-26,

———. *Religion and Science.* New York: Oxford University Press, 1961.
Ryrie, Charles Caldwell. *Neo-orthodoxy.* Chicago: Moody Press, 1956.
Sagan, Carl. *Cosmos.* New York: Random House, 1980.
Sartre, Jean-Paul. *The Transcendence of the Ego: An Existentialist Theory of Consciousness.* New York: Noonday, 1957.
Schank, Roger C. *The Cognitive Computer, On Language, Learning, and Artificial Intelligence.* Reading MA: Addison-Wesley, 1984.
Schleiermacher, Friedrich. *On Religion: Speeches to Its Cultured Despisers.* Translated by John Oman. New York: Harper Torchbooks, 1958.
———. *The Christian Faith.* Vols. 1 and 2. New York: Harper Torchbooks, 1963.
Sheldrake, Rupert. *A New Science of Life: The Hypothesis of Formative Causation.* Los Angeles: Jeremy P. Tarcher, Inc. 1981.
———. *The Rebirth of Nature: The Greening of Science and God.* New York: Bantam Books, 1992.
Shu, Frank H. *The Physical Universe: An Introduction to Astronomy.* Mill Valley CA: University Science Books, 1982.
Simon, Julian L., *The Ultimate Resource.* Princeton NJ: Princeton University Press, 1981.
Skyrms, Brian. *Choice & Chance, An Introduction to Inductive Logic.* 3d ed. Belmont CA: Wadsworth Publishing Co., 1986.
Spielberg, Nathan and Bryon D. Anderson. *Seven Ideas that Shook the Universe.* New York: John Wiley & Sons, Inc. 1987.
Stanley, Steven M. *The New Evolutionary Time Table, Fossils, Genes, and the Origin of Species.* New York: Basic Books, Inc., 1981.
Stephani, Hans. *General Relativity: An Introduction to the Theory of the Gravitational Field.* Cambridge: Cambridge University Press, 1982.
Suppes, Patrick. *A Probabilistic Theory of Causality.* Amsterdam: North-Holland Publishing Co., 1970.
Taylor, A. E. *Varia Socratica.* Oxford: James Parker & Co., 1911.
The Interpreter's Dictionary of the Bible, An Illustrated Encyclopedia. 4 vols. New York: Abingdon Press, 1962. V1.
Thayse, A. Editor. *From Standard Logic to Logic Programming: Introducing a Logic Based Approach to Artificial Intelligence.* Chichester: John Wiley & Sons, 1988.
Tillich, Paul. *Biblical Religion and the Search for Ultimate Reality.* Chicago: University of Chicago Press, 1955.
———. *Systematic Theology.* 3 vols. Chicago: University of Chicago Press, 1967.
Trefil, James S. *The Moment of Creation: Big Bang Physics From Before the First Millisecond to the Present Universe.* New York: Charles Scribner's Sons, 1983.

Turing, Alan M. "On computable numbers, with an application to the *Entscheidungs-problem*," *Proc. London Math. Soc.*, Ser. 2, 42: 230–65.

Tzu, Lao. *Tao Teh King*. Interpreted by Archie J. Bahm. 2d ed. Albuquerque NM: World Books, 1986.

Van Till, Howard J., Davis A. Young, and Clarence Menniga. *Science Held Hostage, What's Wrong with Creation Science AND Evolutionism.* Downers Grove IL: InterVarsity Press, 1988.

Van Tuijl, H. F. J. M., "A New Visual Illusion: Neonlike Color Spreading and Complementary Color Induction between Subjective Contours," *Acta Psychologica*, 39 (1975) 441–45.

Von Neumann, John. *Mathematical Foundations of Quantum Mechanics.* Princeton NJ: Princeton University Press, 1955.

———. *The Computer and the Brain.* New Haven CT: Yale University Press, 1958.

Wallace, Robert A., Gerald P. Sanders, and Robert J. Ferl. *Biology: The Science of Life.* 3d ed. New York: HarperCollins Publishers Inc., 1990.

Watson, John B. "Psychology as the Behaviorist Views It," *Psychological Review* 20 (1913).

Weizenbaum, Joseph. *Computer Power and Human Reason, From Judgment to Calculation.* San Francisco: W. H. Freeman, 1976.

Wesley, John. *The Journal of the Reverend John Wesley, A. M.* Standard Edition. Edited by Nehemiah Curnock. London: The Epworth Press, 1938.

White, Andrew Dickson. *A History of the Warfare of Science with Theology in Christendom.* New York: The Free Press, 1965.

White, Lynn, Jr. *Medieval Technology and Social Change.* London: Oxford University Press., 1962.

Whitehead, Alfred North. *Adventures of Ideas.* New York: Mentor, 1955.

———. *An Enquiry Concerning the Principles of Natural Knowledge.* New York: Dover, 1982.

———. *Modes of Thought.* New York: The Free Press, 1968.

———. *Process and Reality.* Corrected Edition by David Ray Griffin and Donald W. Sherburne. New York: The Free Press, 1978.

———. *Science and the Modern World.* New York: The Free Press, 1967.

———. and Bertrand Russell. *Principia Mathematica To #56.* Cambridge: Cambridge University Press, 1962.

Wilder, Raymond L. *Introduction to the Foundations of Mathematics.* New York: John Wiley, 1960.

Wittgenstein, Ludwig. *Philosophical Investigations.* Translated by G. E. M. Anscombe. New York: Macmillan, 1953.

———. *Remarks on the Foundations of Mathematics.* Edited by G. H. von Wright, R. Rhees, and G. E. M. Anscombe. Oxford: Basil Blackwell, 1956.

———. *The Blue and Brown Books*. Oxford: Basil Blackwell, 1960.
———. *Tractatus Logico-Philosophicus*. Translated by D. F. Pears and B. F. McGuinness. London: Routledge & Kegan Paul, 1922.
Yourgrau, Palle. *The Disappearance of Time: Kurt Gödel and the Idealistic Tradition in Philosophy*. Cambridge: Cambridge University Press, 1991.
Zeller, Eduard. *Outlines of the History of Greek Philosophy*. New York: A Meridian Book, 1955.

Index

A
actuary 167
Adam and Eve 84
ah ha experience 135
allele 70
all-or-none law 119
"Amazing Grace" 90
Anaximander 16, 17, 35, 36
Anaximenes 35, 36
animal experiments 123
anthropic principle 177, 185
anti-gravity force 181
Apocrypha 89
Aquinas 43, 45, 179, 206, 208
arche 36, 37, 38, 189
Archimedes 4, 23, 25, 26, 31, 51, 69, 86, 135, 204
arguments
    emotive 219
Aristarchus 3, 23, 25, 26, 31, 51, 69, 177, 178, 203
Aristotle 3, 94, 95, 179
artificial intelligence 120
astronomy 9, 181, 209, 212
    big bang 143, 155, 175, 176, 183, 188, 191, 194, 196, 204, 212
    big crunch 183
    contemporary 212
    early mathematical 15
atom 43, 44, 158
atomism 32, 43, 45
Augustine 7, 43, 45, 94, 95, 123, 126, 128, 135, 179, 206, 208, 209, 211, 213
    mathematical influence on 96
autogeny 73
Averroës 206, 207, 208

B
Bach 212
baptism 187
Barbour, Ian 9
Barth, Karl 210
basketball 208
behaviorism 123, 124
Bentley, Richard 178
Bethlehem 220
Bible 84, 134, 135, 136, 156, 165, 166, 168, 175, 183, 189, 191, 196, 203, 204, 206, 207, 208, 211, 217
    as word of God 8
    Christianity 165
    cosmology 27
    doctrine of creation 212
    facts of 60
    Fundamentalism 168
    inerrancy 6, 166
    inspiration of 7, 88, 188, 195
    perfection of 89
    resurrection of body 200
    shape of the earth 17, 18
    theories in 60
black hole 177, 204
blackbody radiator 156
body and soul 117, 120
Bohm, David 152
Bohr, Niels 157
Born, Max 159
Bracken, Joseph 190
Brahe, Tycho 28, 86

brain 101
    creates appearance of continuity 103, 104
    hierarchical control functions 102
    left and right lobes 101
    looking for soul in 101
Brook, John Hedley 9
Buber, Martin 209, 210, 211, 212, 213, 214
Buddhism 209
Bultmann, Rudolf 210
burning bush 215, 216

C
calculus 99
Calvin, John 45
Calvinism 85
Carter, Brandon 185
Cartesian coordinate system 143
CAT scans 101
Catholic Church 175, 187
causality 115, 130, 131, 132
    divine 194
    freedom 134
Christ 134, 188
Christian 207, 208
    doctrine of creation 177, 185, 187
    theology 205
Christianity 136, 141, 209
    contributed to secularization 58
    emphasis on physical reality 58
    heart of 2
    meaning of 1
    Newtonian 81
Church-Turing thesis 106

COBE exploration
    first 182
    second 182
cognitive science 88, 108, 119, 127
collapsing universe 178
computer 118
    gate 118
    has no soul 120
    images of 105
    scope of 106
concrete reality 214
consciousness 103, 123, 124, 126, 128, 129, 131, 132, 133, 134, 137, 169, 214, 215
    mystery of 107
    trickery of 131
constants
    universal 183, 193
Copernicus 4, 27, 51, 203
cortex 102
cosmology
    Anaximander's universe 15
    contemporary 17
    Old Testament world 15
counting 99
creation 89, 200
    doctrine of 175, 179, 204
    out of nothing 89, 188, 192
creation science 81, 176
creativity 135, 188
creature-God relationship 215
curvature of space-time 150

D
Darwin, Charles 6, 67, 68
    blending theory 69
Darwinism 81, 204, 213
Davies, Paul 7, 151, 208, 209

Index 241

de Broglie, Louis 157, 158
De Young, Donald B. 18, 19
decision 220
Deists 61
Democritus 44
deoxyribonucleic acid 71
Descartes 94, 123, 126
    his dualism 97
    mathematical influence on 96, 97
determinism 6, 123, 127
Dicke, Bob 182
Dickinson, Emily 5
divinity
    characteristic of spiritualism 38
    in Greek philosophy 33
doppler effect 180
double slit experiment 159, 162

E
earth
    age of 74
    spherical 19
ecstasy 208, 219
Einstein, Albert 4, 135, 142, 144, 157, 158, 177, 181
electric fields 142
electromagnetic
    events 163
    force constant 184
electron 117, 118, 146, 147, 157, 158, 159, 168
    microscope 158
    paths 163
emotion 220
energy
    conservation of 83
    kinetic 83
    position 83

entropy 83
    and sin 84
environment
    early childhood 130
Eratosthenes 20, 21, 31
Escher, M. C. 43
esthetic appreciation 212
ether 142
Eucharist 90, 215
Euclid 144
eukaryotes 73
Evangelicals 175
event 213
    electronic 117, 147, 157, 166, 167
    structures 141
evil 221
evolution 6, 84, 176, 205, 212, 221
    as "bad" science 82
    as artistic creation 74
    assumptions of 66, 67
    philosophy of 65, 68
    scientific 65, 66, 77
    summary of 77
expanding universe 179
experience
    of freedom 133
    religious 206
eyetracking experiments 104
Ezekiel
    shape of the earth 18

F
facts
    in philosophy of empiricism 56
    their ambiguity 64
faith 206
    meaning of 5

faith and reason 46, 210
fear of father 125
feeling 168
Feynman, Richard 159
fields 163
flat earth 16
 biblical position 18
fossil record
 explained by flood 84
four corners of the earth 88
four-space 144, 150
freedom 129, 130, 134, 136, 168, 169, 212
Freud, Sigmund 6, 125, 126, 128
Fundamentalism 81, 85, 88, 90, 175, 203

G
galaxies 177, 178, 180, 181
Galileo 4, 15, 22, 86
Gamow, George 182
gates 118
 electronic 107
gene 70
generality
 characteristic of spiritualism 38
 mathematical and theological 33
Genesis 89, 175, 189, 191
genetics 69
 Mendelian 69
ghost in a machine 114
Gilkey, Langdon 210
Gilson, Etienne 205
Gnostic heresy 165
God 1, 17, 130, 134, 135, 136, 137, 147, 153, 165, 175, 178, 184, 185, 189, 191, 193, 198, 206, 210, 211, 212, 214, 215, 216, 219, 221
 arguments from design 60
 as a society 190
 as immutable 42
 existing within the universe 36
 incarnate 109
 of Hebrews 38
 of the Bible 203
 who became human 45
God's
 causality 136, 192
 creative power 188
 emotions 135
 enjoyment 221
 existence 175, 205
 freedom 192
 grace 198
 power 216
 reason 135
 sustaining power 188
 transcendence 153
 will 135
Gödel, Kurt 164
 incompleteness theorem 155, 164, 170
Gospel 43
 meaning of 2
Gould, Steven Jay 77
Graham, Billy 60
gravitational force constant 184
gravity 149, 150
Greek
 mathematics 86, 206
 philosophy 206
 rationality 46
Griffin, David 152

H

Hawking, Stephen 3, 152, 170, 171, 175, 177, 181, 185, 207, 209
healing 188, 197
    divine 188
Hebrews 211
Heinsenberg, Werner 158
    indeterminacy principle 155, 159, 161, 169
hidden matter 183, 204
historical religions 136
historical theses
    first 21, 22, 27, 31, 46, 54, 82, 86, 87, 94, 109, 175, 185
    second 27, 28, 31, 81, 86, 87, 94, 109
    third 31, 65, 86, 87, 93, 109, 123, 141, 148, 155, 159, 176
history 214
    Newtonian 82, 84
Hobbes, Thomas 99
Holy Spirit 190, 197
Hubble, Edwin 179
Hume, David 94, 99, 126, 132
    doctrine of soul 100

I

Ibn Rochd 206
idolatry 58
I-It 210, 211, 212
images
    cognitive science 109
    computer 107
    design of dice 77, 78
    expression as philosophy 2
    geometric 3, 4
    mathematical 94
    mechanistic 3, 81
    motion picture 111
    of an electron 161
    of computer 117
    of spatialization 152
    projection machine 112
    right triangle 35
    soul 117
    throw of dice 76
    vegetable 2
Incarnation 136, 188, 193, 194, 196, 200
indeterminacy 158
inertial frames 142
infinitesimal 98, 99
infinity
    structural limitations 34
interference pattern 160
Isaiah
    shape of the earth 18
Islam 136, 196
    promotes an infallible Qur'an 8
I-Thou 210, 211

J

Jefferson, Thomas 61
Jerusalem 211
Jesus 4, 46, 85, 90, 109, 135, 165, 194, 198, 200, 214, 215
    as the Word 189
    as word of God 8
    preexistent status 189
    resurrected body of 110, 200
    speaking of the soul 93
    suffering of 211
Job
    earth hung upon nothing 18
John 189, 190
Jordan, Michael 26

Joshua 22
Judaism 136

K
Kingdom of God 203
Koffka, Kurt 104
Köhler, Wolfgang 104

L
laboratory experiments 209
Lamark, Chevalier De 68
Lamarkism 68
Lazarus 198
    his tomb 197
Leibniz 94, 97, 99, 126
    non-mechanical philosophy 55
Leucippus 44, 55
light 141, 150
    speed of 142
limitative theorems 155, 164, 165, 166, 169, 203, 207
Locke, John 99, 126
logic 205
    and God 86
logos 189
Luke 195
Luther, Martin 22, 45, 126, 128, 205

M
Maric, Mileva 148
Mark 195
Mary 194
Mary and Martha 198
mass 150, 187
materialism 6, 75, 78, 87, 213
    nature of 75
mathematical ideas
    as divine 41
mathematics 15, 126, 208
    doctrine of soul 94
    images of 32
    influence on early Christianity 31
Matthew 195
mechanism 60, 159
Mendel, Gregor 69, 71, 75, 204
Messiah 195
metaphysics 110
Michelson, Albert A. 142
microwave detectors 182
Middle Ages 205
milky way 177
Millikan, Robert A. 157
mind 95
miracles 82, 85, 194
    as facts 61
    their ambiguity 62
moral laws
    as image for physical laws 57
Morris, Henry M. 81, 82, 84, 87, 90, 203, 206, 207
Moses 46, 136, 215, 216
Mount Sinai 136
Mozart 219
myth
    nature of 8

N
natural law 193
natural selection 67, 68, 76
    as creative force 68
nature 130
    theological analysis of 39
Neo-orthodoxy 210
neuron 119
    as event structure 120
new birth experience 85, 187

New Testament 85, 189, 197
  philosophcal influence on 45
Newton, Isaac 3, 51, 68, 69, 75, 81, 86, 98, 126, 141, 144, 148, 176, 178
  and theological revival 60
  astronomy 53
  atomism and spiritualism 59
  calculus 52
  laws 52, 132
  mechanism 54, 55
  method 56
  philosophy 54
  Principia 53, 59, 148, 175
  theology 57
Newton, John 197
Newtonian
  mechanics 156
  perspective 166
  principles 203
  science 166, 177, 203, 205
Newtonianism 81
  as common sense 81
Nobel prize 157, 182
nucleus
  of cell 73

O
Old Testament 189
oral traditions 196
ordered quadruples of numbers 144
ordered triples of numbers 144

P
panexperientialism
  as contrasted with pantheism and atomism 39
panspiritualism 39
pantheism 39, 188
Parmenides 41, 44
particle 148, 157
Pascal, Blaise 5, 164
Paul, Saint 32, 126, 128, 131, 135, 193, 198, 199, 205
Peebles, Jim 182
Penrose, Roger 170, 181
Pentateuch 57
Penzias, Arno 182
person events 113
perspective
  biblical 128
PET scan 101
Peter's confession 195, 196
Philippians 193
philosophy 187, 212
  expression of images 2
photoelectric effect 157
photon 157
physics
  contemporary 112
Planck, Max 156
Plato 42, 94, 95, 96
pneuma
  as breath and spirit 37
  as structured 37
Polkinghorne, John 167
pollution
  as example of entropy 83
Pope 175
predestination 85, 134
prehension 168
Principia Mathematica 164
process thought 10, 111, 169, 209, 211, 213, 214, 217
progress
  Darwinian 203
prokaryotes 73
propositions 209
Proverbs 189, 190

psychologism 210
psychology 88
   behaviorist 123
   cognitive 100, 109
   gestalt 104
   Gestalt 107
   philosophical 93
   presystematic 93
   psychoanalytic 123, 126
   scientific 93
Ptolemy 51, 204
   Almagest 26, 52
purpose 76, 124, 125, 129, 183, 219, 221
Pythagorean 33, 35
   ecstasy 35
   point 40
   theorem 33, 96
   unity 43
Pythagoreans 219

Q
quanta 156, 157
quantum mechanics 88, 118, 137, 143, 145, 153, 155, 158, 159, 163, 168, 170, 175, 191, 205, 207
Qu'ran 196

R
random events 220
   meaning of 71, 72
randomness 163, 168
rational choice 127
rationality
   as miraculous 82
real presence 215
reason 206
red shift 179

reincarnation
   Pythagorean 35
relativity theory 88, 137, 145, 153, 175, 191, 205, 207
   general 143, 148, 150, 151, 155, 170, 181
   mathematics of 147
   special 142, 143, 146
religion 165
   biblical 211
religious experience 217
Republic 95
response 124
resurrection of the body 85, 188, 198, 199
   biblical doctrine of 42, 116
revelation 211
Revelation
   shape of the earth 18
Riemann, Georg Bernhard 144
Rolston, Holmes, III 9
Ross, Hugh 177, 183, 204
Rubin, Edgar 104
Russell, Bertrand 55, 131, 164, 184

S
Sagan, Carl 20
salvation 197
Satan 90
scholars
   biblical 195
Schrödinger, Erwin 158
   equations 159, 163
science 212, 220, 221
   classical 82, 207, 210
   its source 216
   limitations of 155
   mathematization of 131

meaning of 2
theory of 216
scientific
    knowledge 219
    theory 216
second conversion 187
seeing
    as discontinuous 103
sense of acceleration 132
serial endosymbiosis 73
sexual exhibitionism 125, 126
Shakespeare 72
sin 126, 130, 136
    as inherited 130
    biblical doctrine of 6
singularity point 175, 193, 199, 204
six-day creationists 175
skating 208
skepticism 5
society
    personal 199
software
    expert system 106
solar system 177
soul 93, 124, 128
    and body 116, 117
    as bodily 110
    as eternal 41, 42
    as sequence of events 111
    as wispy spirit 113
    associationist doctrine of 94
    biblical 109, 110
    classical 94, 99, 100, 109, 110, 111, 123
    continuity of 97, 114, 116, 127
    eternal 86, 94
    examining the 115
    freedom and causality of 115
    history of a 114
    influence on body 120
    influenced by mathematics 98, 100
    logic of 93
    not naturally eternal 113
    objective 100
    subjective 100
    substances without 117
soul event 114, 116, 117, 120, 146, 147, 165, 166, 213
space
    absolute 141
    physical 147
space and time 137
space-time 150
    curvature of 149
spatial intuition 145
spatialization of time 151, 212
speaking
    activities of 117
spectral lines 179
spiritual beings 221
spiritualism 32, 35
stars 177, 178
Stern, Isaac 26
stimuli 124
strong nuclear force constant 184
structure
    characteristic of spiritualism 38
    mathematical and theological 33
subconscious 126, 128, 130
subjective time 152
subjectivity 168, 213
substance 188
    classical 111, 112
sun 177

T

temporalization of space 151, 212
Ten Commandments 6
Tertullian 206, 207, 208
Thales 16, 35, 36, 37
theology
    as logos of theos 45
    as rational description 46
    classical 216
    of religion 216
thermodynamics
    explains God's curse 84
    first law 83, 85, 203
    laws of 82
    second law 84, 88, 132, 203
Thompson, J. J. 157
time 141
    absolute 141
    different views of 116
    Newtonian 116
    non-physical 114
    physical 147, 151, 152
    physical 191
    subjective 151, 152, 191
time and space 191
    Newtonian 82
Torah 57
Trefil, James S. 171
Trinity 190
Trinity Broadcasting Network 175
true-breeding plant 69, 70
truth
    biblical 166
Turing machine 105
    universal 106
Turing, Alan 105
two-space 149

U

ultraviolet catastrophe 156
unity 32, 86
    mathematical interpretation of 40
    philosophical interpretation of 39
universe
    as dead 61
    eternal 179
    static 181

V

variation
    as random 69, 76
Virgin Birth 193, 196, 208
viruses 131

W

Watson, J. B. 123
wave 148
wave particle duality 159
weak nuclear force constant 184
Wertheimer, Max 104
Whitehead, Alfred North 164, 168, 169
Wholly Other 210
Wilson, Robert 182
wisdom 189
world
    eternally existing 207

Y

young earth doctrine 203